International
Library of the
Philosophy of
Education

**New essays
in the
philosophy
of education**

International Library of the Philosophy of Education

General Editor

R. S. Peters
Professor of Philosophy of Education
Institute of Education
University of London

New essays in the philosophy of education

Edited by

Glenn Langford

Department of Philosophy
University of Exeter

and

D. J. O'Connor

Professor of Philosophy
University of Exeter

Routledge & Kegan Paul

London and Boston

First published in 1973
by Routledge & Kegan Paul Ltd
Broadway House, 68–74 Carter Lane,
London EC4V 5EL and
9 Park Street,
Boston, Mass. 02108, U.S.A.
Printed in Great Britain by
C. Tinling & Co. Ltd
London and Prescot

ISBN 0 7100 7690 8

Library of Congress Catalog Card No. 73-83120

Contents

v

Contents

General editor's note

There is a growing interest in philosophy of education amongst students of philosophy as well as amongst those who are more specifically and practically concerned with educational problems. Philosophers, of course, from the time of Plato onwards, have taken an interest in education and have dealt with education in the context of wider concerns about knowledge and the good life. But it is only quite recently in this country that philosophy of education has come to be conceived of as a specific branch of philosophy like the philosophy of science or political philosophy.

To call philosophy of education a specific branch of philosophy is not, however, to suggest that it is a distinct branch in the sense that it could exist apart from established branches of philosophy such as epistemology, ethics, and philosophy of mind. It would be more appropriate to conceive of it as drawing on established branches of philosophy and bringing them together in ways which are relevant to educational issues. In this respect the analogy with political philosophy would be a good one. Thus use can often be made of work that already exists in philosophy. In tackling, for instance, issues such as the rights of parents and children, punishment in schools, and the authority of the teacher, it is possible to draw on and develop work already done by philosophers on 'rights', 'punishment', and 'authority'. In other cases, however, no systematic work exists in the relevant branches of philosophy—e.g. on concepts such as 'education', 'teaching', 'learning', 'indoctrination'. So philosophers of education have had to break new ground—in these cases in the philosophy of mind. Work on educational issues can also bring to life and throw new light on long-standing problems in philosophy. Concentration, for instance, on the particular predicament of children can throw new light on problems of punishment and responsibility. G. E. Moore's old worries about what sorts of things are good in themselves can be brought to life by urgent questions about the justification of the curriculum in schools.

There is a danger in philosophy of education, as in any other applied field, of polarization to one of two extremes. The work could be practically relevant but philosophically feeble; or it could be philosophically sophisticated but remote from practical problems. The aim of the new International Library of Philosophy of Education is to build up a body of fundamental work in this area which is both practically relevant and philosophically competent. For unless it achieves both types of objective it will fail to satisfy those for whom it is intended and fall short of the conception of philosophy of education which the International Library is meant to embody.

This volume of essays which emanates, in the main, from the University of Exeter has two distinctive features. First, it attempts to explore what is meant by 'education' and 'educational theory'. In part it does this by containing articles which are critical of what many regard as the current orthodoxy in British philosophy of education as represented by R. S. Peters and P. H. Hirst. Replies by Peters and Hirst are included.

Second, an attempt is made to open up discussion about the main spheres of education—i.e., moral, religious, aesthetic, mathematical and scientific education. This is very much to be welcomed; for philosophers of education in Great Britain have tended to concentrate more on central issues. Although they have done a lot of work on moral education and on indoctrination, they have tended to neglect the other spheres of education dealt with by this volume.

It is to be hoped, therefore, that this volume will be influential not only in continuing the controversy about the nature of education and of educational theory, but also in opening up discussion about more specialized forms of education. There has been a great deal of work, of course, in philosophy generally, on aesthetics, philosophy of religion, philosophy of mathematics and philosophy of science but little investigation of the educational implications of the positions adopted. The relevance of such detailed studies to problems of the curriculum is obvious enough. They fit very well into the concept of philosophy of education underlying the International Library which is to link established branches of philosophy with educational issues.

Preface

It seems advisable, in order to avoid possible misunderstanding, to explain our policy in compiling and editing this book. The intention was to collect together newly-written essays on the concept of education and related topics such as indoctrination and theory of education; and on aspects of education of particular interest, such as moral education, or which, as a matter of fact, are reflected prominently in the curricula of schools and colleges. The most regrettable omission, from this point of view, relates to history and the social sciences. Contributors were informed of this general plan but beyond that were left to develop their own views in their own ways. Though contributors therefore share roughly the same view of philosophy and roughly the same view of education, since all are writing within the same philosophic and educational traditions, no further agreement than this suggests is to be expected from them. Indeed we are of the opinion that the philosophy of education is an embryonic field of enquiry in which no orthodoxies have been established. It would be a mistake therefore to expect the essays to support one another in dealing with different aspects of a single underlying theme.

G. L.
D. J. O'C.

Acknowledgments

We would like to thank all the contributors for their chapters.

Early versions of Professor O'Connor's and Professor Hirst's papers were published in *Proceedings of the Annual Conference, Philosophy of Education Society of Great Britain*, 6 (1), January 1972, reprinted here with the permission of the editors and Messrs Blackwell.

Professor Daveney's paper is an amended version of an inaugural lecture published by the University of Exeter; we are grateful to the university for permission to include it here. An early version of Mr Langford's paper 'Education and values' was read at a meeting of the London branch of the Philosophy of Education Society of Great Britain in March 1972.

Education

part **I**

The concept of education   I

Glenn Langford

I

In this chapter my main concern will be to elaborate and defend the view that to become educated is to learn to be a person: I am therefore offering a definition of the words 'to become educated'. My reasons for concentrating on this phrase rather than on the word 'education' will, I hope, become apparent in due course; later I will also say a little about what one is doing in offering a definition of this sort.

I will begin by making a distinction between *formal* and *informal education*. In *formal education* two parties may be distinguished, one of whom, the teacher, accepts responsibility for the education of the other, the pupil. *Informal education* is defined negatively as education in which this condition is not met. In these definitions the word 'education' is left undefined; this is in order at this stage. I would like to make two points about the definition of formal education. First, it points to what is sometimes called a logical or conceptual connection between formal education and teaching, in that the definition of formal education mentions teachers, i.e. those whose role it is to teach. By contrast there is no such connection in the case of informal education. Second, the word 'responsibility' included in the definition is ambiguous. In its primary sense, which I will call *causal responsibility*, an event or person may be responsible for the occurrence of a second event, involving a change in either a person or thing, in the sense that it causes or brings it about. The second sense of responsibility is that of being held accountable for what one is causally responsible for; I will call this *social responsibility*. To say that somebody is socially responsible for some happening pre-supposes, or takes for granted, that that person was causally re-sponsible for what happened, and suggests that they are liable to praise or blame for what they did. Social responsibility is attributed only to people; it makes no sense to attribute it to natural events. For example we might say either that the cloudburst was responsible for the flooding of the road or that Albert, by leaving the bath taps running, was responsible for flooding the bathroom; but only Albert, and not the cloudburst, could be held socially responsible for the flooding which occurred. Social responsibility arises in a

3

number of different ways. A person may be morally accountable for certain of his actions in being a member of a particular moral community; he may be legally responsible in being a member of a particular legal community, i.e, a citizen of a sovereign state; or he may acquire additional responsibilities in accepting or coming to occupy a particular role such as that of teacher or parent. To say then that in formal education the teacher accepts responsibility for the education of others is to presuppose or take for granted that teachers are, typically, causally responsible for the education of their pupils and to assert that in accepting the role of a teacher they have accepted social responsibility for bringing about that education.

Having distinguished between formal and informal education I will now look more closely at formal education. 'Formal education', I suggest, is the name of the purposive, self-conscious practical activity which goes on in schools and other educational institutions. The word 'name' is not used here simply as a synonym for 'word'; it is used deliberately to suggest that the phrase 'formal education' normally functions as a referring expression. For example to say that the education (i.e. the formal education) in this town is not very good is to refer to, or talk about, the practical activity referred to above, and to say of it that it is not very good.

The suggestion that education is the name of a practical activity relies on the notion of an activity. This is a complex notion and I will try to indicate the main elements in it by means of a diagram (see Figure 1).

| *things that people do* (as contrasted with things that happen to them) | *act or perform actions* Intention involved: bringing about change. Example: sharpening pencils as a result of which pencils become sharp | *activities* actions and observation are grouped together in more complex activities by reference to their overall purpose as either: | *theoretical activities* Overall purpose: to discover truth. Examples: physics, psychology |
| | *observe or make observations* Intention involved: finding out what is the case. Example: watching John, so finding out that he is digging his pencil into his neighbour's back | | *practical activities* Overall purpose: to bring about change. Examples: gardening, farming, teaching |

Figure 1

4

This schema for 'activity' covers much philosophical ground with unavoidable brevity. Some points must, however, be made. First, it is concerned with the things which people do *as persons*; and these include both performing actions and making observations. On my view the most important of the differences between actions and observations lies in the intention with which they are done. In acting the intention is practical; it is to bring about change. In observing the intention is theoretical; it is to discover what is the case. In daily life action and observation are inextricably interwoven; when people do things they do not in a temporal sense first observe and then act; rather both action and observation continue throughout the period of their activity. Moreover, although this may be a contingent matter so far as observation is concerned, actions are necessarily monitored by observation; nothing would count as an action, as understood here, unless what was done was based on the person's observation of the situation in which he acted. Second, many, though not all, of the things which people do form part of some more or less elaborate plan or pattern of activity in which the person is engaged. Individual actions and observations, each picked out by its own immediate goal or intention, form part of some more general, temporally extended activity. The more general activity itself has an overall purpose, and the actions and observations which form its parts are seen as parts in virtue of their contribution to that purpose. Activities themselves are divided into either theoretical or practical, insofar as they aim at truth or at change. Both theoretical and practical activities involve both actions and observations; this follows from the remarks made above about the intimate relation between action and observation. It would in any case be obvious in the case of practical activities, since change would not be purposive if not based on knowledge of the relevant facts. In the case of theoretical activities also the search for truth is often overtly active in, for example, changing the facts experimentally in order to observe the consequences of such change. Third, there is no reason to expect any particular human activity to be either wholly theoretical with no practical taint, or wholly practical with no theoretical taint. For example, scientific experiments, though aimed at truth, do incidentally change things. Conversely, experience gained in pursuing practical ends is often used as a guide to future practice. This is especially the case in social activities such as education, in which experimenters have difficulty in controlling variables and face moral objections about gambling with individuals' futures. But guidance is sought for educational practice through pilot schemes such as 'experimental' schools and through comparative study of practice elsewhere. Fourth, the use of the term 'intention'

5

in connection with actions and observations and the term 'purpose' in connection with theoretical and practical activities is intended to mark only the restricted scope of the former. A particular action or observation is undertaken with the intention of achieving some immediate end, such as putting a usable point on a pencil or seeing what John is up to. Both, however, may form part of a more complex activity such as teaching in being directed to a common, though more remote, end which I have called the overall purpose of the activity. Finally, the diagram may suggest an atomistic view of an activity, according to which individual actions and observations retain their individuality unmodified in joining together to form activities. If so this is misleading; the overall purpose of the activity, which provides its principle of unity, is reflected in its parts. This point is developed in the next paragraph. 'Formal education', then, is the name of an activity distinguished from other activities by its overall purpose; and that purpose is that someone should become educated. Since its purpose is to bring about change, it is a practical and not a theoretical activity. To say that it is an activity which is undertaken self-consciously adds little except, perhaps, to suggest that the active participants in it are, to some extent at least, aware of or have knowledge of that purpose. It should, I hope, now be clear why I suggested earlier that it is primarily the phrase 'to become educated' which requires elucidation rather than the word 'education' itself; 'education' is the name of a practical activity the unity of which depends on its overall purpose, and that purpose is that somebody should become educated.

This is a suitable place to consider briefly what one is doing in offering a definition of the phrase 'to become educated'. It follows from what I have said that my intention is to provide an account of what those engaged in the practical activity of formal education see themselves as doing. It also follows, insofar as that activity is undertaken self-consciously, that those best qualified to provide such an account are those actively engaged in the activity itself; the provision of such an account by a philosopher therefore requires explanation. This lies, I think, in the fact that the activity of education is a sophisticated and complex one. Those engaged in it may be conscious of the fact that their practice is unified in serving an overall purpose without being as clear as they might wish as to what that purpose is. Therefore, though teachers do in a sense know what they are doing in acting as teachers it does not follow that they will find it easy to give explicit expression to their knowledge. It is relatively easy to formulate and express proximate goals; indeed some intentions are so obvious that they cannot be expressed without triviality. The immediate intention of a teacher correcting a child's spelling, for example, is simply to correct the child's spelling; the description of what is done and of the intention with which it is done are the same. A teacher may, however, describe what he is doing from either a very limited perspective, as in this example, or from a broader point of view. He may, for example say that he is sharpening pencils; teaching children to form their letters correctly; teaching them to write; or teaching them to express themselves in writing. If so one can say that the purpose of sharpening the pencils or correcting the spelling is to teach the children to express themselves in writing; and this would not be a trivial thing to say. The teacher's immediate intention in sharpening the pencils and in correcting the spelling were quite different; the difference, indeed, between sharpening pencils and correcting spelling. The two actions are related, however, in sharing a common purpose and, therefore, forming part of the same activity. It is only when that purpose is understood that the individual actions which are combined in the activity become intelligible to us and lose the appearance of triviality which they possess when seen as independent atoms of activity.

It cannot be claimed that the move from sharpening pencils to teaching children to express themselves in writing presents special difficulty. Other moves, such as that from correcting sums to the achievement of numeracy, might be more difficult to spell out. My present concern is with the overall purpose which lies behind, and gives unity to, all educational activities; and it is notoriously difficult to express this explicitly and clearly. The test of the accuracy of an account of it lies in the reaction to it of those engaged in the activity itself, i.e. of those whose purposes it claims to express. There may, of course, be genuine and substantial disagreement amongst professional teachers, some thinking of their role as close to that of a social worker whereas others think of it in a more traditional way. Since the overall purpose of an activity serves also as a principle of relevance governing the selection of proximate goals such a difference would be reflected in radical disagreement about the adoption and relative priority of such goals, and about the way in which their choice is to be justified. Teachers do in fact disagree about the extent of their concern, as teachers, with such things as children's mental and physical welfare and juvenile delinquency. If such disagreement were sufficiently deep-rooted one would have to conclude, I think, that there is no single activity referred to by the word 'education'. This is a possibility which ought to be borne in mind, though I will not consider it further here. If such disagreements do exist then clearly they cannot be resolved by philosophical analysis, or by saying what the word 'education' *really* means,

7

though the nature of the disagreement may be clarified by analysis. Whether or not the details of my own account of what it is to be educated are correct, *some* view of the overall purpose of education is necessary if anything is to count as a specifically educational reason for doing anything. It is therefore of the greatest practical importance that views of that overall purpose should be given as explicit expression as possible.

Formal education, then, is the name of a practical activity involving two parties, one of whom, the teacher, accepts responsibility for the education of the other, the pupil. The overall purpose which gives this activity its unity is that of the teacher, while those to be educated are the pupils. The words 'teacher' and 'pupil' here refer to roles rather than individuals. In Hardy's novel *Jude the Obscure*, for example, Jude Fawley acquired most of his education whilst driving his aunt's bread cart in the lanes and by-roads near Marygreen.

> As soon as the horse had learnt the road and the houses at
> which he was to pause awhile, the boy, seated in front, would
> slip the reins over his arm, ingeniously fix open, by means of a
> strap attached to the tilt, the volume he was reading, spread
> the dictionary on his knees, and plunge into the simpler
> passages from Caesar, Virgil, or Horace . . .

Jude was both student and teacher; his education was therefore formal, since he accepted responsibility for it himself, although, since the colleges at Christminster would have nothing to do with him, it took place outside the explicit institutional arrangements normally involved in formal education.

Earlier I contrasted formal education, in which two parties could be distinguished, with informal education in which this condition was not met. The party which remains I will call the pupil, although since 'teacher' and 'pupil' have been used as correlative terms this is strictly inappropriate. Since the purpose which lends formal education its unity is that of the teacher, informal education is not an activity. It is possible to speak of it as education, however, because the results which teachers consciously and systematically seek to achieve may occur in the absence of, or even in despite of, their efforts. An analogy may make this clear. Farming is a practical activity the point of which is to produce food and other organic raw materials. It is possible, however, to have the end product of farming without the farming. A simple gathering community, for example, may subsist on the fruit, nuts, edible roots and small animals which are freely available in its locality. As numbers increase, however, the need for food may become too great to be satisfied in this way, and organized efforts become necessary to see that supplies are adequate. Though it would be appropriate to speak of farm produce only in the latter case, what was produced might differ only in quantity from the food which was originally available freely. Similarly in a simple society formal education may be unnecessary: children learn informally what they need to know in order to become fully-fledged members of that society. In a complex modern society, however, we cannot assume that this will be so, and, accordingly, make specific arrangements directed to that end. The introduction of such arrangements necessarily brings with it some awareness of the ends towards which they are directed. With such awareness comes the possibility of reflection about the ends to be pursued; and with reflection, in turn, the possibility of discarding some ends, of selecting others as of high priority, and of introducing new ones. Once this position is reached, ends can be identified as educational, and it becomes possible to see that the same results occur informally. The most interesting possibility is that some things, such as learning to talk, normally occur informally; but exceptionally may not do so, or may do so only inadequately, for example in the case of children suffering from a disability such as deafness, very low intelligence, or extreme emotional withdrawal. It is then considered important, that is educationally important, to provide special provision; indeed, the phrase 'special education' is used in this connection.

There is, then, room for a concept of informal education in educational discourse in order to refer to the achievement of educational ends outside the formal educational system. The most important area involved is probably that of the family, especially the infant's contact with his parents and, later, with siblings and children of neighbouring families. I do not think it is stretching language unduly to apply the term 'education' to infants. If it is, then I think that there is a strong case for changing the concept of education to allow it, based on the psychological and sociological evidence of the importance of the very early years of a child's life for both intellectual and social development. This is a case in which our concepts either have been or should be influenced by empirical evidence. One reason for making provision, within educational discourse, for talking about this stage of a child's development is that chance provision, though it may in favoured circumstances excel the best efforts of art. is unevenly distributed and may be almost wholly absent. Most homes, for example, provide an adequate opportunity for a normal child to acquire language; in others, however, the opportunity offered may be less than, on reflection, is thought desirable in the light of modern social ideals of equality. If

9

so there is a case for extending institutional provision in the form, for example, of nursery schools.

What is now required is an analysis of 'becoming educated' which is relevant to both formal and informal education; as I have already indicated my suggestion is that to become educated is to learn to be a person. Of the terms contained in this definition, the concept of a person has, one way or another, attracted a great deal of attention in the history of philosophy. 'Learning' has not itself attracted attention; but, as I shall explain later, my principal point about 'learning' is that it is an epistemological concept; and philosophers have always concerned themselves with questions about knowledge. Since any attempt to answer the question 'what is learning?' or 'what is a person?' is bound to be philosophically controversial, it is tempting to stop at this point, leaving the proposed definition of becoming educated as a sort of philosophical blank cheque. For it would be possible for two people to accept the proposed definition whilst disagreeing radically about the further analysis of the terms contained in it. I think it is desirable, however, that anyone who accepts such a definition should at least indicate their commitment on the main philosophical issues even if detailed consideration is not possible. In section II, therefore, I will consider the concept of a person and in section III the concept of learning.

II

One way of cataloguing the sorts of things which the world contains is to divide them into persons on the one hand and physical objects, or mere things, on the other. The catalogue would probably be incomplete unless it included also the relations which hold between things; but this is a complication which can be ignored for the moment. There is, then, a fundamental contrast between persons and physical objects or mere things; the philosophical problem is to say what that contrast is.

Two things seem obvious; first, that persons are conscious and capable of thought; and second, that persons are agents and capable of rational choice. I will say a little about each of these in turn. To say that persons are conscious is to say not merely that they experience sensations such as pains and tickles but also that they are conscious of, or aware of, their environments. Consciousness is consciousness *of* something and, moreover, of something as being of a certain sort; to put it another way, a person's awareness of his environment is conceptually structured. To stress the fact that such awareness involves the use by a person of his eyes, ears and sense of touch, it might be called perceptual awareness; although, importantly, persons are also conscious of, or aware of, what they are doing. In being conscious in this way persons form beliefs about the world they live in; a belief is something like an awareness of how the world is which is remembered after the initial encounter. In forming beliefs persons come to live in a more extended time span and to form an increasingly comprehensive and complex picture of the world. A principal feature of that complexity has already been indicated: the distinction between persons and mere things. Persons become aware of a physical world consisting of physical objects and the relations between them and of a social world consisting of persons and the relations between them. Though change occurs in both worlds, it occurs only against a background of relative stability; both physical objects and persons retain their individual identities for varying periods despite changes in their surroundings and minor changes to themselves. A man, for example, remains the same person even though the community in which he lives changes and he himself grows older. Persons also come to distinguish between their experience of the world and the world they experience; the things of which they have experience, the particular things which the world contains, are thought of as continuing to exist independently of their observation of them. If this were not so a person's awareness of how the world is could not extend beyond his immediate experience of it; belief, as defined above, would be impossible. Finally persons come to form a conception of themselves as the subject of those experiences; that is, of themselves as persons living among persons.

The second thing about persons is that they are agents and as such capable of rational choice. In general to act is to act on something and so to change it; in this broad sense physical bodies act on one another, bringing about mutual change. Persons, however, have some conception of the world in which and on which they act; they are able to anticipate the changes which their actions will bring about and act with the intention, which may be consciously formulated, of doing so. They are therefore able to bring about changes relevant to their wants, needs and interests. They choose to bring about one state of affairs rather than another because they have a reason for doing so.

We think, then, of persons as both centres of consciousness and as agents. We think also that our treatment of persons should differ radically from our treatment of what, by contrast, we regard as mere things; it is persons to whom we accord respect and who may properly be said to possess rights. Respect for persons is based on the belief that persons are unique centres of consciousness or perspectives on the world having a sense of their own identity as persons.

Similarly, persons are held responsible for what they do; that is, they are held socially responsible for what they are causally responsible for insofar as they fail to accord to others the respect due to them. Our willingness to ascribe responsibility to persons but not to animals, plants or inanimate objects is based on the belief that persons are capable of consciously controlling the changes they bring about. Consequently to refuse to hold someone responsible for what they do, or to refuse to respect them, is by implication to withhold from them the status of a person.

This necessarily brief account of what a person is stands in need of considerable expansion; even so, it is incomplete. No mention, for example, has been made of the way in which persons respond to encountered situations not by trying to change them but with an internal emotional response; or of the way beliefs become articulated in language. Nevertheless the account must suffice for the present purpose, which is primarily to indicate a direction of philosophical commitment.

This account of what a person is follows Descartes in its emphasis on consciousness or thought. On Descartes's view, however, a person may come to know of his own existence as a person by reflecting on the fact that he thinks or is conscious. Since to reflect is to think, and since persons are characterized as thinking beings, a person cannot doubt that he exists. This suggests two things: first, that an entity either thinks and is therefore a person or it does not think and therefore is not a person, rather as a switch is either on or off, so that being a person is not a matter of degree; and second, that persons are isolated individuals who may, perhaps, enter relations with others but who do not need to do so in order to be persons. The Cartesian view, therefore, suggests a sharp break between men and other animals. On my view, however, being conscious is not an all or nothing affair; it is a matter of degree, since the conceptual scheme by means of which experiences are structured may be simple, making few distinctions, or it may be sophisticated and complex. One may think, with Russell, that an amoeba might regard the use of the word 'sophisticated' as question begging, but it is relevant that the amoeba is not equipped to argue the matter. I have already mentioned one important direction of complexity: the distinction between physical objects and persons. I am inclined to stipulate that in order to be a person one must not merely be conscious but also think of oneself and others as persons; and one cannot think of oneself as a person unless one is prepared to think also of others as persons. Both F. H. Bradley and, more recently, Professor P. F. Strawson offer arguments for this conclusion. If this is so then persons are primarily social, not isolated, individuals, in that in order to be persons they necessarily have to enter into relations with other persons. This may involve no more than the recognition that persons other than themselves may exist; but, since other persons do exist, it is likely to involve much more. It may involve a shared conception of the world—for example a shared concept of a person—or shared purposes as when persons co-operate to bring about common ends, as in formal education. This, in essence, was the Greek view of persons as citizens.

From what I have said it will be obvious that the concept of a person is not that of a particular biological species. Animals, including men, are grouped into species on the basis of bodily and anatomical form and of their ability to produce viable offspring and, therefore, to reproduce their kind. Locke, for example, contrasted persons, or 'rational selves', with men, those of a certain bodily form. 'When the abbot of Saint Martin was born', he says, 'he had so little the figure of a man, that it bespake him rather a monster.' But, Locke comments, 'there can be no reason given why, if the lineaments of his face had been altered, a rational soul could not have been lodged in him.' Indeed, since in due course he became the abbot of Saint Martin, a rational soul presumably was lodged in him. Similarly when, in Kafka's short story 'Metamorphosis' Gregor Samsa awoke one morning to find that he had changed into a large beetle, he was clearly no longer a man, since he had changed into a beetle. But his personality was unchanged, at least at first; he remained the same person. On the other hand, as Locke points out, 'some, though of approved shape, are never capable of as much appearance of reason all their lives as is to be found in an ape, or an elephant, and never give any sign of being acted by a rational soul.' The concept of a person, therefore, is not that of a member of the biological species *man*. Though we tend to assume that all men, and only men, are in fact persons, it follows that a rational parrot would be a person but not a man; and that an idiot would be a man but not a person. A man might be defined as a hairless ape or a featherless biped or in some such way; the precise definition to be adopted is a question for biology. Here I have been concerned with the philosophically problematic question of what a person is.

The contrast between men and persons lends support to the view, expressed earlier, that being a person is a matter of degree. Since 'men' are defined in biological terms it is obvious that men come into existence by being born. New-born babies, however, are not, strictly, persons in the relevant sense, though they normally possess the capacity to become persons; they have to learn to be persons. It is this fact which provides the scope and need for education. Since learning takes time it follows that the process of becoming a person is a gradual one and, therefore, that being a person is a matter of degree.

This conclusion, however, seems to be inconsistent with the fact that, whereas we are willing to diminish the extent to which we hold persons responsible, for example young children and those acting under stress or psychological compulsion, we are unwilling to qualify or reduce the respect due to them as persons. We regard even new-born babies, idiots and, on some views, foetuses as persons even though they do not possess the complex, conceptually structured awareness of the world which, according to my definition, they need in order to qualify as persons. This might be taken as grounds for saying that an individual either is, or is not, a person and, therefore, that being a person is not a matter of degree.

Though I share the liberal attitudes which this way of thinking reflects, I think it is extremely difficult to justify in any but a pragmatic way. I will try to bring out what I mean by this by considering the difficulties involved in applying a rule prohibiting vehicles in the park. The problem is to decide which things are vehicles and therefore are to be refused entry to the park. Cars and motor-bikes clearly are vehicles but other cases are less obvious; cases which might be thought doubtful include go-carts, children's push chairs and scooters, pogo sticks and wheel-barrows. Therefore, though there are some things which clearly are vehicles and some which clearly are not, other cases are doubtful. If we draw up a list of the features which lead us to say that something is a vehicle we will see that motor-cars, perhaps, possess all of them—they are mechanical, move about on wheels, are used for transport, are self-propelled and so on—whereas pogo sticks possess only one. One vehicle may therefore differ considerably from another and whereas we have no hesitation in calling the first a vehicle, we agree to call the second a vehicle only after hesitation and thought. Once the decision is made, however, both are treated alike in being excluded from the park. For the purpose of the rule everything must be treated as though it either is or is not a vehicle and either admitted or refused admittance to the park.

I suggest that the position with regard to persons is analogous. One person differs from another just as much as one vehicle differs from another. There is no sharp line between persons and mere brutes any more than there is between steamrollers and pogo sticks. In the case of persons we tend in practice to adopt a biological criterion and assume that one man is as much a person as any other; this may be justified by pointing out that any attempt to discriminate rationally would inevitably lead to abuse. It is also convenient since it is almost always clear whether something is or is not a man; unnatural unions do not produce viable offspring and chance mutations are rare. It has some bizarre consequences; for example a child born without a cerebral cortex is regarded as a person whereas a chimpanzee, which may have the sensitivity and intelligence of a normal three-year-old child, is not. In the present connection what is most relevant is the impression which this practice produces that there is a sharp line between persons and those who are not persons; it is this impression which I have been trying to explain.

Not everybody, I am sure, will accept this explanation; they will insist that it is not a question of agreeing to regard one man as though he is as much a person as any other; each person really is as much a person as any other, including of course new-born babies, idiots and, possibly, foetuses. It is not simply a question of having to draw a line somewhere and allowing a generous margin for error; all men are, equally, persons. I find the claim that all persons are equal, in some non-empirical sense, unintelligible, unless understood as prescribing the practice I have outlined. I conclude, therefore, that no intelligible objection, based on the way we ordinarily think and talk, can be sustained against the view that to be a person is a matter of degree. On my view we agree to treat every man as if he were as much a person as any other; though, since being a person is a matter of degree, this is not really so.

This conclusion is relevant to what might be thought of as a difficulty for my account of education. We do occasionally refer to persons as uneducated; but if, as I have suggested, to become educated is to learn to be a person, the idea of an uneducated person is, on the face of it, self-contradictory. If, however, being a person is a matter of degree, the phrase 'uneducated person' can be taken as meaning either 'a relatively uneducated person' or, even more straightforwardly, 'a person who has not had the benefit of a formal education'. A serf in Czarist Russia, for example, might be uneducated relative to the standards appropriate to a landowner, but not, surely, relative to the animals in the forest.

On the other hand allowance must be made for the fact that we speak of people as continuing to mature after their education would be said to have been completed. There is, it is true, an acceptable sense in which a person of any age may be said to be continuing his education. Formal education may be continued in adult life by extra-mural classes or at the Open University; and what Jude Fawley did can be done at any age. Similarly, the knowledge and experience which a newly-qualified teacher or doctor gains when he begins to practise his profession may be regarded as an informal continuation of his education. But not all personal development can be looked on in this way. For example, the sort of maturity which allows a writer or painter to produce his best work only late in life cannot be attributed to education. Moral maturity, too—for example the maturity which led to Rommel's eventual disillusionment with Hitler—is not a product of education. Education may make creative living possible; it cannot dictate the form it should take. It provides the social heritage without which a person would not be a person; but the use to be made of that heritage must be left open in a society which allows for the possibility of change and progress.

III

To become educated is to learn to be a person. I have said a little about what I think a person is. Before turning to the concept of learning I will make some factual remarks about human learning.

Most animals are born with complete, fixed behavioural repertoires or with the ability to learn to do only a limited number of specific things such as fly or build nests. They learn to do these things quickly and easily once the appropriate physiological state is reached but are very limited in their ability to learn anything else. This is a crude generalization which is more accurate for some species, for example most birds, than for others, such as chimpanzees and monkeys. Human beings—that is, members of the species *man*—on the other hand are able to do very little when first born but possess the ability which itself matures to learn to do a great variety of things. This difference between specific and non-specific learning abilities is of the greatest importance, though it does not seem to be reflected in the concept of learning itself. In saying what a person is I have already tried to describe the basic minimum which has to be learnt before a man becomes a person; very briefly, all persons have to acquire the concepts of a physical object and a person. The learning involved starts, for the normal child, as soon as it is born. What has to be learnt is complex; it is not simply a matter of learning to respond differentially to different stimuli currently present. For example I have suggested that what is basic to the concept of a physical object is continued existence whilst unobserved. (The hardness, or impenetrability, of some objects is relatively unimportant.) It also follows from this that the concept of a physical object involves that of a person, i.e. of one who is not currently observing the object in question. What has to be learnt, indeed, is the complex of concepts and beliefs which we have about the physical and social worlds in which we live. It is obvious therefore that there is room for big differences in the content of what is learnt. Men differ in the details of what they learn and, consequently, in the sort of persons which they become and the sort of societies which they form. The ability to learn makes possible both the richness and the variety of human life. It also provides both the scope and need for education, in which differing ideals of the sort of person it is desirable to become are reflected.

The content and extent of what is learnt by a particular person will depend on a variety of factors in addition to the opportunities offered to him. The most important fact is individual genetic differences in ability to learn. It is fashionably 'liberal' to deny this, though the classical liberalism of John Stuart Mill does not require anyone to deny well-supported empirical facts because they are inconsistent with a dogmatically held 'liberal' position. Other genetic differences affect aspects of personality, such as emotional stability, though it is not easy to distinguish the effects of learning and heredity. At the moment genetic factors are regarded as outside human control, though one day genetic engineering may supplement education in consciously producing certain sorts of person rather than others.

I will turn now to the concept of learning. First, it is obvious that it is a psychological concept. Psychological concepts are, roughly, those introduced into language to talk about people rather than physical objects; they include, for example, 'thinking', 'believing', 'wanting', 'hoping', 'trying' and so on. They are, therefore, part of ordinary, everyday language; they are not confined to the language used by psychologists in their attempts to understand human behaviour scientifically.

Psychologists do use psychological terms, of course, often borrowing them from ordinary language. When they do so, however, they often change or modify their meaning in accordance with their own theoretical requirements. One such requirement is that the terms should be applicable to animals, which are the subjects of many psychological experiments. But it might be asked whether it makes sense to say that animals other than man think, believe, want, hope, try and so on. We do apply these terms to animals; for example, we might say that a beetle which has fallen into a smooth-sided bowl was trying to get out. But though to speak in this way would not be to misuse language, it would be a mistake to suppose that beetles try to do things in the sense in which people do. To say that a person is trying to do something means, roughly, that he has some conception of what he is trying to do, that he wants to do it, that he realizes that he cannot do it without special effort and that he is supplying that effort. If, therefore, somebody insists that the beetle is trying to get out of the bowl in exactly the same sense as a person might be said to try to get out of prison, he is making a mistake either about the concept of trying or about the facts concerning beetles. He is either unaware of the full conditions which have to be satisfied before someone may properly be said to be trying; or is mistaken in supposing that beetles ever satisfy them. Psychologists and biologists have therefore tended to modify the meanings of the psychological terms which they have borrowed from ordinary language so that their application to animals does not involve them in unjustifiable assumptions.

Something of this sort has happened in the case of 'learning'. The noun 'learning' applies to typically human skills and accomplishments, such as knowledge of Roman history or the ability to read classical Greek; and a learned man is one who has such skills and accomplishments. There is, therefore, little temptation to speak of animals as learned; it is very obvious, even to the most unsophisticated observer, that pigs know nothing of history and cannot read. Animals do have their own skills and accomplishments; but it was not realized until very recently that many of them are acquired in a manner which is similar to, if not identical with, that in which human learning is acquired. The fact that a great deal of animal behaviour is learnt, and its importance for their survival, was an empirical discovery made under the influence of Darwinism. It was probably a consequence of this discovery, rather than because it initially seemed natural to do so, that the concept of learning came to be applied extensively to animals. When this happened it quickly became a technical term, becoming theory-laden and acquiring a connection with the biological concept of adaptation. In its technical sense the word 'learning' has come to refer to the family of processes whereby animals adapt their behaviour to changes in the environment in ways which increase their chances of survival. The technical sense of 'learning' is of course not unrelated to that used in ordinary speech; it was based on it and, no doubt, has subsequently influenced it. Nevertheless the two senses are different. Here I am primarily concerned with the use of the term 'learning' in educational discourse, where it retains its unmodified, everyday meaning, rather than in psychology and biology; though the specialized use of the term is instructive.

My first point, then, is that 'learning' is a psychological concept, both as it occurs within psychology and in the non-technical sense relevant to education. Second, learning is a temporal process involving a change in the learner. To say that somebody has learnt something is to compare, at least implicitly, some aspect of their condition after learning has taken place with that before it. It follows that you cannot learn to do what you can do already, just as you cannot want what you already have. Once you have learnt to ride a bicycle or to speak French you cannot learn to do so again unless you have first forgotten what you have learnt. You can of course become a more skilful cyclist or learn new French words or phrases; but that does not involve learning what you can do already. Similarly an animal born able to swim cannot learn to swim, unless at some stage it loses the ability to do so. It is important, in this connection, not to confuse logical with psychological and physical possibility. Human beings can, logically, learn to control the rate at which their hearts beat though, as a matter of fact, most of them are unable to learn to do so.

Third, the change which takes place must not simply be a change in the state of the learner's body; it must be a change connected with the learner as a functioning, living organism or person. It is tempting to follow psychological practice and say that the change must be a change in behaviour; if so, however, 'behaviour' must be interpreted broadly to include skilled performances and ways of thinking about and looking at the world. Much human learning consists in the acquisition of beliefs, and beliefs cannot, on my view, be reduced to dispositions to act. What is clear is that though changes in behaviour may involve bodily changes, bodily changes themselves cannot be said to be learnt. For example, it may be necessary for a weight lifter, in the course of learning to lift heavy weights, to acquire good muscles. Nevertheless what he learns is how to lift heavy weights; he does not learn to have good muscles. Similarly, learning that the toads in Lake Titicaca are found nowhere else in the world may involve the establishment of certain neural connections; but what is learnt is that the toads in Lake Titicaca are unique and not to have those neural connections. Attempts by psychologists to define learning in terms of changes in neural circuits serve only to show how far the meaning of the term 'learning' in psychology has departed from its ordinary meaning, and the extent to which it has become theory-laden.

Fourth, 'learning' involves restrictions on the way in which the change is brought about. This condition is important for both the technical and non-technical concepts; but it is difficult to formulate precisely. Basically the change which occurs in learning must be a consequence of the learner's past experience; it must be related to the way the learner functioned in the past as a living organism or person. Since the effects of learning are contrasted with those of heredity, this condition is primarily intended to rule out changes due solely to the maturation of bodily organs and neural pathways; that is, changes which occur independently of the learner's inter-action with the environment.

We would probably be reluctant to say that learning had taken place if the change in the animal or person had been brought about solely by the use of drugs or surgery. For example, if an animal was injected with a drug which modified its nervous system in such a way that, thereafter, it avoided fire, we would be reluctant to say that it had learnt to avoid fire. Similarly if a child acquired mathematical competence by some form of direct physical, chemical or electrical interference with his brain, we could not deny that he had acquired that competence; but we would be reluctant to say that he had acquired it by a process of learning.

Both being injected with drugs and subjected to brain operations are, however, part of the person's interaction with the environment and, therefore, of their past experience in a broad sense. Changes brought about by them may be contrasted with those due to maturation. They can be excluded as learning processes only by a further requirement that the experience which brings about the change in the learner must be related to that change not simply in bringing it about but in some further way. It is not easy to state this requirement in a satisfactory way; the relationship must in some sense be a natural one. More precisely, the relationship must be internal in that the descriptions of what is learnt and of the way in . which it is learnt overlap in containing the same propositional core. This condition is easily satisfied in the case of learning that something is the case either by seeing or being told that it is so. For example, you may learn that the toads in Lake Titicaca are exceptionally large either by being told that they are or seeing them for yourself. What you are told or see is that the toads are large; what you learn, also, is that the toads are large. Similarly you may find that the toads in Lake Titicaca are good to eat by having them for dinner and finding that they are good to eat. It is worth noting, however, that you will learn that the toads are large by being told that they are only if you understand what you are told; and this will be so only if your experience in being told is conceptually structured in the relevant way. In the same way, you will learn that the toads in Lake Titicaca are good to eat by eating and enjoying them only if you have some conception of what you are doing in eating and enjoying them. A lion, for example, would not, in eating a zebra with whatever passes for enjoyment in lions, thereby learn that zebras are good to eat. It does not have the conceptually structured awareness of what it is doing that a person has; even if it has something corresponding to our conception of a zebra it certainly has nothing corresponding to our complex, though ill-defined, notion of 'good'.

It is less easy to see that the requirement that the way in which learning takes place must be internally related to what is learnt is satisfied in the case of learning to do something. What it amounts to in this case, however, is that you learn to do something by doing it, that is, by practice. It may be necessary, as a matter of fact, to do it repeatedly before learning takes place; or one practice, or trial, may be sufficient. In the case of drugs or surgery, however, there is no practice and this prevents competence acquired in this way from being said to have been learnt. Consideration of psychological paradigms of learning such as classical and operant conditioning, support the view that you learn to do something by doing it. For example, a hungry dog salivates in the presence of food; this behaviour is unlearnt and part of its inherited behavioural repertoire. In order to produce a conditioned response repeated presentations of food are paired with the sounding of a bell. Eventually the dog salivates if the bell is sounded even though no food is presented to it. The dog is then said to have become conditioned to salivate in response to the bell. It learns to salivate when the bell is sounded by repeatedly salivating when the bell is sounded. There is therefore a connection between the descriptions of what is learnt and of the way in which it is learnt. A more homely example is that of the animal which learns to avoid fire. It does this by touching something which is burning and, therefore, hot and immediately withdrawing, avoiding further contact with it; this is an unlearnt response. If it subsequently avoids fire without first getting burnt we would say that it has learnt to avoid fire. It therefore learns to avoid fire by avoiding fire.

The requirement that the description of what is learnt and of the way it is learnt should overlap in containing the same propositional core is therefore satisfied in the case of classical and operant conditioning. Indeed, in a sense it is more easily satisfied than in the case of learning that something is the case; for the dog being conditioned to salivate in response to the sound of a bell does not need to understand the description of what is learnt or of the way in which it is learnt. There is no requirement, in other words, that the experience by which learning is brought about should be conceptually structured in any way. The moral to be drawn from this is that animals which do not possess a conceptually structured awareness *can* learn in these ways; not, as philosophers are sometimes tempted to claim, that persons who do possess such a structured awareness *cannot* learn in this way. Later I will argue that the use of a conceptual scheme, and indeed its extension, *is* involved in what I will call typically human learning. This is a conclusion, however, which I will arrive at only indirectly by considering a paradox which seems to arise out of what I have already said.

To say that you can learn to do some things only by doing them verges on a paradox if what I said earlier is correct, i.e. that you cannot learn to do what you can do already. If you can learn to do arithmetic only by doing arithmetic and to swim only by swimming it seems as though it would be impossible to learn to do them. For if you can do arithmetic already you not merely do not need to learn to do it but cannot do so; and if you can swim already you cannot learn to swim. One way out would be to say that what you learn is not to do something which you could not do before, but to do what you could already do in new combinations and circumstances. The dog in the classical conditioning experiment, for example, was already able to salivate; what it learnt, therefore, was not to salivate but to salivate in response to the bell.

It could plausibly be argued that learning to swim also does not involve learning to move in wholly new ways; you were previously able to make all the movements involved in swimming and have to learn only to combine them in the appropriate way. But this cannot be generalized; many of the things which people learn to do are wholly new to them. This is especially so for the typically human learning most relevant to education, such as learning mathematics or how to speak a foreign language. Learning to make marks on paper with a pencil may involve no more than using existing skills in new ways—the ability to grasp things in the hand, to move the arm and use visual and tactual cues to orientate the movement precisely, and so on. A chimpanzee can learn to do this. But it would be absurd to argue that learning to set out a mathematical proof involves no more than using the existing skill of being able to make marks on paper in a new way.

The ability to learn things wholly new to them which people, but very few animals, possess, is very important from the point of view of education. Animal learning is, in general, specific; it is an ability to learn to do only a limited range of things. Human learning, by contrast, is non-specific; it is an ability to learn to do a virtually unlimited range of things. In terms of content rather than ability, the content of animal learning is closed; whereas the content of much human learning is open-ended. The paradox with which I am concerned arises most obviously in the case of open-ended learning.

People can learn to do some things by being told how to do them (i.e. by being told that this is the way to do them) or by seeing how to do them (i.e. by seeing that this is the way to do them). Teachers, for example, often tell or show their pupils how to do things. It is not an infallible method of bringing about learning, but it does succeed on occasion. No practice is necessary to bring about learning, although we would not admit that learning had taken place unless it was demonstrated in performance. No paradox arises, therefore in these cases.

This method of bringing about learning, however, is not effective, or not wholly effective, in other cases. It is in fact out of the question in cases in which the content of the learning is not merely new to the learner but wholly new; for example when a mathematician learns what the proof of a particular theorem is by discovering it for the first time. (I do not think that there is a separate 'discovery' meaning of 'learning'.) These cases require practice, and it is practice which gives rise to the paradox.

The paradox, I suggest, can be avoided only by introducing the notion of trying. When the content of the learning is open-ended, you learn to do something not by doing it but by trying to do it. I suggested earlier that to say that a person is trying to do something means, roughly, that he has some conception of what he is trying to do, that he wants to do it, that he realizes that he cannot do it without special effort and that he is supplying that effort. The most important point in the present context is that a person who is trying to do something has some conception of what he is trying to do. Children learn to do sums not by doing them but by trying to do them; though of course retention of what they have learnt may be achieved by doing them. The first step, therefore, in teaching children arithmetic is to give them some idea of what it is all about; only then will they be in a position to learn to do arithmetic by trying to do arithmetic. How this is to be achieved is a psychological question, but it seems obvious that verbal explanations have an important part to play. It is clear therefore that a great deal of typically human learning involves consciousness in the sense in which persons were said earlier to be conscious of, or have a conceptually structured awareness of, themselves and their environments, whether what is learnt is that something is the case or how to do something.

A further question which might be raised is whether the learner is also necessarily conscious or aware of the fact that he is learning what he is learning and, therefore, is able to report that he is engaged in learning it. But though the introduction of notions like trying suggest this, it would be quite implausible to claim that this was so. Self-consciousness is not involved in what is called incidental learning. Indeed, some human learning may take the form of operant or classical conditioning in which consciousness is not in any way involved.

I have suggested that both learning that something is the case and learning to do something of a typically human sort, such as arithmetic, both involve concepts. Concepts, too, have to be learnt; or rather persons have to learn to structure their thought using concepts. Can the requirement that the way in which learning occurs must be related to what is learnt be satisfied in this case also? To answer this question one would need a description of the way in which young children acquire concepts; to that extent it is a factual question. If they acquire them wholly through a process of maturation—independently of experience—then they do not learn them at all. If they learn them through experience, then the relevant experience almost certainly consists, at least in part, of direct acquaintance with instances of the things the concept of which is being acquired. This is simply to say that persons acquire the concepts of physical objects such as chairs, plates, etc. partly through contact with the relevant objects, the concept of a person through contact with persons, and so on. If this is so, then again there is an internal connection between the descriptions of what is learnt and of the way in which it is learnt. If it is not so, then concepts are not learnt but acquired in some other way, analogous to brain surgery or drugs, such as absorbed through mother's milk.

To summarize, my fourth point is that the change which occurs in learning must be a consequence of the learner's past experience. Also, in order to exclude changes due to drugs, brain surgery, etc. the experience which brings about the change in the learner must also be naturally or internally related to the change, so that the descriptions of what is learnt and of the way in which it is learnt share the same propositional core.

My fifth and final point is that the concept of learning is an epistemological one. Since my first point was that it is also a psychological one, this means that it is both epistemological and psychological. There is no reason why this should not be so; other concepts share this feature, such as those of belief, seeing and understanding.

To make this point is to direct attention from the process of learning to its content. To talk of the content of learning is not, quite, to talk about the change brought about in learning, though the two things are closely related. If I learn that the toads in Lake Titicaca are good to eat, the change which occurs in me is that I now believe something—that the toads in Lake Titicaca are good to eat—which I did not believe before. The change which occurs when learning takes place is personal; it is a change in the learner. The content of learning is not personal in this way; what I learn—that is, the content of my learning—is that the toads in Lake Titicaca are good to eat. And this is so whether anyone learns that it is so or remains in ignorance of it. The content of learning does not change in being learnt, so that several people can learn the same thing. Since to describe the change which occurs in learning necessarily involves stating the content of the learning, it may seem pointless to insist on this distinction. It does, however, mark a difference of approach; to talk of the content of learning rather than the change which occurs in the learner is to adopt an epistemological rather than a psychological approach.

Psychologists, not surprisingly, are interested in the psychological aspects of learning; that is, in the processes whereby the changes involved in learning take place. They are not interested in the content of learning as such; consequently many of the learning tasks which they set their subjects are trivial, such as, for example, the sequence: 'biv, ril, tig, tud, mov, laz'. Even in this case the learning has a content, the sequence just quoted; and the psychologist cannot say that learning has taken place unless it has been mastered. Nevertheless the direction of interest in psychology may be reflected in the technical concept of learning, which may have no epistemological implications at all. This would be so, for example, if 'learning' is *defined* in terms of the formation of neural circuits or receptor-effector links, or in terms of the processes involved in experimentally defined paradigms such as classical or operant conditioning.

So far as the non-technical concept of learning is concerned, however, the epistemological aspect is of primary importance. An important part of what we say when we say that someone has learnt something concerns the content of their learning. If the content of the learning is a belief the proposition expressing the belief must be true; if it is a performance, that performance must be skilled, reflecting an ability on the part of the performer. Accordingly a person could not be said to have learnt that the toads in Lake Titicaca are good to eat if in fact they are inedible. Similarly a person could not be said to have learnt to swim if, after jumping in at the deep end, he simply thrashed about and drowned. Nor does this point depend on the meaning of the word 'swim'. Thrashing about and drowning is of course not swimming; but neither is it any other sort of skill.

Some support for this view of 'learning' is provided by the *Concise Oxford Dictionary*; the entry for 'learn' begins: 'Get knowledge of (subject) or skill in (art etc.) by study, experience or being taught.' Indeed, insofar as acquaintance with the relevant evidence is a condition of knowledge it sets the epistemological standard higher than I have been prepared to. The epistemological condition is also prominent in what might be called 'discovery contexts', which range from learning that your long forgotten uncle in Australia has left you a fortune to learning about the effects of insecticides on the balance of nature or how to send a rocket to the moon.

Whether a belief is true, or a performance skilled, and whether, therefore, learning can be said to have taken place, is independent of the circumstances in which the belief or skill was acquired. Beliefs are true if what is believed is in fact the case. For example, the belief that the toads in Lake Titicaca have no natural predators is true if in fact the toads in Lake Titicaca have no natural predators. And whether the toads in Lake Titicaca have any natural predators can be decided, ultimately, only by studying the toads in Lake Titicaca. Whether someone who has come to believe this may properly be said to have learnt anything, therefore, depends not merely on facts about that person such as the way in which the belief was acquired, but also on facts which are wholly independent of him, such as whether the animals that live in and around the lake eat the toads. Similarly, whether a performance is skilled depends not simply on what the performer does, but on the standards for performances of that sort; and these are laid down prior to and independently of particular performances. To say this is not to be committed to an absolute view of truth; the claim is only that 'So-and-so has learnt that the toads are good to eat' entails 'The toads are good to eat.'

The position outlined in the previous paragraph requires elaboration to allow for the fact that beliefs acquired in certain ways tend, in general, to be true. If this were not so there would be no point in studying the toads in Lake Titicaca in order to decide whether certain beliefs about them were true and whether, therefore, those who had come to hold them could be said to have learnt anything; indeed if it were not so we would have no concept of truth, or, therefore, of anything else. We might, therefore, agree that somebody had learnt that something was so on finding out that they had acquired their belief in an appropriate manner. For example, we might agree that somebody who came to believe that the herons which live near Lake Titicaca eat the toads had learnt that this was so if we found out that they had acquired their belief by watching the herons eating the toads. We do not say that they have learnt, however, simply because they acquired their belief in that manner but because we accept that a belief acquired in that manner is likely to be true. There are, however, no infallible ways of arriving at truth, although philosophers, notably Descartes, have thought that there were. It remains possible, therefore, that a belief acquired in the appropriate manner may nevertheless turn out to be false. Consequently the requirement that the belief acquired in learning be true cannot be reduced to the requirement that it be acquired in a particular manner.

In order to exclude being injected with drugs or subjected to brain operations as learning processes, it was stipulated earlier that the experience which leads to learning must be related to the change which it brings about not simply in bringing it about but in some further way. The relationship, it was suggested, must be in some sense natural or internal; for example, coming to believe that the toads are good to eat by eating and enjoying them. What was then called the natural way is related to what was referred to in the previous paragraph as the appropriate manner. The appropriate manner of acquiring a belief is the manner which, in general, leads to the acquisition of a true belief. If I come to believe that the toads are good to eat as a result of eating them with enjoyment, for example, my belief is likely to be true. On the other hand, if I acquire a belief because somebody has been interfering with my neural circuits, there is no particular reason why that belief should be true. The difficulty in giving a satisfactory account of the relationship between the change involved in belief and the way in which the change must be brought about, therefore, was due partly to trying to abstract from the epistemological aspect of learning and treat it as a wholly psychological concept.

It could be argued, with some plausibility, that our ordinary way of talking does not support the view that to say that somebody has learnt something is, in part, to make an epistemological claim on their behalf. For example we might say that someone had learnt bad habits; or even that they had learnt that something was the case, even though we ourselves know that it is not. In some cases an epistemological claim is being made by a third party; for example, we might say that John learnt from his teacher that toads like to sleep in a damp place. We may know that they like to sleep in a dry place; but the use of the word 'learnt' is sanctioned by the fact fact that the teacher, and now John also, think otherwise. Similarly we do not, on the basis of changes in knowledge, retrospectively claim that the word 'learning' was used inappropriately in the past. We are prepared to allow, for example, that biology students at one time learnt that the coelacanth was extinct because it was generally accepted at the time that this was so, although we now know that it is not. What is involved in the use of the word 'learning' is not timeless certainty but merely a claim to knowledge.

Counter examples can easily be produced, however, which cannot be dealt with in this way. A child may acquire the habit of starting his tens and units adding sums with the tens column, as a result of which he always gets them wrong if carrying is involved; twenty-six and twenty-nine, for example, become four hundred and fifteen. But, some might wish to say, though in acquiring this habit he has not learnt any arithmetic, he has learnt something; he has learned to add incorrectly. To me this seems an odd, almost self-contradictory, way of talking; but some people appear to favour it. The appearance of contradiction can be avoided only by interpreting them as saying that the process by which the child acquires the incorrect habit is the same as that by which he acquires correct habits; and this may often be so. They are therefore thinking of 'learning' as the name of the process or processes involved in learning. The inclination to talk in this way may be a result of a spillover of the technical, psychological term into ordinary language.

If this way of using the word 'learning' is accepted it has the odd result that a child who gets his sums wrong may be said to have learnt just as much, or perhaps more, than a child who gets them right, although the content of what he has learnt is different. (Learning would be quantified, presumably, by counting the newly-formed neural connections, or in some such way.) In the context of education, however, it seems more appropriate to say that he has not learnt anything but has acquired some bad habits which may, in fact, interfere with future learning, i.e. to speak of learning only when the epistemological condition is satisfied.

There are of course learning processes, i.e. those processes whereby learning takes place. Several such processes have been investigated and labelled by psychologists; they include imitation, habituation, classical conditioning and operant conditioning. That learning takes place in these ways, however, is an empirical discovery; it is not a fact about language. No restrictions are placed on the sorts of processes which can count as learning processes by the word 'learning'. In this learning differs from perception. If I see a table in a room then the process whereby I see must involve my eyes, light waves and so on. I may also, in seeing a table in a room, be said to have learnt that there is a table in the room. If so the process whereby I learnt that this was so was a perceptual one; it involved no *sui generis* learning process, though there was a process whereby I learnt. In referring to what has taken place as learning, attention is drawn, not to the process involved, but to factors such as my not having previously known that this was so and the fact that I did not immediately forget what I had seen. We would not normally have occasion to say 'I learnt that there was a table in the room' unless what I learnt was of special interest or relevance to me; unless, for example, the room is the prison cell in which I will spend the next twenty years; but the use of the word 'learnt' is quite in order in this context.

28

The view that 'learning' is the name of a process has implications for 'teaching' if a teacher is thought of as one who accepts responsibility for helping others to learn. According to Professor C. D. Hardie (in C. B. J. Macmillan and B. Paul Komisar (eds), *Psychological Concepts in Education*, p. 153), for example, 'all learning must belong to one or other of the two types just described', i.e. classical and operant conditioning. If this were correct it would follow that a teacher can teach only by conditioning his pupils. This is a consequence which Professor Hardie might be willing to accept. So far as I know, however, no teacher training institution trains its students to condition rats, let alone children; and conditioning rats is a skilled operation which certainly cannot be undertaken successfully without special training. On the other hand, the view that 'learning' is not the name of a process leaves the way open for an eclectic approach to the question of teaching method.

I have tried, in this essay, to elaborate a definition of 'becoming educated'. The first step was to point out that the word 'education' itself is the name of a practical activity, the overall purpose of which is that somebody should become educated. To become educated, it was claimed, is to learn to be a person. The second part of the essay was therefore concerned with the content of what has to be learnt in order to become educated; that is, with what it is to be a person. What was emphasized most about persons was their conceptually structured awareness, or consciousness, of the world, enabling them to acquire knowledge of the world and to adopt and intelligently pursue ends and purposes. The third part of the essay was concerned with the concept of learning; what was emphasized most about learning was the need for its content to conform to epistemological standards; for beliefs to be true and performances skilled. The two halves of the account combine, therefore, to give an account of the overall purpose of education.

IV

Finally, and briefly, I would like to compare the account of education put forward here with that offered in *The Logic of Education* by Professors P. H. Hirst and R. S. Peters. Teachers, insofar as they 'are concerned about education', strive 'to initiate others into a form of life, which they regard as desirable, in which knowledge and understanding play an important part'. There are therefore two 'logically necessary conditions . . . for the use of the term "education" ' (p. 20). First there are 'desirability conditions'; ' "educating" people suggests a family of processes whose principle of unity is the development of desirable qualities in them.' Second there are 'knowledge conditions'; ' "education" suggests not only that what develops in someone is valuable but also that it involves the development of knowledge and understanding' (p. 19). And later they add that *'public forms of experience* ... are absolutely central to the development of knowledge and understanding' (p. 32).

They also contrast the concept of education outlined above with an 'older and undifferentiated concept which refers just to any process of bringing up or rearing in which the connection either with what is desirable or with knowledge is purely contingent' (p. 25). 'We distinguish now between "training" and "education" ', and between "socialization" and "education", whereas previously people did not' (p. 23). Accordingly we now find it more natural to speak of training animals and birds rather than of educating them. Whereas educators direct their efforts towards 'the all-round development of a person morally, intellectually and spiritually' (p. 24), training is 'a more narrowly conceived enterprise' (p. 25) directed towards 'more limited and specific goals' (p. 24) such as 'toilet training, getting children to be clean and tidy, and to speak with a nice accent' (p. 25).

What Hirst and Peters call the desirability condition is reflected in my account, though it has not been stressed. On my account 'education' is the name of an activity to which individuals devote their lives and nations sizeable fractions of their incomes. Their willingness to do so is evidence—indeed I agree with John Stuart Mill that it is the sole evidence which it is possible to produce—that they value the end achievement of which is the purpose of that activity. My view therefore is that education is valued by those engaged in it but that there is no question of independent or 'objective' justification. This point is developed later in this volume in my chapter 'Values in education'.

Turning now to what Hirst and Peters call the knowledge condition, I have stressed not so much knowledge itself but the conceptually structured awareness which makes belief and therefore knowledge possible; it also makes possible the development of feelings about, and attitudes to, the world. (It is along these lines, if at all, that the reference in Hirst and Peters to understanding is to be explicated.) This point is reinforced by the epistemological condition for the use of the word 'learning'. Hirst and Peters's 'knowledge condition', therefore, is also reflected in my account. I agree also that knowledge is connected with public forms of understanding, provided that this refers only to the need for 'shared concepts' and 'objective tests for what it is claimed is experienced, known or understood' (p. 62). The further claim that 'modes of experience and knowledge' can be divided into 'some seven areas'—

logic and mathematics, the physical sciences, knowledge of people, morals, aesthetics, religion and philosophy—I regard, however, as no more than a philosophical dogma which should on no account be incorporated into the concept of education. My account of 'education' is less committed, also, in a second way. According to orthodox philosophical accounts of 'knowledge' a person is said to know something if he not only truly believes that it is so but also has evidence for his belief. To reflect Hirst and Peters's knowledge conditions fully, therefore, I would have to amend my account so that to become educated is to learn to be a rational person. This, however, would be unduly restrictive; for there are many different ideals of what a person should be. The production of rational persons remains, of course, as a possible and, on my view, desirable educational aim insofar as it is practicable.

Finally I accept the need to distinguish between a more specific concept of education which allows a contrast to be drawn between education and both socialization and training and a looser usage which does not. The way the contrast is drawn will depend not only on the account given of 'education', but also on that of 'training' and 'socialization' respectively. Hirst and Peters's suggestion that training 'is a more narrowly conceived enterprise' directed towards 'more limited goals' appears to be on the right lines. The words 'more narrowly' and 'more limited' are however relative; the training which a person receives, therefore, may also form a part, perhaps the major part, of their education. For example, a legal education, in the course of which criminology, philosophy of law and comparative law are studied, may be contrasted with a legal training which leads only to a detailed knowledge of part of the existing statutes of a particular country. Similarly, a scientific education, which includes a study of history and philosophy of science and of the social consequences of technological change, may be contrasted with a scientific training confined to one branch of science. But legal or scientific training necessarily form the core of a legal or scientific education, just as teacher training must play a central part in the education of teachers. The aim of both legal education and legal training is that somebody should become a lawyer; and to become a lawyer is to take a further step in the process of learning to be a person. But they differ in reflecting different ideals of what a person should be and also, therefore, of the sort of society which people should form.

According to my account, there is more that might come within the scope of the term 'education', though less that must, as compared with that offered by Hirst and Peters. But on any account not everything which children learn in the course of growing up in a particular society counts as part of their education. The fact that formal education is a self-conscious purposive activity serves to some extent to distinguish it from socialization. As soon as practical steps are taken to inform people of the health dangers of casual sex or cigarette smoking people start talking about sex or health education. And I have already tried to give an account of informal education earlier in this chapter. Nevertheless, some of the things which children learn cannot be regarded as contributing to either their formal or informal education. No sharp line can, I think, be drawn; we tend to exclude those things, like learning to wiggle one's ears, which are trivial or unimportant from the point of view of learning to be a person. But many things are important, from this point of view, which do not at first glance appear to be. For example, the importance of learning to control your bowels is disguised by the low failure rate. But anyone who failed in this respect would, in our society, be severely handicapped as a person. Children are not normally admitted to nursery school, for example, until they have achieved bowel control; whilst an adult who failed in this way would be rejected by all society. Failure to acquire the relevant musculature control, of course, would not be an educational failure, though no less disastrous.

Two more obvious points of difference are, first, that on my view the word 'education' is the name of an activity, whereas on Hirst and Peters's view it is not. This point is developed in detail in my subsequent chapter in this volume, 'Values in education'. Second, I draw attention to the connection between 'education' and 'learning'; whereas Hirst and Peters appear to rely on the notions of 'initiation' (into worthwhile activities) and (personal) 'development'. 'Learning' enters their account only when they begin to talk about teaching.

V

In this chapter I have elaborated the view that 'education' is the name of an activity, the point of which is that someone should become educated and that to become educated is to learn to be a person. Not everyone will want to accept this account in its entirety. It has, however, provided the occasion for discussions of the concepts of a person and of learning; and these surely are of central importance for the philosophy of education.

The concept of indoctrination

2

Patricia Smart

As long as we are using the words prescriptively rather than descriptively there is little difficulty in distinguishing education from indoctrination. We can assume that 'Education is initiation into what is worthwhile with the provision that what has been transmitted has been taught in a morally unobjectionable way.'[1] Indoctrination might be described as the transmission of doctrines of which we are suspicious by teaching methods which we regard as morally objectionable. We might perhaps get a little closer to stating our objection to indoctrination if we attempt to say a little more about what makes a teaching method 'objectionable' within an educational context.

It is often assumed that indocrination should be eradicated from education altogether. Other writers have thought that some degree of indoctrination was permissible at the early stages.[2] Snook has tried to distinguish between 'pejorative and non-pejorative forms of indoctrination'.[3] But Russell saw 'propaganda' as an integral part of education.[4, 5]

> In all education propaganda has a part. The question
> for the educator is not whether there shall be propaganda but
> how much, how organized and of what sort; also at some
> stage during education an attempt should be made to free
> boys and girls as far as possible from the influence of
> propaganda by teaching them methods of arriving at impartial
> judgements.

Russell's position on indoctrination is clear if paradoxical. Education must inevitably contain some degree of indoctrination. But ultimately it is only by the process of education that the effects of indoctrination can be ameliorated. The effects of indoctrination are minimized by the process of enabling pupils to make 'impartial judgments'. If this is not accomplished, then indoctrination becomes the dominant factor in our educational system.

The close connection between indoctrination and education cannot be overlooked. Education, on anyone's definition, tends to lead one into those areas where we are most suspicious of indoctrination. Education has been variously described as 'bringing people

33

into contact with what is excellent', 'initiation into what is worthwhile', 'transmitting the values of society' and so on. It is just this aspect of education which has made some writers think that all education is, *ipso facto*, indoctrination. But it might be remembered that education covers a much wider area than indoctrination. Activities such as learning to play cricket cannot properly be described as indoctrination, though they might be regarded as part of education. Even so, critics might argue that one was bringing a boy to 'middle-class values' merely by teaching him cricket at all. But to insist that all education is really indoctrination turns our attention from those distinctions which it is necessary to make when trying to embark upon a system of education rather than one of indoctrination. A genuine attempt to distinguish between education and indoctrination cannot be accomplished so easily.

However, we might throw some light on the concept of indoctrination by examining some of the essential qualities of education with which it is so often contrasted. Martin Buber[6] has summed up the dilemma of the educator when confronted with the child he is to educate. 'In every hour the human race begins. We forget this too easily in the massive fact of past life, of so-called world history, of the fact that each child is born with a disposition of "world-historical origin".' The child is born into a world with pre-established values, standards and knowledge. But he himself is new, unique. The educator has to take account of both these factors. He has to remember the uniqueness of the individual child, while acknowledging the child's membership in society.

These two aspects of education have been epitomized in what has become known as the 'moulding' and 'growth' models of education. As Scheffler has pointed out, the differences between these two notions break down.[7] But nonetheless these two metaphors manage to convey two attitudes towards the child and towards education. The growth metaphor tries to dissociate education from the notion that the child is there to be moulded into the existing pattern of society. This has led the advocates of the 'growth' metaphor to encourage what are often described as 'activity' methods. The child is not told what to believe or what he should think. He is encouraged to think for himself and to formulate his own beliefs. Of course, such a theoretical framework does not exclude the occurrence of indoctrination at a practical level. But such attitudes do at least try to overcome the possibility of the teacher regarding the child as an entity to be filled with pre-established opinions. If the child can somehow be prevailed upon to 'think for himself' or 'come to see for himself' the teacher feels that he can be absolved from the accusation of foisting his own opinions upon the child. There has been a switch from the notion of 'hydraulic injection' to the notion of 'teaching how to'.[8]

But when we consider indoctrination we are not merely suggesting that the teacher is presenting his own opinions to the child. We are suggesting in addition that he is putting over his own point of view more strongly than he should to the detriment of other possible viewpoints. We are also suggesting that the teacher may be deliberately obscuring other opinions in order to get the child to believe what he wants him to believe. He is, in short, using 'morally objectionable methods'. This particular type of 'moral objectionableness' occurs not only because a person tries to disguise the truth but because he contravenes the kind of standards one requires from a teacher in his role of teacher.

There is a *prima facie* tautologous relationship between such words as 'to teach', 'to learn', 'to know' and 'to be true', which is perhaps misleading. For example, if I have taught John X (achievement) then John must also 'know X'. But if John knows X, then X must be true, for I cannot 'know' what is not the case. It is odd to say 'John knows X, but X is not true'. It is tacitly implied that what a teacher teaches is true. A teacher who deliberately teaches what is known to be false or not quite true, seems to be abandoning a claim to professional integrity. This is something over and above the censure extended to people who are liars and tricksters, whether political or commercial. When we speak of indoctrination we seem to be assuming that the teacher is misusing his position as a teacher in order to influence his pupil in the acceptance of certain beliefs.

But what exactly does the indoctrinator do which the teacher does not do? What methods of teaching does he employ which the genuine teacher does not utilize? By and large a case can be made out for suggesting that the teaching methods of the indoctrinator must differ radically from that of the educator. But John Wilson[9] raises an objection to this view. He points out that if identical teaching methods were used in mathematics and in the teaching of religious or political opinions it is only in the latter case that we could sensibly speak of indoctrination. 'Suppose,' he says, 'we could teach four-year-old children all their mathematical tables while they were asleep, or by hypnosis. Or suppose that a boy could master "A" level physics simply by having an electric charge passed through his brain cells.' Wilson believes that whether or not we called this practice 'indoctrination' would be 'arbitrary'. But if these methods were used to instruct boys in political or religious beliefs, we should have no hesitation whatever in saying that indoctrination had occurred. And he goes on, 'What is the difference between hypnotising a boy to believe in communism and hypnotising him to master

"A" level physics? Plainly, it is not a difference in method; it is rather a difference in subject matter.'

Wilson is possibly correct in implying that we should not call such methods 'indoctrination' as far as mathematics is concerned. Though it might be hoped that we should not call them 'educational' either. There are, for example, a few questions which one might need to ask. One might want to ask whether the boy *chose* to have an electric charge passed through his brain. If he did not, then we should have a case of assault, rather than indoctrination. On the other hand, if the boy asked to have an electric current passed through his brain so that he could learn more easily, one might have to have discussions at examiners' meetings as to whether marks should be deducted for laziness! Whether hypnosis could ever be admitted to the sacred circle of educational activities would largely depend upon empirical evidence about what actually happens in hypnosis. If, during hypnosis, it were possible to teach without the conscious or unconscious co-operation of the pupil, then again this activity would have to be excluded from legitimate educational activities. Or again, we might argue whether 'unconscious co-operation' came within the concept of education.

We seem to be faced with the following position. Identical teaching methods can be used on separate occasions. On the one occasion, we have a process which we call 'indoctrination' and on the other occasion we do not. Is Wilson correct in assuming that it is, therefore, subject matter and not method which constitutes indoctrination? If we look a little more closely at the cases taken by Wilson and the subject matter involved, we shall perhaps see why it is that we are prepared to say that indoctrination is, or is not, involved. It is chiefly because the logical status of mathematics and of politics is radically different. Whether a proposition is, or is not, open to the process we call 'indoctrination' depends ultimately upon the logic of that statement.

First, when we speak of indoctrination we are not discussing methods *per se*, but methods which are used in getting people to believe certain propositions. It is implied, second, that the indoctrinator uses these methods to prevail upon the pupil to adopt beliefs which he would not adopt had he been taught by other (more honest) methods. It is possible, then, for indoctrination to occur whenever it is legitimate for a pupil or for another individual to hold another opinion. The indoctrinator puts over one opinion more strongly than the other; or he might omit to mention the other opinion altogether. Indoctrination can occur in every area of enquiry, except for elementary mathematics, simply because other opinions are not evidently excluded by the available evidence.

There may be historical reasons for maintaining that indoctrination is less likely to occur in the physical sciences than, say, in religion, but the work of Kuhn should prevent too much complacency on that score. It would be much more honest to admit that indoctrination does occur in the physical sciences from time to time and it occurs (a) when one point of view is put forward to the exclusion of another equally legitimate point of view and (b) when matters which are in dispute are put forward as established.

If, then, we accept the suggestion that indoctrination can occur whenever an alternative point of view is justified logically, we shall see equally well why it is that mathematics cannot be indoctrinated. If I am indoctrinated in religious matters while under the influence of hypnosis I may become a Jehovah's Witness. Or I might have been brought up by a family of Plymouth Brethren and come to to accept their beliefs. I then have cause to complain that if I had not been indoctrinated by these people I would not have accepted their beliefs. Had other religious teachings been put before me I might have become a Seventh Day Adventist or an atheist. But this kind of reasoning does not make sense when applied to mathematics. I cannot complain that if I had been differently taught I would not have accepted that $2+2=4$, or $9 \times 9=81$ and there is no sense in complaining that if I had not been indoctrinated, I would have come to a different conclusion. Tables taught by hypnosis must be the same as tables taught by other methods. We could not make sense of the allegation that someone had a different version of Pythagoras's theorem because they had been taught under hypnosis, or by indoctrination.

However, to say that indoctrination does not occur in mathematics is not to say that indoctrination does not occur *about* mathematics. Indeed the history of mathematics would provide an interesting cautionary tale for those writers on indoctrination who seem to think that indoctrination can occur only in religion, history or politics. The most famous example of indoctrination must be the Pythagoreans who threatened death to all those who dared to propagate the irrationality of the square root of the number two. It is interesting that they did not deny the irrationality of root two itself or the validity of the proof. They suppressed the transmission of this to the uninitiated. The history of the development of non-Euclidean geometry during the early nineteenth century gives further instances of this tendency.

To talk of indoctrination is to suggest that the teacher uses unfair means to induce the child to come to conclusions which he himself intends him to make, but which the subject matter does not necessarily demand. One cannot properly be permitted to have alternative views about how many threes make nine. The logic is too definite, too certain for the indoctrinator to tamper with.

Many writers have felt that indoctrination can be avoided by giving evidence for beliefs. Indoctrination occurs when evidence is absent or insufficient for the degree of belief accredited to it. The educator is concerned with offering reasons, the indoctrinator with offering rationalizations. He is a trafficker in faulty logic, while the educator is only concerned with sound reasoning. He makes it his business to see that the child understands the nature of the evidence and appreciates why X is evidence for Y. Wilson, for example, writes.

> If we are to avoid indoctrination, therefore, the beliefs we
> teach must be rational. They need not be certain. . . . It may
> only be that the general weight of evidence is in their favour.
> They *may* be certain or they may be highly probable, or
> probable, or just likely on the whole. What they *must* be, is
> backed by evidence; and by 'evidence' of course, we must mean
> publicly-accepted evidence, not simply what sectarians regard
> as evidence.

There are a number of criticisms which need to be made of this passage. It is not so easy to distinguish between reasons and rationalizations and this most certainly cannot be done in the method suggested by Wilson. One certainly cannot draw the line between what is a reason and a rationalization by means of what is 'publicly accepted', or, better, 'publicly acceptable'. Whether a proposition is to be accepted as evidence must be decided, on this view, by counting heads, which is not the usual way of assessing an argument. No doubt at the trial of Galileo most people would have rejected his heliocentric theory. He was, after all, putting forward a minority view, not a view which was publicly acceptable. To both the Church and the Aristotelians, Galileo was putting forward a 'sectarian' point of view. The proposition 'only sectarians are engaging in proper reasoning' would be contradictory on Wilson's suggestion. Again, many of the propositions with which Wilson is concerned could more sensibly be thought of in terms of 'justification' rather than 'evidence . If we are to follow Wilson's reasoning, it would be impossible to indoctrinate children with communism in Russia because the evidence would be 'publicly accepted'. Trying to put forward an alternative point of view would be the work of 'sectarians'.

But the mention of evidence with reference to indoctrination brings us to the crux of the matter. Outside formal logic and mathematics where we are concerned with a tight system of deductive reasoning, evidence for a particular belief or hypothesis is always incomplete. The more speculative our area of enquiry, the greater the possibility of indoctrination. It is interesting to note that as the possibility of proof, in a strong sense, recedes, persuasion, with its appeal to emotion, takes over. It is for this reason that we ignore the possibility of indoctrination in mathematics. There is little room for manoeuvre between premises and conclusion, which the indoctrinator can make and still retain any degree of credibility. Indoctrination can occur in the sciences because there is in all non-deductive inference a logical jump between hypothesis and evidence for the hypothesis.[10] If indoctrination does not occur in the sciences, it is not the logic of the propositions themselves which prevents this, but other qualities of reasoning and procedure which we connect with 'scientific method'. Where the logic is less determined, and where justification for ethical and religious beliefs is often open to question, the possibility of indoctrination increases. The indoctrinator has little difficulty in enabling the pupil to take a specific line of reasoning.

But to try to distinguish the notion of indoctrination by talk of specious arguments does not work satisfactorily, on account of the simple fact that we are frequently mistaken about the strength of our evidence. Medieval thinkers did not conclude that the world was flat because they ignored the evidence. On the whole, Bellarmine showed a greater respect for genuine argument and canons of proof than Galileo. Many examples of a similar nature can be found. It is the occurrence of incidents such as this, which have led writers on indoctrination to retract their original suggestion that indoctrination consists of teaching false beliefs. Snook, for example writes, 'A person indoctrinates P (a proposition or a set of propositions) if he teaches with the intention that the pupils or pupil believe P, regardless of the evidence.'[3] This is intended to circumvent accidents of history where people are genuinely mistaken about the strength of their evidence. 'To accuse the medieval teacher of indoctrinating his pupils with the belief that the world was flat, when there was no contrary evidence for this belief would be like accusing a seventeenth-century doctor of malpractice because he did not use penicillin.'

The implication of this is that indoctrination must be intentional. One cannot indoctrinate by accident. One must want one's students to develop unshakeable beliefs, even though one is aware of the inadequacy of the evidence one is propagating. But this has the interesting consequence that neither fanatics nor the 'simple-souled' believer can indoctrinate, for neither are *aware* of the inadequacy of their evidence. Indeed, to them there is no other point of view. Now although we might be prepared to excuse the 'simple-souled' believer from indoctrination on the grounds that he himself was conditioned it would be much more difficult to do so for the fanatic.

It is sometimes supposed that some light can be thrown on the idea of indoctrination by elucidating the concept of a *doctrine*. If there are 'high' and 'low' risk areas, then doctrines must present a 'high risk' zone. Professor Peters has suggested that 'whatever else indoctrination may mean it obviously has something to do with doctrines, which are species of belief'.[11] But though etymology may be interesting, it can also be misleading and is rarely philosophically enlightening. It might, for example, be dangerous to assume that only doctrines can be indoctrinated. On the other hand there is little point in extending the term 'doctrine' to cover every proposition which is capable of indoctrination. Nonetheless it may be that our insistence upon retaining the word 'doctrine' for propositions of religion and politics may throw some light on the nature of indoctrination.

Two kinds of propositions seem to be exempt from the possibility of being doctrines or of being open to indoctrination. We do not generally talk of indoctrinating mathematics or describe theorems of geometry as doctrines. Nor do we usually talk of indoctrinating plain observational statements, though here we are on more dangerous ground. An indoctrinator may certainly use observational statements for his own purposes to provide 'evidence' for his doctrines, even if he cannot change observations themselves. No one would seriously try to maintain that a cat had two tails or that a cow had seven horns, though various people have made out a case for the divinity of both these animals. If observations are not indoctrinated it is because no semblance of credibility can be maintained. Indoctrination cannot occur because we cannot have different opinions about how many tails a cat has, or how many ears a donkey has. But, of course, when we begin to be concerned with *inferences* from observations, then we are concerned with a different type of statement and once again may be treading within the area of indoctrination. It may be a 'plain fact' that the heart is on the left side of the body and there would be little point in denying it. But there could be room for difference of opinion concerning how the heart pumps the blood round the body. The indoctrinator may, indeed, want us to accept as plain fact what are inferences from observations, e.g. is 'the sun goes round the earth' an observation or an inference from observation? But observations in themselves are not usually thought of as doctrines, though on occasions, inferences from them might become doctrines.

Various attempts have been made to delineate a doctrine by utilization of the principle of verifiability or falsifiability. It would, indeed, be very convenient if it could be established that propositions which are 'unverifiable' in principle can be safely described as 'doctrines'. But difficulties with the criterion of verifiability (or falsifiability) are notorious. Some writers[12] have, indeed, proceeded along these lines. But the result seems to be that a criterion which is stringent enough to exclude metaphysics also excludes propositions of science and a criterion which includes scientific statements also includes metaphysics![13] This is often taken to be some form of condemnation of the verification principle. But perhaps it should make us more sensitive to the logic of scientific statements.

But before we abandon the criterion of verification or falsification it may be useful to look much more closely at two different types of falsifiability. It is well known that some of the basic assumptions of scientific theories are not falsifiable in any real sense. We might consider, in this respect, the atomic theory of matter which had such far-reaching effects both in science and philosophy. If we consider this theory, we see that the atoms involved are by definition beyond the scope of observation. But this is a different kind of un-falsifiability from the type described by Popper:[14]

> These theories appeared to be able to explain practically everything that happened within the fields to which they referred. It was precisely this fact—that they always fitted, that they were always confirmed—which in the eyes of their admirers constituted the strongest argument in their favour of these theories. It began to dawn on me that this apparent strength was in fact their weakness.

The atomic theory was a metaphysical theory because it dealt with entities which were essentially unobservable. But the theories which Popper had in mind were unfalsifiable because the theories had deliberately been constituted so that nothing could falsify them. This is an important difference between the two types of theory. The one happened to be unfalsifiable. The other was so constructed that it never could be falsified. That is, from the theory itself, it had an inset mechanism for dealing with any state of affairs which might appear to falsify it. Because of this factor, the theory must always remain 'true'. With this mechanism there can be no escape from the scope of the theory and nothing can be permitted to count as evidence against it. Basically, then, a doctrine is a proposition which socially or intellectually influential groups have decided shall be true for all time. If this outlook were consistently maintained, there is no reason why the propositions of science should not become 'doctrines'. It is, I think, immaterial whether we talk of the 'theories of psychoanalysis,' 'the doctrines of psycho-analysis' or the 'dogma of psychoanalysis'. Similarly, in Europe the

atomic theory of matter remained a theory while in Islam it became
a doctrine, because it was not permitted to challenge it. It is not
that nothing can count against the theory in a logical sense but that
there has been an accepted determination to formulate the theory
so that it cannot be falsified. (Something *should* be able to count
against the theory of psychoanalysis. But the theory has been
constructed so that this cannot occur.) A doctrine, then, cannot
adequately be distinguished from a scientific statement on the
grounds of logic alone, i.e. in terms of verifiability. For neither a
doctrine nor a proposition of science need be verifiable or falsifiable.
Metaphysics cannot be eradicated from science, but this does not
make such propositions doctrines. A doctrine can be distinguished
from other forms of unverifiable statements by the attitude which is
reflected towards evidence against that proposition. Whereas
propositions of science are tentative and provisional, doctrines must
be true and immutable. Whether a proposition is to be afforded
doctrinal status depends upon how far we are prepared to allow it
refutability. On the whole 'scientific method is distinguished by a
willingness to allow refutability. Doctrines are constructed so that
they are immune from refutation.'

But even if considering the notion of 'doctrine' may throw some
light on the kind of reasoning involved in indoctrination the specific
linking of 'indoctrinate' with 'doctrine' might be a little too facile.
That is, one feels that one requires an appropriate internal object
for 'indoctrinate' and 'doctrine' appears as a suitable candidate!
One thinks thoughts, drinks drinks and by the same token, indoctrinates doctrines. But the point is really whether 'indoctrinate'
requires an internal object any more than 'educate'. As far as
education is concerned, one just educates people. Similarly, a case
might be made out for suggesting that one just indoctrinates people
also. Thus one indoctrinates John *in* certain beliefs, rather than
'indoctrinating beliefs'.

So far, then, we have considered indoctrination in regard to
subject matter and the methods which are open to the indoctrinator
but not to the educator. The indoctrinator is prepared to teach half-
truths as whole truths by either giving only one point of view or by
suppressing other possible points of view. The teacher is willing to
distort the way in which the pupil can come to make 'impartial
judgments'. But basically what enables the indoctrinator to adopt
this method of teaching, is his attitude towards the pupil he is
teaching. This point was made, obliquely, by R. M. Hare in his
discussion with Wilson:[15]

The educator is waiting and hoping all the time for those whom he is educating to start *thinking*. . . . The indoctrinator on the other hand, is watching for signs of trouble, and ready to intervene to suppress it when it appears, however oblique and smooth his methods may be.

To Hare, the difference between the educator and the indoctrinator can be explained in terms of method. But, of course, it is only because educator and indoctrinator differ fundamentally in their attitude towards the person that they are teaching, that differences in teaching methods can occur. (The indoctrinator who suppresses a person's beliefs need not hesitate to suppress the person.)

The indoctrinator regards the pupil as a 'thinking thing' to be pushed into his own patterns of thinking. The educator, on the other hand, is concerned with the individuality and growth of the individual. To use a Kantian phrase, the indoctrinator can regard the pupil as a means and not as an end in himself. He is not concerned with the individual simply as a person, he is only bent upon getting him to accept a particular set of beliefs.

But the educator, on the other hand, must have respect for the individuality of the pupil he is teaching. A teaching method which is 'morally objectionable' is the kind of method which permits the teacher to disregard the individuality and the rationality of the person he is teaching. To set out to instil one's own beliefs into a child is to use the child as a means instead of treating him as an end. This kind of situation, in which the teacher is tempted to 'use' the pupil for his own ends, rather than treating the child as an end in himself has been portrayed by Martin Buber.[6] He asks us to

consider, for example, the relationship of doctor and patient. It is essential that this should be a real human relationship experienced with the spirit of the one who is addressed; but as soon as the helper is touched by the desire, however subtle in form, to dominate or enjoy his patient . . . the danger of falsification arises, besides which all quackery becomes peripheral.

It is because this kind of falsification has occurred in the situation between the pupil and the would-be indoctrinator, that any form of deceit regarding reasoning and subject matter, is also inevitable.

In his essay 'The fixation of belief'[16] C. S. Peirce makes some valuable comments on the nature of indoctrination and the kind of relationship this attitude entails both towards other people and towards oneself. There is, he says, a 'method of tenacity':

Let an institution be created which shall have for its object to keep correct doctrines before the attention of the people, to reiterate them perpetually and to teach them to the young; having at the same time power to prevent contrary doctrines being taught advocated or expressed. Let all possible cases of a change of mind be removed from men's apprehension.

But despite these efforts those who hold tenaciously to beliefs find sooner or later others who hold beliefs contrary to their own.

It will be apt to occur to him, in some saner moment, that their opinions are quite as good as his own and this will shake his confidence in his belief. This conception that another man's thought and sentiment may be equivalent to one's own, is a distinctly new step, and a highly important one.

But this process by which a man begins to lose confidence in his own beliefs and to consider that 'another man's thought and sentiment may be equivalent to his own' is a step someone who is thoroughly indoctrinated in a set of beliefs cannot make. It is a step which the indoctrinator must ensure that his pupils cannot make. Respect for the ideas of another is normally associated with a respect for persons. This is something again which the indoctrinator tries to avoid. It is, therefore, part of the ploy of the indoctrinator to insist that one cannot have respect for people who hold opinions contrary to one's own. This again is very convenient for him, because it absolves him from having to consider the opinions of others.

But there must be different degrees of indoctrination as there are different degrees of education. All 'good education' is alleged to be 'self-education'. But what of indoctrination? There is the opinion that in indoctrination the pupil soaks up opinions in a passive kind of way. This, indeed, is the kind of indoctrination which Spinoza has in mind when he wrote:[17]

Whence it follows, that such things as no one can be induced to do by rewards or threats, do not fall within the rights of the commonwealth. For instance, by reason of his faculty of judgement, it is in no man's power to believe. For by what rewards or threats can a man be brought to believe that the whole is not greater than its part or that God does not exist. So, too, by what rewards or threats can man be brought to love one whom he hates or hate one whom he loves.

Some indoctrination may well be superficial. But in the last resort indoctrination must be self-indoctrination. If Hume is correct, the indoctrinator is aided in his task by basic tendencies of the human mind. It may well be easier to 'indoctrinate oneself' than to 'educate oneself'. Hume suggests: 'All these opinions and notions of things to which we have been accustomed from our infancy take such deep root that 'tis impossible for us by all the powers of reason and experience, to eradicate them.'[18]

It is here that the force of the 'in' of indoctrinate becomes apparent. For to be indoctrinated is to become enmeshed within a web of doctrines from which there can be no escape. One cannot extricate oneself because one sees no need for doing so. Usually we change our opinions in the light of experience or because of inconsistencies which arise from commitment to particular beliefs. But if we are presented with a set of beliefs which can explain away alleged inconsistencies and maintain that experience is irrelevant there remains nothing which can challenge our beliefs. Change is dependent upon some kind of falsification, and this possibility has been excluded from the outset.

The possibility of indoctrination may indeed increase in those areas of enquiry where the logic of the subject is less definite. This seems to suggest that indoctrination will not occur in mathematics but will be more likely to occur in religious and political matters. But having said this, it is well to remember that there have been occasions in the history of mathematics when propositions of mathematics have been suppressed by methods which resemble indoctrination. And if this can occur in mathematics, then what of the sciences?

It is interesting to note that though considerable lip service is paid to 'scientific method' and the logic of the sciences there is very little general agreement about what the precise nature of this logic is. Writers agree about the nature of mathematical reasoning, even if they do not agree about the nature of mathematics, in a way in which there is little agreement about the logic of the sciences. Following Popper it has become customary to place the 'logic of discovery' outside logic altogether, and there is no general agreement concerning the 'logic of testing'.

But if the 'logic of discovery' lies outside logic, so must 'the scientific method' itself, because basically the scientific spirit depends upon the maintenance of a particular attitude of mind being shown towards new discoveries and new discoverers. One of the characteristics of the sciences has been its commitment to evidence, change and revision and not to a set of beliefs based upon authority and sacrosanct dogma. But the 'scientific approach' and 'scientific method' has often been obliterated by a desire to suppress particular beliefs, or an individual holding those beliefs. It has been one of the happier characteristics of science that it has paid more attention to evidence and testing than to 'revelation' and beliefs dependent upon authority. Any system of beliefs can only escape from indoctrination by allowing these beliefs to be challenged. And a ready hearing of contrary opinions is not anything which logic can guarantee, either within the sciences or elsewhere.

Notes

1 'What is an educational process?' in R. S. Peters (ed.), *The Concept of Education*, London, 1967.
2 R. F. Atkinson, 'Instruction and indoctrination' in R. D. Archambault (ed.), *Philosophical Analysis and Education*, London, 1965.
3 I. Snook, *Indoctrination and Education*, London, 1972.
4 B. Russell, *Education and the Social Order*, London, 1932, ch. 15.
5 G. Langford, *Philosophy and Education*, London, 1968, pp. 127–30 gives an account of the differences between propaganda, advertising and teaching.
6 Martin Buber, *Between Man and Man*, London, 1947.
7 I. Scheffler, 'Educational metaphors' in *The Language of Education*, Springfield, Illinois, 1960.
8 G. Ryle, 'Teaching and training' in R. S. Peters (ed.), *The Concept of Education*, London, 1967.
9 J. Wilson, 'Education and indoctrination' in T. B. Hollins (ed.), *The Aims of Education*, Manchester, 1964.
10 Most writers would deny that there is a logical connection between observations and the hypotheses purporting to explain them. See K. R. Popper, *The Logic of Scientific Discovery*, London, 1968.
11 R. S. Peters, *Ethics and Education*, London, 1966.
12 Gregory and Woods, *Proceedings of the Annual Conference*, Philosophy of Education Society, 1970.
13 A. J. Ayer, *Language, Truth and Logic*, London, 1946.
14 K. R. Popper, *Conjectures and Refutations*, London, 1963.
15 R. M. Hare, 'Adolescents into adults' in T. B. Hollins (ed.), *The Aims of Education*, Manchester, 1964.
16 C. S. Peirce, 'The fixation of belief' in *Essays in the Philosophy of Science*, New York, 1957.
17 Baruch Spinoza, *Theologico—Political Treatise*, New York, 1951.
18 David Hume, *A Treatise of Human Nature*, Book 1, Part 3, 8, New York, 1888.

The nature and scope of educational theory (1)

3

D. J. O'Connor

'Poor dear Psychology' wrote Professor Broad in 1933, 'has never got far beyond the stage of medieval physics, except in its statistical developments, where the labours of the mathematicians have enabled it to spin out the correlation of trivialities into endless refinements. For the rest, it is only too obvious that, up to the present, a great deal of Psychology consists mainly of muddle, twaddle and quacksalving, trying to impose itself as a science by the elaborateness of its technical terminology and the confidence of its assertions.'[1] This was of course a libel on psychology even in 1933 but if we replace 'psychology' by 'education' in this passage we have a very fair summary of the state of education in 1972. A major share of the blame for this state of affairs must rest on the inadequate theoretical background of education.

The word 'education' has, as is well known, at least two well-marked senses. In the first sense, it refers to a social institution like marriage, the law or the economic system. It is in this sense of the word that we say, for example: 'X per cent of the gross national product of Great Britain is devoted to education.' In the second sense of the word, 'education' is an inter-related set of studies devoted to the understanding of this social institution. We could draw a tentative analogy here with economics. Economics is a scientific study devoted to understanding, explaining, predicting and controlling that part of the world under its investigation. The study of education (or 'educational theory' in a wide sense of the phrase) differs from this and from most scientific studies in several ways. Although it draws its factual basis from scientific disciplines, it does not, like most other such disciplines, have a clearly marked and well-defined subject matter. This is perhaps due to our present lack of knowledge. It may be that we shall learn in the future what parts of human knowledge are relevant to the study of education. At present we have only a rather vague idea. In this, as in other fields of human interest and welfare, we have to wait upon relevant developments in the appropriate sciences.

But, second, what are the appropriate sciences? So far as we know, educational theory in this wide sense relies on a number of such sciences—psychology, economics, sociology, human biology are the most obvious ones. But along with these, there are non-scientific components—value judgments of varying kinds, religious concepts, political and social ideals and so on. It is one of the basic tasks of the educational theorist to show how these different components can be related in general and how in fact they are related in any particular educational theory which he may recommend. This, as we shall see, is not an easy task.

But the objects of educational theory are not simply the goals of explanation, prediction and control which can be seen in ordinary scientific activities. (Indeed such goals are not as yet even approximately realized in educational theory.) There is also an essential relation to human welfare built into the concept of education and which has to be taken account of in educational theory. Here again there is a kinship with economics. Both studies deal with human satisfactions and their maximization; education, like economics, aims at optimizing the efficient use of scarce resources—time, teaching skills, intelligence, intellectual curiosity and so on, as well as the purely material ones like money, land and buildings. We might perhaps regard the educational system of a given society as the product of social engineering whose construction is guided by the currently accepted concept of human welfare and made possible by knowledge of the sciences which make it possible to realize this ideal, however imperfectly. (Such analogies are imperfect, as we shall see, but they offer a framework for discussion.)

I will assume then that the term 'educational theory' in a wide sense can be taken to refer to those rational enquiries which have as their aim, first, the explanation of the workings of the educational process and the system in which it operates, and second, their improvement in the light of our knowledge of these workings and of the ends which the institution purports to serve.

When I wrote some years ago on this subject[2] I tried to give an answer to the question 'What is an educational theory?' My answer consisted, briefly, in sketching the standard senses of the term 'theory' and showing that educational theories did not conform at all closely to these standard senses. I concluded that 'the word "theory" as it is used in educational contexts is generally a courtesy title'. Naturally enough, this conclusion was not well received by all of those whose interests lie in these fields. It seemed to some critics to be, at best, unduly restrictive and, at worst, wildly perverse to take scientific theories as a model for theories in general and for educational theories in particular. I would like to offer some justification of my earlier view with special reference to the criticisms offered by Professor Hirst. It is he who has put forward the most careful and competent criticisms of what I said, and I feel confident that if I can meet his objections, I shall not have much to fear from anyone else.

We can start by noticing two obvious features of the term 'theory'. First, it is a vague term and is applied to a wide field of intellectual frameworks which are designed to bring organization and explanatory power to some field of interest or activity. Second, it is a term infected with emotional overtones, both favourable and pejorative. We need notice this second point only to put it aside. Some people find the terms 'theory' and 'theoretical' reassuringly reminiscent of the reliable and practical findings of the laboratory; others contrast unfavourably what is 'merely theoretical' and 'all very well in theory' with workaday down to earth practical activities. We need not be misled by these emotive echoes. Let us consider the question of vagueness.

When any term is used to indicate a wide domain of referents which differ among themselves, it is natural to try to find some property which all such referents have in common. The history of philosophy has shown that this can be a dangerous error. It may be true that it can be done in suitable cases. Chemistry can show us why the term 'carbon' is properly applied to certain types of material which differ from each other very widely—for example, diamond, soot and graphite. And biology can tell us, though not quite so convincingly, why Great Danes, dachshunds, Yorkshire terriers and chihuahuas are all properly called 'dogs'. But it is not necessarily the case that all those intellectual constructions which have been called 'theories' can be shown to have a common core of properties which justify the application of the term. Where disputes arise in cases of this kind, we have to proceed carefully.

Let us recognize first of all that there is, and can be, no final and objectively demonstrable answer to the question 'what is a theory?' There is no final and conclusive answer to questions like 'what is a gentleman?' 'what is a scientist?' or even 'which colours are properly called "red"?' But that there are no such definite answers available to these questions does not justify us in applying the terms just as we like. Some applications of vague terms can be shown to be correct, some can be shown to be marginally plausible and some simply absurd. That some questions can be answered more or less judiciously rather than simply by 'Yes' or 'No' does not mean that there are no criteria for assessing the answers.

Definitions of the type found in a dictionary purport to state the way in which the term to be defined (the *definiendum*) is used in the language community. Often such dictionary (or *lexical*) definitions as they are called are unenlightening. The Concise Oxford Dictionary, for example, defines 'theory' as 'a supposition explaining something'. This is wide enough to enable us to say that explaining the squeaking behind the wainscot by the presence of mice is to propound a theory. So when we are trying to explicate a concept in the interests of clear thinking we often have to supplement such descriptions of common usage by *recommendations*, definitions of a stipulative or persuasive kind. In my earlier account of educational theories, I was proposing a stipulative definition of 'theory' and supporting my proposal by pointing to certain basic or standard uses of the term 'theory'. There is, in the literature of the philosophy of science, a great deal of discussion about the nature of theories. What I say here does not try to beg the complex issues raised in these discussions but seeks merely to outline a definition of 'theory' which is consistent with the general position which most of the various *detailed* accounts of theories take for granted as a common framework.

My stipulative definition is that a theory is a logically interconnected set of hypotheses confirmed by observation and which has the further properties of being both refutable and explanatory. What I have to do here is to try to show that this definition is rationally acceptable in the context of educational thinking.

One way of doing so is by showing that alternative proposals are, for one reason or another, not rationally acceptable. In fact this is the most direct way of defending my own view since no one denies that scientific theories are genuine and indeed standard cases of theories. So that if I say that educational theories are properly so-called insofar as they conform to the standard scientific type, critics can object only that my proposed definition is too narrow. They will admit that educational theories are like those of the scientist in that they perform *some* of the tasks that theories in science perform. But they may say that they do other things as well or that they take into account other kinds of statement than the purely factual ones which interest the scientist.

Before we look at some of these points in detail, it may be useful to consider the generous abandon with which the word 'theory' is used in apparently respectable contexts. As an extreme example, we may take Professor Wellek, a well-known literary critic, talking of 'the theory of literature'. He explains that 'literary theory' is 'the study of the principles of literature, its categories, criteria and the like'[3] and is careful to distinguish literary theory from literary *criticism* or *history*. Such a use of 'theory' is of little use, except as a warning, to those who are trying to analyse and clarify educational concepts. It is too wide, too vague and lacks any reference to what most people would agree to be the central criterion of a genuine theory, its *explanatory* function.

But it is easy to cite examples of theories which purport to have an explanatory function but which would not generally be admitted to be genuine claimants to the status of theory. There are many bogus sciences—graphology, astrology, phrenology, palmistry, for example—any one of which will have a theoretical background which sets out to explain particular facts in the light of general laws. For example, an astrologer might claim to explain someone's character or even his destiny in the light of the exact configuration of the heavens at the time of his birth. Such theories would generally be rejected on the grounds (a) that they fail to give correct explanations in a significant number of cases and (b) that they are so stated that they do not admit of any possibility of refutation. No astrologer would ever admit that the outcome of his predictions refute astrological theory. He would blame the discrepancy on the inaccuracy of his observations or his calculations. And the same general criticism applies to theoretical systems like psychoanalysis or some forms of Marxist theory. These have achieved some intellectual respectability in the present century but experience has shown them to be of the same unfalsifiable type as superstitions like astrology, and so equally useless. All such claimants to the title of 'theory' seek to claim the benefits of science, its corroboration by experience, without its burdens, the danger of finding that facts run against you. But they can be regarded, however inadequate, as a first approximation to a genuine theory in that they recognize that a theory has an *explanatory function*.

Nearer to the standard, we have the instances of theories which were, in their day, admitted as genuine and later discredited by the discovery of facts which they could not accommodate. Such are the phlogiston theory of combustion and the Ptolemaic theory of the solar system. These have the merit not only of being genuine attempts at explanation but also, since they have been refuted, of being refutable by experience. It is an occupational risk of any genuine theory that it may come, in time, to be rejected in the light of further discoveries. And this requirement applies even to the most respected theories of twentieth-century science. And so it is a prerequisite of the model that I am proposing for theories in education. If they are not, in principle, open to disproof they are not candidates for the title. I propose then as a minimum set of criteria for a genuine theory that it should be (a) explanatory and (b) refutable. A part of the justification for these minimum criteria is that we cannot reasonably demand of any theory that it should be *true*. We do, of course, hope and intend that our theories will be true; but we cannot know that they are. And by requiring that they shall at least be explanatory and refutable we come as near as we can in general terms to making them candidates for truth. For if they are explanatory, they will link what we are hypothesizing to what we already have good reason to accept; and if they are refutable, they retain that essential connection with objective fact that their truth will require. It may indeed seem paradoxical at first sight that falsifiability is a necessary condition for truth in empirical matters. But reflection removes the appearance of paradox.

This account of a theory, sketchy as it is, needs completion in at least two ways. First, the concept of explanation has to be unfolded a little. Second, we have to ask what, if anything, must be added to the necessary conditions, either to complete the set or to make them into a set of sufficient conditions, sufficient, that is, for an educational theory. I shall pay attention chiefly to the second of these two questions, as it is to this point that Professor Hirst has directed most of his criticisms.

On the first point it is necessary only to draw attention to some well-known facts. Explanation is a concept with two components, one psychological and the other logical. To explain something (a fact, an event, a theory) is to link it in some intelligible way with what we already believe. It follows that an explanation of some puzzling and anomalous item of experience may be a 'good' explanation, in the sense that it is subjectively satisfying to one person without being so to another. This may occur for either or both of two reasons (1) Two people may have different background beliefs so that the explanation offered may be intelligible to one of them and unintelligible to the other. For example, we find by experience that it is much quicker to cool a bottle of wine in a bucket of iced water than in a refrigerator even though the temperature of the refrigerator may be lower. Someone who knows a little physics and the respective thermal conductivities of gases and liquids will explain this phenomenon. To someone without this knowledge, it will be an unexplained and perhaps puzzling fact. (2) An intelligent schoolboy will explain this fact by deducing it from the theory of heat that he has learned at school. His less intelligent classmate may fail to hit on the explanation because, although he knows about the conduction of heat and its relation to molecular structure, he cannot apply that knowledge to the case before him. These instances emphasize two important facts about explanations. (i) No true explanation can be given to one who lacks the necessary background knowledge. The biblical dictum 'To him that hath shall be given' applies to knowledge as to other things.

(ii) An explanation is a conclusion[4] arrived at by inference and so must conform to the requirements of any valid inference. That is to say, for the conclusion to be true, we must know (a) that the premises are true and (b) that the inference is a valid one, made in accordance with the rules of logic.

If educational theories did no more than conform to these standards, they would indeed be just a kind of scientific theory. And perhaps they are—or rather, perhaps they should be. For it is clear that no known large-scale educational theory conforms to such criteria at the present time. But Professor Hirst has brought forward serious objections to this account which I must now consider.

His first objection is that the scientific ideal which I have sketched above is, in his words, 'thoroughly false and artificial'.[5] And this is because theories of practical activities like education are 'radically different' from scientific theories. 'The theories of science and the theories of practical activities are radically different in character because they perform quite different functions, they are constructed to do quite different jobs.'[6] In science, theories are the end product of the scientific activity; in practical activities however they are constructed to guide the activity. I do not think that I need to disagree with this; indeed, it would hardly be defensible to do so. Some explanatory gloss is needed, however, if we are to see how far Hirst and I disagree on this point.

There is clearly a sense in which scientific theories do guide practical activities. Physical theory is the outcome and justification of the physicist's work; but it is a guidance system for the applied physicist and the engineer. Economic theory is the end product of the work of the theoretical economist; but it is used to guide and correct economic policy. Physiology and pharmacology are sciences in their own right; but they lay down guide lines for the day-to-day work of the practising doctor. So too, psychology and sociology are studies undertaken for their own intrinsic interest. But they have fields of application in practical activities of various kinds, including education.

So far, then, I agree with Hirst that there is the difference he mentions between theories in science and in practical activities. But the difference, so far at least, lies not in the nature of the theories themselves but in the way that they are regarded. So too a map may be looked on as a product of the science of cartography or as an aid to finding one's way around. But nothing that I said in my original account of theories in education tended to deny this. Indeed I said that the use of the word 'theory' in educational contexts 'is justified only where we are applying well established findings in psychology or sociology to the practice of education'.[7] And as these words occur in a passage which Hirst singles out for criticism, it is clear that simply to recognize the difference between the place of theories in science and in practical activities does not bridge the gap between us.

That gap exists because Hirst believes that, at least as far as educational theory is concerned, the necessary conditions that I mentioned above, explanatory power and falsifiability, are not a complete list. Other ingredients are also required. I would agree that these conditions tell less than the full story. But where Hirst and I disagree lies in the additions that we would make. (I am assuming that he would agree that the two that I have listed are in fact necessary for educational as for other theories. If not, then our differences are wider and less remediable than I had supposed.) What then are these additions? And how are they to be justified?

In criticizing the passage that I have quoted from above, Hirst says that I have failed to do what I set out to do, namely, 'to discover the job educational theory performs'.[8] But to put the matter in this way presupposes that we actually have *an* educational theory in the way that we have one physical theory. We do not have any such theory. And this indeed is part of the trouble. For if we had such a theory, we would be in a much better position to see what it was like and what job it actually did do. All we do have is a number of fragmentary contenders for the title and some rival blueprints for filling out the fragments. It is an important function of discussions of this kind that they enable us to get our ideas clear on what we should look for in an educational theory, if indeed we should ever succeed in constructing one.

What other ingredients does Professor Hirst want to prescribe for educational theory? And what function are these additional elements to perform? After saying that a theory in a practical activity like education is 'constructed to determine and guide the activity' he goes on to add: 'The function of the theory is to determine precisely what shall and what shall not be done, say in education.'[9] And this is to say more than that they are constructed to 'guide the activity' as scientific theories do. However, the phrase 'to guide the activity' is ambiguous. It can mean 'to indicate the limits of what *can* be done in the field'. And it is in this sense that scientific theories guide the activities of politicians, doctors, educators, engineers and others in their respective roles. But it can also mean 'to indicate what *ought* to be done'. This is of course a very much stronger sense of 'guide'; but it is, I think, the sense which Hirst intends in his use of the phrase 'to guide the activity'.

It might be said that this second sense of 'guide' introduces a value concept. But it need not do so. A violinist who is teaching a pupil to play the violin may be said to guide the pupil's activities in a stronger sense than that of merely indicating the limits of possible performance. He is demonstrating and recommending practices which tend to produce results generally accepted as desirable among violinists and their audiences. Is this a sufficiently strong sense for Hirst? If it was, educational theory for him need contain no more than purely empirical components. And indeed, I do not see why he should not be satisfied with this sense—for to acquiesce in this would save him from unmanageable logical problems. There is no reason why a satisfactory scientific background to education should not enable us to bring about those educational outcomes which are accepted as desirable in a given community. It is to this type of end that doctors and engineers use their scientific knowledge and that politicians seek, less successfully, to use the frailer weapon of economic theory. Indeed, it is for this purpose that teachers and administrators use *some* of the methods of educational psychology to achieve *some* of the aims of education.

But Hirst wants to import value components into the theory itself. This is a step that seems to me to be both unnecessary and logically disastrous. Let us, first of all, look at his claims. In education:[10]

> it is a fundamental task of the theory to determine the ends
> and goals to be pursued as much as the means to be employed.
> Thus whereas engineering consists almost entirely of the use of
> scientific knowledge in determining efficient means to agreed
> ends, educational theory in large measure depends on the
> making of value judgments about what exactly is to be aimed
> at in education.

And he goes on: 'In doing this, of course, it relies on the logic of moral reasoning.' But unfortunately there is no agreed 'logic of moral reasoning'. Indeed, the very use of the word 'logic' is question-begging here. For it suggests that there is an agreed and recognized procedure of reasoning about moral questions. If there was, moral philosophy would be a completed and uncontentious subject. But, on the contrary, it is a difficult and highly contentious subject just because it is not at all clear how we justify value judgments or how we argue, if indeed we can, from facts to values.

Second, suppose that these questions were settled and that value judgments could appear in a theory of education side by side with empirical statements. What would the relations be between them? Only if we have first answered this question can we understand how the theory could be any sort of unity. But we cannot

55

answer the question until we have antecedently solved the central problems of moral philosophy and, moreover, solved it in a manner favourable to the highly disputable claim that there can be logical relations between statements of fact and statements of value. I do not wish to claim that such a happy outcome will never be achieved. But in the present state of philosophy there is no reason at all to suppose it likely and good reason to suppose that it cannot occur.

We can indeed, if we wish, import our educational values into our theory and claim in consequence that 'it is a fundamental task of the theory to determine the ends and goals to be pursued as well as the means to be employed'.[11] But then they serve exactly the same purpose (namely, guiding actions) as they would serve if they were extrinsic to the theory. So by constructing such a logical hybrid we gain no advantage that we would not gain by leaving our value premises outside the theory. And we incur, as penalty, the logical odium of begging disputed questions that are central to moral philosophy. It must be remembered that a theory is not just a collection of propositions; it is a set of propositions made into a unity by logical relations between the members. A theory is a *structure*, not an intellectual salad. And until logical relations can be demonstrated between statements of value and statements of fact, the importation of value statements into theories is unjustified. Hirst says indeed that 'educational principles are justified entirely by direct appeal to knowledge from a variety of forms, scientific, philosophical, historical etc. Beyond these forms of knowledge, it requires no theoretical synthesis.'[12] If by 'educational principles' here, he means 'educational value judgments', he is begging the question. And if he does not include value judgments under educational principles, he leaves them unjustified. Perhaps indeed that is the way to leave them. But then it is prudent to give them no spurious prestige by making them parts of the theory. I can summarize my main point here by stating rather starkly the alternatives open to Hirst: either the value components of his theory are proved from its factual components or they are not. If they are, let us see the proof (which would indeed be a philosophical landmark). If they are not, there is no point in making them integral to the theory. For they can do their work of prescription and guidance just as well outside it.

It is clear from Professor Hirst's reply to an earlier version of this paper that he and I differ profoundly on the role to be assigned to reason (and so to its associated activities such as explanation). He thinks that I take a narrow logico-scientific view of reason while he accepts a wider and more generous connotation. I do not think, however, that this is a field in which broadmindedness and generosity are necessarily virtues. To be sure, 'reason' like most general words has a penumbra of vagueness that makes it unprofitable to try to decide just where its border lies. But as with 'theory', we can delineate the agreed central area of meaning. To say that the function of reason is the critical evaluation of evidence for statements is to propose an uncontroversial minimal connotation. But exactly what content such a prescription has for us can only be determined by the successes and failures of reason in the past. We have no other guide. And these successes and failures are recorded in the history of human thought and, in particular, the history of science.

Hirst says that 'it would be unwise to be too definite about what can and what cannot be regarded as valid inference'.[13] It is hard to believe that he means that established and accepted inference patterns may be shown in the future to be invalid. No doubt he means rather that new patterns of acceptable argument remain still to be discovered; and that such patterns may validate, for example, inferences from facts to values. To this one can only reply that it is imprudent to base one's beliefs on a bare possibility of novel and indeed revolutionary developments in logic for which its past history and its present state offer no evidence. In this field the fact that no one can foretell the future is as good a reason for caution as for optimism. And when Hirst says of fact and value 'I do not accept that there is no logical connection between them that is important in determining educational practice'[14] one can only reply that where logical connections exist, they can be demonstrated. Perhaps this demonstration lies in the future. If so, Hirst's faith will be justified; but this is a field in which faith must be justified by works.

It may perhaps be useful to indicate what developments in logic might be taken to vindicate Hirst's belief. The accepted notion of validity requires that a valid argument form does not permit the deduction of a false conclusion from a true premise. If we are to allow the possibility of deducing value statements from factual premises we need at least one of two things: (1) a totally new concept of validity which is not tied to the notion of truth or falsity or (2) acceptable tests for assigning truth-values to value statements. I mention this only to indicate just how considerable a revolution must be contemplated even to make sense of Hirst's conjecture.

Hirst further objects that to restrict the activity of reason to a scientific paradigm is to neglect the fact that we can properly speak of reasons for action. 'Is not the process of reasoning here one that must involve the logical horrors Professor O'Connor finds so distasteful?'[15]

The answer to this is twofold. In the first place, it is simply not the case that all cases of giving reasons are properly described as reasoning. Nor, without extending the application of the word 'reason' (in the sense here in question) well beyond its usual denotation can we describe all cases of reasoning as involving the giving of reasons. At best, the giving of reasons may be said to include reasoning, if the reasons are of a special kind, such as, for example, rules of inference or the premises of an argument (including previously established conclusions). At worst, the two classes overlap without either including the other. And second, reasons for action may be good or bad but they are objectionable only if they are bad reasons. The pattern of argument here was sketched by Aristotle.[16] I desire X; Y is an efficient means of getting X; therefore I choose Y. Whether this is good or bad reasoning depends simply on the truth of the premise 'Y is an efficient means of getting X'. But such cases have nothing to do with possible logical links between fact and value.

Of course, there are moral problems central to education as there are to any large-scale social institution like marriage or the law or the political framework. And there are day-to-day moral decisions called for in teaching and in administering the system as there are in medicine or politics or in marriage. We deal with such problems as best we can by allowing our values an appropriate weight in determining the outcome. But this does not mean that the values of the teacher must, in some mysterious way, be given a status as part of a theory any more than the values of a doctor are a part of the theory of medicine.

I conclude therefore that Professor Hirst's attempt to integrate value concepts into educational theory is both unsuccessful and unnecessary; and that, in consequence, we have no good reason to suppose that a purely empirical basis for educational theory would be inadequate. I do not claim indeed that such a theory actually exists or that it ever will. But it could do any job that we could reasonably require of a theory. However, I am reassured by this examination of Hirst's claims. For it seems to me that if he cannot succeed in such an enterprise, it is unlikely that anyone else will do so.

I know that suggestions that the methods of science are adequate to solve human problems are commonly regarded as a symptom of intellectual philistinism; and that many people distrust such proposals. But their value is that they rest on the belief that reason (that is, tested methods of assessing and evaluating evidence) is our only guide in problem solving. There are no 'higher' or 'better' methods that rational ones; there is only guessing. And even that can be used more efficiently on rational principles. (Witness, the theory of games.)

58

II

So much for the nature of educational theory. What can we say about its uses? If we grant, as most people would, that theory does not, at the present time, play the part in guiding and controlling the educational system that a developed theory might be expected to play, can we make any rational conjectures about its possible uses in some ideal future?

I will start by trying to develop the analogy between education and technological applications of scientific knowledge like medicine and engineering and by indicating where the analogy breaks down. This may give us some guide towards a rational reconstruction of educational theory, at least in its general outlines. The *prima facie* necessity for educational theory rests on the analogy between education and other scientifically based activities of great social import like medicine and engineering. No one, I suppose, believes that education is itself a science or even a group of sciences. It is rather a focus for the application of various sciences in an important social context, a set of practical activities with a common group of aims. Like any other craft of this sort, teaching and the auxiliary organizational activities that together make up what we call 'education' have their theoretical background. And at least part of this theoretical background consists of scientific knowledge about human behaviour and development and the working of communities. In the same way, the art of medicine has its related sciences, anatomy, physiology, biochemistry and the rest. And engineering depends for its effectiveness on the application of mathematics and physics to the design of machinery.

This analogy is not quite so straightforward as it looks. But even if it were, the problems presented by education differ from those of medicine, engineering and other applications of science to technology in some very important ways. I shall discuss some of these ways below. But the analogy is itself misleading for two different reasons. (1) Effective education is quite possible without any of the theoretical background of the kind offered by psychology, sociology and the rest of the relevant sciences. And this is not the case with medicine and engineering. (2) The social sciences which are, if anything is, the 'theoretical basis' of education differ from the natural sciences in several ways. One of the important ways in which they differ is that their findings are less recondite and more obvious to common sense than those of physics, chemistry and biology. I will say a little on each of these points in turn.

(1) Education is a social institution which is an essential part of any reasonably developed society. And we can see in the social

history of Europe effective educational institutions at work for two-and-a-half thousand years. The products of these systems were in no way inferior to the products of our system. The evidence for this is simply the history of literature, music, art, science, mathematics and philosophy from early Greek times to the present day. Not until quite recently were the findings or the speculations of the psychologists and the rest brought to the aid of the teacher. I shall look in a moment at the question of how far they have helped teachers in their job. But it is surely quite obvious that the help they have given to teachers in their classrooms has been minimal compared to the enormous efforts that have been made to develop these sciences over the past hundred years. Diminishing returns, to use the economists' phrase, are manifest very early in this sphere of application. But the case is quite different if we look at the history of medicine. There simply was no effective medicine until the sciences of physics, chemistry and biology had become well established. There was no effective surgery until the discovery of antisepsis and anaesthetics in the nineteenth century. Nor was there any specific treatment of diseases (smallpox and scurvy in the late eighteenth century apart) until the early experiments on anti-toxins in the 1880s. Prior to the nineteenth century, medical men took the credit due to the healing powers of nature, as they still do to a large degree. And the same can be said, *mutatis mutandis*, for the development of engineering. My claim is therefore that education does not really stand in need of a theoretical background, if we mean by that phrase, a background of developed scientific theory. Medicine and engineering, on the other hand, could not exist without it. Nor could a complex industrial economy.

The real difference between the education of the twentieth century and that of previous centuries is simply a matter of the extent of its application. We have decided, rightly or wrongly, that the benefits of literacy and numeracy are such that no one must be spared them. And this enormous extension of the range of application of the educational process has brought with it difficulties that teachers in previous ages did not have to face. When only a few children are selected, by talent or rank, to be educated, there are enough or more than enough naturally gifted teachers to go round. When everyone has to be socially processed in this way, we are faced with the sort of difficulties that arise when skilled handicrafts are replaced by factory mass production. We are faced with administrative difficulties—those of organizing and financing a great social project—and profound and little understood social consequences which have to be discovered and slowly adjusted to. We are also faced with increasing shortages of good quality materials both to fill our classrooms and to fill the colleges where teachers are trained. But these are not difficulties of educational principle; they are problems of social adjustment similar to those consequent on setting up a nationalized health service in a previously under-doctored community. It might indeed by claimed that just because education on a national scale necessitates our processing sub-standard materials with sub-standard operators, we have all the more need of whatever help a theoretical background of the relevant sciences can offer us. There is, I believe, something in this claim.

For example, we do now have to train our teachers (or most of them) where previously we did not have to do so. But this training amounts less to imparting any newly discovered psychological principles than to indoctrinating them with the traditional lore of the craft. The psychological principles are, of course, added for good measure. They may be expected, at least to provide intellectual satisfaction to the curious by showing how the traditional skills of the teaching profession are vindicated by the advance of science in the way that traditional herbal remedies may be vindicated by the advance of pharmacology. But they may do more than this. I discuss below some of the special difficulties created for the practical teacher by the spread of formal education from a small privileged class to the population at large. Scientific psychology offers some promise of help in these difficulties though it is early to say whether the promise can be honoured.

(2) Whether we are justified in expecting more from the supposed scientific background of education turns to a large extent on the truth of the second point I made above—the obviousness of the truths of the social sciences. It is clear enough, I believe, that the broad pattern of the sciences of man is more obvious or at least less surprising than those of the sciences of nature. I have suggested elsewhere[17] that the social sciences might be satirically but not unfairly described as those sciences that tell us nothing that we do not already know. Being human, we have excellent opportunities for becoming acquainted with the main trends of human experience and behaviour. And since we live in societies, we cannot help seeing in rough outline how societies work, provided only that we are reasonably curious and observant. Indeed, the fact that most of us acquire a morality is some evidence of this. This rough and ready knowledge of primitive psychology and sociology is necessary to us if we are to live successfully in a social environment. It is also sufficient for us to teach successfully as long as our classes are not too large or our pupils too stupid and, if not anxious to learn, at least tolerant of being taught. But once education becomes universal, we make teaching a much more difficult task. Large classes containing

pupils of all grades of intelligence provide vastly more intractable material than teachers were faced with in the days when education was the privilege of a few. And the very fact that literacy, since it is now supposed to be a prerequisite of citizenship, no longer confers any social cachet removes the main inducement for becoming literate. Only those stages of education which are restricted to privileged minorities still offer incentives to the average pupil. It is in these very daunting circumstances that educators look to science to provide the help that unaided skill and intelligence can no longer give the teacher. The pessimists believe, in other words, that since much of education is nowadays little more than the manufacture of artificial silk purses from real sows' ears, we need the help of science to enable us to effect such a transmutation.

But even if we conceded that the pessimists were right, is scientific theory equal to the tasks that the popularization of education has created? It is worth noting that the analogy with medicine and engineering breaks down at another important point. The fact that scientifically based medical treatment and engineering achievement are so widespread and so integral a part of our civilization is itself a consequence of the scientific revolution. It is not just a consequence of a *social* revolution that decided that these benefits should be extended to all. For there could have been no such benefits but for the scientific discoveries that made medicine and engineering possible. But in education, it is the other way round. The democratization of society was the cause of the spread of education; and then, by positive feedback, education furthered the extension of democracy. And it is the spread of education that has raised the problems that send educators to the social sciences in the hope of increasing the efficiency of the educative process by giving it a basis in science.

These hopes are perhaps easy to understand but not so easy to share. The history of the social sciences is a short one. Experimental psychology, the science from which education has most to hope, has a history of no more than one hundred years. Since no one can foresee how far it may progress, may we not hope that when these sciences have reached the stage now achieved by physics and chemistry they may provide a basis for the same sort of spectacular achievement in education that we have seen in medicine and engineering over the past eighty years? Perhaps the education of the twentieth century is in the same primitive condition that medicine and engineering were in up to two hundred years ago and from which the development of their theoretical background has now freed them.

Of course, nobody can say with assurance that these hopes will not be fulfilled. But if we look at the differences between the sciences of man and the sciences of nature, on the one hand, and the kind of educational problem with which science might conceivably help us, on the other, there seems little *prima facie* reason to indulge in any utopian hopes for the future. Such educational problems can be divided into two main classes, problems of administration and problems of teaching.

Under problems of administration, we can class questions about the organization of different stages and levels of education. Of these, the controversy about comprehensive education is the best-known contemporary example. The answer given to such questions in fact is largely determined by judgments of value embodied in political and social attitudes and not by objectively established findings of scientific investigation. It is not, in principle, impossible to bring scientific methods to bear in solving such problems, if only they are regarded as questions of educational efficiency. Selection procedures were indeed so determined for some years by such scientific methods. At the present time, they are less used, partly because they are considered to be 'undemocratic' (that is to say, they provide objective evidence of human inequalities) and partly because the currently available procedures have proved to be of less perfect prognostic value than was at one time hoped for. We may see in this single instance a double danger that imperils all attempts to apply the theoretical background of education to its day-to-day working: (i) the scientific theories and results are too fragmentary and imperfect to offer a completely reliable guide (although they are the best and indeed the only rational guide we have); (ii) there is a strong prejudice, rooted in popular ignorance, against the application of science to human affairs. Men like to believe that they are not a part of nature in a way that makes them invulnerable to reliable classification, prediction or control.

Under problems of teaching, there are three main sub-problems where scientific knowledge might be expected to help us: improving the curriculum, improving incentives to learning and improving presentation. These three sub-problems are, of course, closely interconnected but they are all questions on which psychology and sociology might be expected to help us. In fact, of course, experimental procedures in the classroom using only superficial and common-sense knowledge of the human sciences continue to give as much help with such questions as the findings of the specialists. (Consider, for example, the disappointing development of the one notable application of psychology to education in the past twenty years, programmed learning and its application in teaching machines.)

There are two chief reasons for this. The first is that the human sciences are still in too undeveloped and controversial a stage to give us unambiguous directions; the second is that their findings, even where they are well established, are too remote from the practical situations for which we seek their help. Many of the difficulties arise not because the educational situation is too complex to form a suitable field of application for science but rather because it is too remote. I can perhaps illustrate what I mean here by comparing the application of science to weather prediction with its application to cookery. The physical principles of meteorology are fairly well understood but their application in concrete situations is still imperfect enough to make weather-forecasting a fairly hazardous art. The variables involved are so numerous, their changes so rapid and the calculation of the results of their interaction so complex and time-consuming that we have to be satisfied with fairly rough predictions. We have no analogous situation in the explanation, prediction and control of educational situations. The underlying scientific laws are very imperfectly understood. And we do not really know what would be involved in applying these laws to our material if we knew what they were. The situation is much more analogous to explaining success or failure in cookery in terms of physics and chemistry. We could, if it were worthwhile, determine the chemical consequences of mixing ingredients in certain ways and in certain proportions and submitting them to various changes of temperature. But it is simply not worthwhile to do this for the coarse empirical methods of cooks in their kitchens are entirely adequate to ensure the advance of their art. So, too, the crude empirical methods of teachers in their classrooms may well be more efficient, for the present at least, in solving the problems of teaching than the hit-and-miss application of imperfectly formulated psychological theories.

The conclusions of my argument may be summarized as follows: (i) The construction of educational theories, insofar as it is a rational activity, is subject to the same standards as the paradigm instances of theorizing that we meet in science. (And insofar as it is not a rational activity, it is a pretentious and contemptible waste of time.)

(ii) Nevertheless, even if theories of education did meet these exacting standards, it is doubtful if they would yield the same kind of practical advances that technology, medicine and economic organization owe to their respective theoretical bases.

But is it not inconsistent both to demand rationality of educational theory and at the same time to doubt the likelihood of its profitable application? I do not think so. It is not in the hope that their results will find some useful employment that scientists play the game of reason. If it is found that our theories can be put to some beneficial use, then it is a piece of uncovenanted good fortune for which the rules of the game that we play against nature give us no warranty. And if it is asked why I insist so pedantically on the necessity for rational methods in educational thinking, there are two answers. The minor one is simply that education is a field in which cranks and charlatans do get (and always have had) an audience unhealthily receptive of superstition and absurdity. And anything that might tend to discourage that is surely to be supported. But the important answer is simply that, whether our problems are theoretical or practical, we have to rely on proved rational methods to solve them. For if we abandon reason, we have nothing else to turn to.

Notes

1 Broad, *Examination of McTaggart's Philosophy*, Cambridge, 1933, vol. 1, p. 270.

2 D. J. O'Connor, *Introduction to the Philosophy of Education*, London, 1957, ch. 5.

3 R. Wellek, *Concepts of Criticism*, New Haven, 1963, p. 1.

4 For a clear elementary account of explanation and the idea that the statement to be explained is the conclusion of a deductive argument, see D. M. Taylor, *Explanation and Meaning*, Cambridge, 1970, chs 1–3.

5 P. H. Hirst, 'Philosophy and educational theory', *British Journal of Educational Studies*, vol. 12, no. 1, 1963, p. 60.

6 P. H. Hirst, 'Educational theory' in J. W. Tibble (ed.), *The Study of Education*, London, 1966, p. 40.

7 O'Connor, *op. cit.*, p. 110.

8 Hirst, 'Educational theory', p. 39.

9 *Ibid.*, p. 40.

10 *Ibid.*, p. 52.

11 *Ibid.*

12 *Ibid.*, p. 55.

13 P. H. Hirst, 'The nature of educational theory: a reply to D. J. O'Connor', *Proceedings of the Philosophy of Education Society of Great Britain*, vol. 6, no. 1, January 1972, p. 112.

14 *Ibid.*, p. 116.

15 *Ibid.*, p. 114.

16 Aristotle, *Nicomachean Ethics*, Book 3.

17 O'Connor, *op. cit.*, p. 99.

4   The nature and scope of educational theory (2)

Reply to D. J. O'Connor[1]

Paul H. Hirst

In his initial discussion of the nature of educational theory in his book *An Introduction to the Philosophy of Education*, Professor O'Connor distinguished a number of different senses in which we use the term 'theory'. One of these, contrasts theory with practice, the word referring to 'a set or system of rules or a collection of precepts which guide or control actions of various kinds'.[2] In this sense, it was suggested, educational theory consists of 'those parts of psychology concerned with perception, learning, concept formation, motivation and so on which directly concern the work of the teacher'.[3] The word 'theory' was, however, said to have another sense, in which it is used as it occurs in the natural sciences, where it refers to a single hypothesis or a logically interconnected set of hypotheses that have been confirmed by observation. In this sense, it was suggested, we have standards for judging the value of theories put forward by writers on education. Commenting on Professor O'Connor's account in my paper 'Educational theory'[4] I argued for the importance of conceiving educational theory along the lines of the first of these two senses, when it is seen as producing rational principles for educational practice, but I rejected the claim that it will then consist simply of parts of psychology and other relevant sciences. I maintained instead that it would necessarily have to draw also on other quite different forms of knowledge and understanding, on for instance judgments of moral value, philosophical beliefs and historical knowledge. I argued in fact that the theory of a practical activity must, logically must, involve a concern for more than scientific knowledge. Of course I did not wish to suggest, and took care to make this explicit,[5] that the term 'educational theory' could not also be used as a label to cover simply work in those sciences which conform to the criteria of Professor O'Connor's second sense, insofar as it occurs in the study of education. Rather I wished to bring out the very complex character of the theory the practice of education must draw on, in opposition to any reductionist suggestion that the sciences alone are sufficient for this purpose.

In very general terms Professor O'Connor and I do not disagree.

That decisions about the aims or ends and the means of education involve value judgments as well as empirical considerations, is not in dispute. At a superficial level, therefore, we might seem to be arguing merely about the best use of certain words. But that this concern for the best use of words does in fact stem from issues of substance comes out starkly in Professor O'Connor's paper 'The nature of educational theory'[6] for he not only focuses most clearly the very real agreement between us, but also brings to the fore a range of terms that, having more than one meaning can give a sense of agreement where little might in fact exist. That education must be seen as a 'social institution' and that the study of education is concerned with solving the problems of education by the use of 'reason' alone, I accept entirely. That educational theory seeks to 'explain' and that its claims must be 'refutable' we agree, and also that it is concerned with 'improving' and 'guiding' practice, and promoting human 'welfare'.

Yet one by one these very agreements between us can be seen to mask what are probably fundamentally different points of view. The social institution of education in which we are interested is not, of course, a natural object and what makes it the thing it is, cannot be set out merely in terms of its observable features. Because it involves deliberately planned activities, education is only characterizable by attending to the way those involved in the institution conceive what they are doing, and though it may have features of which they are quite unaware, it is only in relation to the purposes it is thought to serve that we can hope to satisfactorily describe the institution and its activities.[7] From the start then I find myself somewhat at variance with Professor O'Connor. For if the delineation of education as an institution requires an understanding of human purposes, which I do not consider reducible to an understanding of what is observable, we can say right away that the study of education must involve more than a study of relevant sciences, unless the term science is being used in a very broad sense.

Clearly there is much about the activities both formal and informal which we at present label education that we do not understand. Much of this understanding will only come by scientific investigation. But any adequate explanation of what is going on cannot, as far as I can see, stop there. Explanation in terms of beliefs and values, of reasons as well as causes, seems to me logically necessary, and explanations of this kind do not to my mind fall within the pattern of explanation in the sciences—by means of universal generalizations.[8] Insofar as the logic of mental concepts differs from that of scientific concepts, such a conclusion is to be expected. When, therefore, Professor O'Connor and I agree that educational theory is concerned with explanation, I must not be taken to be agreeing to any suggestion that scientific explanation is its only concern. Indeed I would argue that just because educational theory is concerned in part with the explanation of human activities, it must involve more than the sciences. I see no reason to limit the use of the term 'explanation' to its scientific form and for that reason amongst others wish to refrain from any restriction on the use of the term 'theory'.

To argue in this way is in no way to reject the claim that for a true explanation the premises must be true and the inferences valid. But I am maintaining that statements of reasons are just as capable of being true or false as statements of causes, though the grounds may be very different, and that it is unwise to be too definite about what can and what cannot be regarded as valid inference. Though the logic of explanation in terms of reasons may not be half as clear as we would like, I see no reason for doubting that true explanations are possible and that we can know they are true. In much the same way I am perfectly happy with the idea that refutability is a necessary feature of theories. But I do not accept that the only form of refutation possible is that employed in the sciences. That a theory as to why X did Y can be refuted by X without any scientific appeal, is I think sufficient to indicate this.

Professor O'Connor might argue that we can hope that eventually such sciences as psychology and sociology will provide the form of explanation I am insisting is necessary. If so we certainly disagree sharply. But he holds as strongly as I do, indeed much more strongly, that even these sciences can never alone justify the value judgments educational practice must involve. That educational theory is concerned with 'improving' and 'guiding' practice, with promoting human 'welfare', we both insist. But his account of the guidance the theory offers is that of the technical means the sciences can provide for realizing ends coming from outside the theory—from society at large and its 'currently accepted concept of human welfare'. To my mind, as Professor O'Connor rightly stresses, the theory is itself concerned with determining the ends as well as the means of education, the answers to *all* questions about what ought to be done, moral as well as technical.

Professor O'Connor's defence of his point of view rests primarily on his reading of the current state of moral philosophy and the impossible problems it lands on the plate of anyone taking my stand. There being no agreement that we have the right even to speak of the logic of moral reasoning, let alone to indicate what that logic might look like, and having therefore no agreement on how to justify value judgments and good reason to suppose that it is impossible to give an account as to how scientific facts and values might be related within the theory as I conceive it, he advocates excluding from it altogether the determination of values. To do otherwise, he sees resulting in something being called 'theory' which is a logical confusion. Educational problems he insists can only be solved rationally by looking to the development of the sciences, working within the framework of currently accepted ideals.

My first objection to this position is that the fear of having a theory whose logic we cannot at present satisfactorily elucidate, is being allowed to override the fact that, as no judgments about educational practice escape direct or indirect value commitments, they *must* figure in any *adequate* statement of reasons for action. And that being so, any adequate theory of practice must be involved in debate about such judgments, seeking whatever rational basis for them it is possible to obtain. To do otherwise is to my mind to produce theory quite inadequate for practical judgments, something which, with its emphasis on scientific fact, is better referred to as, say, psychology rather than educational theory. Professor O'Connor seems to restrict the activity of reason to scientific reasoning, but do we not equally speak of reasons for actions and activities, and is not the process of reasoning here one that must involve the logical horrors Professor O'Connor finds so distasteful? To insist that theories are concerned with providing reasons in no way supports the contention that science alone can give us reasons and therefore must comprise the theory of a practical activity.

But clearly I am far from sharing Professor O'Connor's pessimism about the search for the logic of moral reasoning and indeed I think it is in part self-induced by his insistence on too narrow a view of logical relations. It may well be that no pattern of reasoning can be elucidated within the confines of the logic of scientific reasoning. The relationship between fact and value is I agree, not likely to be analysable in terms of the relationships that hold between different scientific truths. But I see no reason to side, at this point in time, against the possibility of such a logic and the mapping of the fact-value relationship. The relationship between statements about mental states and statements about related observable behaviour, do not conform to the pattern of relationships that can exist between different statements simply about such behaviour, but that in no way persuades me that there is no logical relationship. I am encouraged by philosophical work on both mental and moral concepts. The features of moral discourse that give it at least the appearance of a form of rational discourse make me think that the onus of proof rests with those who maintain otherwise. The old argument that there were valid syllogisms before their logical features were teased out, is not without force. I therefore see no reason to reject the idea of rational educational theory concerned with determining ends as well as means, because we cannot at the moment give an adequate philosophical account of moral discourse in general and of the fact-value relationship in particular. After all, the development of science as a rational pursuit did not wait on the development of a satisfactory logic of scientific explanation. Indeed it developed in spite of gross confusion.

In commenting on the arguments I have outlined above, Professor O'Connor elaborates further our disagreements on the role of reason.[9] As can no doubt now be anticipated, I do not accept that in our careful use of the term we should be limited by 'the successes and failures of reason in the past . . . recorded . . . , in particular, in the history of science'. A great deal of contemporary philosophy has served to show that our serious use of the term goes well beyond the confines of science and its instrumental application. So much so, that to take the logic of scientific reasoning as a restrictive paradigm is to my mind no longer helpful. It shows a confidence, as well as a pessimism, I cannot share. If the elucidation of new forms of inference is proving difficult, that does nothing to remove the inadequacies of the older forms. There is a point beyond which one's absolute faith in the old gods cannot be retained.

The insistence on the old gods ties Professor O'Connor to the Aristotelian account of reasons for actions in terms of desire and efficient means. To my mind such an account merely uses the term 'desire' to hide or beg all the questions about the justification of actions that I am interested in, questions which cannot be dealt with in traditional terms and which are at the heart of educational issues. Similarly, even the developments in logic I am concerned about Professor O'Connor wishes to force into a traditional mould. Must we accept that the logical relationship between fact and value must be expressed deductively? I am no longer convinced that the issue is characterizable in such 'simple' terms. And even if it is, it is not clear that the concept of truth, to which the notion of validity is tied, can be anchored as Professor O'Connor wants without begging the whole question. I do not accept that scientific truth is the only form of truth, and I am not at all horrified at the idea that value statements may come to be assigned truth-values. An insistence on scientific norms, if they are alien to our discourse, will not help us to elucidate the character of reasons for action and it is this any adequate account of educational theory necessitates.

In view of this ethical theory, Professor O'Connor seeks to take a stand for educational theory along lines that make it uncommitted on the nature of value judgments. Yet in one crucial respect his position is very much committed. His view that the value judgments educational practice calls on can do their job just as satisfactorily from outside educational theory or from within, assumes an ultimate dissociation of fact and value that seems to me contrary to their relationship in the actual conduct of educational debate. The ends-means distinction is notoriously difficult to draw in many contexts and in educational affairs ends and means are frequently logically inter-related. The means often involve activities that must be assessed not merely as efficient means but also in moral terms as ends in their own right. The means can be constitutive of certain ends and so on.[10] To this must be added the fact that society's notions of general welfare are far too general to enable those in education to derive detailed principles from them granted all the science in the world. The conflict of values too creates endless problems on which even individual teachers must make value judgments for themselves. If the inter-relation of fact and value cannot at present be mapped, I personally cannot accept the very particular feature of dissociation Professor O'Connor seems to assume. In the present state of philosophical knowledge, I prefer to accept as legitimate in educational theory all the elements that must occur in it if it is to fulfil its function for educational practice, including the rigorous critical discussion of values, even when this calls in question prevailing ideas of human welfare. To restrict the notion of educational theory to the relevant sciences is to my mind to encourage a totally inadequate critical appraisal of both ends and means.

From what I have said it will I think be clear that I refuse to be impaled on Professor O'Connor's fork. He insists that either the value components of educational theory are proved from its factual components or they are not. If they are, then I should produce the proof; if they are not, there is no point in making them internal to the theory. My answer is that though I do not for one moment think the value judgments can be 'proved' from the factual components, I do not accept that there is no logical connection between them that is important in determining educational practice. The values cannot to my mind act equally from without or from within the theory. What can be obtained from without is totally inadequate to the job. Value assessments that are significant in deciding to do A rather than B must be made from within and are not simply derivable from value assessments taken from without.

Professor O'Connor's stipulative definition I therefore reject, not because a group of sciences is not worthy of the title theory on the grounds of some form of irrationality, but because it does not seem to me able to provide what educational practice needs and I see no necessary irrationality inherent in the domain of critical discussion that would be adequate. It is the latter I prefer to label 'educational theory'. I agree that the logic of this discourse is unclear, but it does not follow that it is simply a 'salad' of disconnected items. That would be to assume again certain forms of dissociation between the elements which I am not prepared to take on board. Professor O'Connor's collection of sciences is certainly at present itself a 'salad', though presumably unifying concepts may someday be found. I am however not at all clear about the place Professor O'Connor's account allows to such other elements as philosophical beliefs, a knowledge of persons and historical understanding. The unity I hope we might elucidate is precisely the unity that comes from the use of these sciences, and other elements, including philosophical beliefs and value judgments, in providing reasons for actions. I have elsewhere been at pains to stress that educational theory is not merely a collection of logically disparate elements, of the kind found in many fashionable curriculum units.[11] But to my mind the unity must be found by examining the theory itself, not by reducing that theory to elements that conform to an already recognized unity of a different character. What I am concerned with is educational theory in Professor O'Connor's 'wide' sense, for in spite of its only partially scientific character, it is through the development of theory in this sense alone that I can see hope for any thoroughly rational educational practice.[12]

One might have expected Professor O'Connor's concern for a thoroughly scientific concept of educational theory to go with a firm belief in the benefits science would in due course bring to educational practice. That on this front he sees so depressing a prospect is disheartening indeed. What is more, I had certainly hoped that in spite of our persisting disagreements about the nature of educational theory itself, we might agree about the significance of scientific advance. Our disagreement this time, however, focuses on the import of recent work in educational theory as much as on philosophical matters.

The analogy between, on the one hand, the dependence of medicine and engineering on their contributory sciences and, on the other, the dependence of education on its sciences may be partial, but I am not convinced that Professor O'Connor has shown this. Where terms like 'medicine' and 'engineering' are taken as labels of scientifically based pursuits and contrasted with 'education', which is not so conceived, it is a mere tautology that education can occur without a scientific basis in the way that medicine and engineering can not. But if we look below the use of these terms, is it not the case that there was much effective curing and impressive road and bridge building based on trial and error, long before the relevant sciences developed? And is it obvious that teaching ever was more successful? That across the centuries certain forms of learning have in certain circumstances been passed on successfully, is doubtful evidence that the relevant sciences are in some ways less important in this area than in the areas of curing and road building. Of course in certain areas the problems differ in character and at the elementary level more problems in one area may be capable of solution than in another. But what follows at more complex and sophisticated levels? In all areas, more difficult problems reveal the need for sophisticated theoretical knowledge, and perhaps that is definitionally the case. To say that 'effective education is quite possible without any of the theoretical background. . . . And this is not the case with medicine and engineering' is, I suggest, true only if one specifically restricts oneself to those relatively elementary educational problems that seem capable of solution in these terms, contrasting them with sophisticated and complex medical and engineering problems. That this kind of restriction of educational issues is in Professor O'Connor's mind is suggested when he comments on the development of universal comprehensive education, for the problems that brings, he seems loath to accept as genuine educational problems. But can we really be as happy as Professor O'Connor seems with the seeming success naturally gifted teachers have had with naturally gifted pupils using traditional methods based on the lore of the craft? Many would claim, and with good reason, that (a) the 'platitudinous' social sciences have cast such serious doubt on notions of natural giftedness that to operate with these is to fail to understand the very nature of social and educational processes, (b) the precise significance of traditional methods in achieving such apparent success is not obvious, and (c) the criteria of *educational* success being used ought to be called in question. In fact I see little reason to think that even in the past educational lore got us any further in dealing with educational problems than medical lore got us in dealing with medical problems. To think otherwise is to be in danger of attributing to seemingly successful teachers abilities they do not actually possess.

Professor O'Connor thinks there is at least something in the view that the coming of mass education has produced the problems that cannot be dealt with by the old lore. There is thus now a need for a scientifically based approach to education where previously there was none. Clearly he is right that mass education has provoked new and difficult problems for teachers, but this recent recognition of the need for a more scientific approach in no way shows that such an approach was previously unnecessary. In education, as in medicine, people operating on the folklore with apparent success may be unaware of the need for making rational judgments on appropriate scientific evidence. But that in no way makes the folklore an adequate basis for past practices, and of course does not justify simply continuing with those practices where relevant scientific information is available. To my mind the necessity for a background of scientific knowledge for rational educational practice is no more a product of mass education than the necessity for a scientific background for rational medical practice is a product of the national health service. The difference in the cases, if any, is in our awareness of that necessity.

In commenting on the contemporary situation one must agree that educational psychology and sociology have not so far provided many of the principles that rational practice demands. But Professor O'Connor is surely being a little ungenerous. The complexity of educational situations and the difficulty involved in applying remote scientific truths to practical issues do indeed cause enormous problems. But I am not convinced that the present state of affairs or the future prospect is as black as he makes out. If we take the areas he refers to, it seems to me that we now know quite a lot about learning processes and that traditional lore, assessment procedures and organizational problems are inhibiting the development of more rationally based teaching methods. The great deal of evidence there is on the effects of selection and streaming is at last having significant influence on our practice. When Professor O'Connor suggests that selection is ending because the related tests show objective evidence of human inequalities and are prognostically imperfect, he is giving only part of the picture. There can now be little doubt that selection procedures are in numerous ways educationally destructive for significant numbers of those involved and that other more rational, more scientifically based, organizations are available. In both these areas I should have thought that we are now acquiring scientific knowledge which is neither impossibly remote nor platitudinously obvious. Indeed if what we know is so obvious, why exactly does the dissemination and application of this knowledge arouse such opposition?

Professor O'Connor may be right in his prognostications, but his is not the only view of the situation. If one is not too ambitious about what one expects to be achieved in a relatively short space of time, might it not be that our lore-riddled educational practice will, bit by bit, become more rational? Indeed to my mind that process has now got under way. The problems ahead are enormous, but I see no cause for gloom. The achievements of reason are indeed our only hope in education; they may be hard to secure, but then when was it otherwise?

Notes

1 The substantial part of this paper was published under the title 'The nature of educational theory: a reply to D. J. O'Connor', *Proceedings of the Philosophy of Education Society of Great Britain*, vol. 6, no. 1, January 1972.

2 D. J. O'Connor, *Introduction to the Philosophy of Education*, London, 1957, p. 75.

3 *Ibid.*, p. 75.

4 P. H. Hirst, 'Educational theory' in J. W. Tibble (ed.), *The Study of Education*, London, 1966.

5 *Ibid.*, pp. 40–1.

6 D. J. O'Connor, 'The nature of educational theory', *Proceedings of Philosophy of Education Society*, vol. 6, no. 1, January 1972.

7 See A. P. Griffiths, 'A deduction of universities' in R. D. Archambault (ed.), *Philosophical Analysis and Education*, London, 1965.

8 See D. M. Taylor, *Explanation and Meaning*, Cambridge, 1970.

9 See D. J. O'Connor, 'The nature and scope of educational theory' (1), published in this volume, pp. 47–65.

10 See H. Sockett, 'Curriculum aims and objectives: taking a means to an end', *Proceedings of the Philosophy of Education Society*, vol. 6, no. 1, January 1972.

11 Hirst, *op. cit.*

12 In chapter 2 of her book *Educational Thought: an Introduction*, Macmillan, London, 1969, Mrs Brenda Cohen makes several of the points made by Professor O'Connor. On the tight connection between 'reason' and 'science' she is however rather extreme (pp. 23–4):

> By deliberately cutting off education from anything resembling scientific standards of truth or validity, Hirst is, in fact, returning the subject to its traditional status as a field where all may propound their ideas with as complete a freedom and as much imagination as in the past. . . . This cleavage between scientific theories and the theories which determine practical decisions in education or politics or private life, is very far from the outlook of the empirically-minded man in any field, for whom the term 'unscientific' implies a root criticism of the standards and criteria that are being applied, even in such areas as education or politics.

I trust I have made it clear that I am in no sense cutting off education from the most stringent standards of truth and validity. The question is how far scientific standards are applicable. To my mind only to scientific statements. But that is not to throw open educational theory to the unfettered imagination. To subject to scientific criteria what is not of that character would be disastrous. To limit one's critical attention to the merely scientific elements of the theory would be to let loose just the horrors Mrs Cohen fears. To suggest scientific and practical theories differ in character is only to be unscientific where science is in any case inadequate. And the point then is, of course, to promote rational criticism of the proper kind, not to limit critical appraisal in the interests of speculation.

Education and values

part 2

Education—a moral concept   5

T. F. Daveney

I

In this chapter it is my aim to consider the concept of education as it is employed in ordinary speech and argument, and try to demonstrate that it is a normative or moral concept. My main thesis can be stated quite simply: when we speak of education, there is presupposed either an ideal of a person to which the education is leading; or alternatively an ideal of a society for which the education fits the individual member. But in any case—and this is the important part—lying behind the concept of education is the notion of a norm or set of norms which gives the education its purpose.

Now when I speak of this notion 'lying behind' or 'being presupposed by' the concept I mean by that 'logically implied'. So if my thesis is correct, then it follows that it is nonsense to talk of a system of education which implies no ideal of man, or society. Consequently we cannot claim to fully understand a given educational system, unless we are aware of the particular moral or normative view which is presupposed, and by reference to which we are able to give an ultimate answer to the question, 'What is the education for?'

Let me give an example: in Plato's *Republic* the rigorous training of the Guardians in philosophy and mathematics can only be understood as part of their education if we know something of Plato's views on the ideal state, and the role which the Guardians play. Given that information, we can see how philosophy must be an essential ingredient in their education; for their ability to rule, and the part they have to play in the state generally, leans heavily on their philosophical training. If we know nothing of Plato's ideal state, but are merely aware that certain citizens are instructed in these disciplines, then it is as impossible for us to be certain in what sense these are educational, as instruction in ping pong, however inspired our guesses might be.

What this amounts to is that education endeavours to fit people for something. And my claim is that despite some appearances to the contrary, what it tries to fit them for is either membership of a given society valued for its own sake; or alternatively a way of life, equally valued for its own sake.

Some educationalists have of course already insisted on a tie-up between education and values, a point which is noted by Professor D. J. O'Connor in his book *Introduction to the Philosophy of Education*, p. 5 *et seq.* And Marxists, Platonists, Christians, and Humanists would no doubt all claim that education must be based on a certain set of values, i.e. their own particular set. But they are making a hortative point rather than a logical one; and one which would convince us only if we accepted their particular normative viewpoint. I, in contrast, am making the general logical point that if we use the concept of education, then values are necessarily implied.

The plan which I employ in trying to prove this thesis is to take four apparently different uses of the term 'education', which I think are collectively exhaustive, and show the moral implication in each case. I then try to illustrate my analysis, and in a sense to test it, by reference to current argument. My method is that of analytical philosophy. It is a technique we all employ. If you can talk you can do it. A child of three who claims that the teapot can't be a pussycat, because it doesn't have a furry coat, has already mastered the basic principles. If he were just a little more sophisticated he might say that the concept of pussycat embraces the concept of possessing a furry coat, so the teapot, not having a furry coat, can't be a pussycat.

However, let me try to give an example of the technique by referring to a piece of philosophical analysis quite unrelated to the problem under discussion: it is fairly obvious that the concept of 'choosing' has something to do with the concept of 'alternatives'. For example, if I offer you the last chocolate in the box, and you take it, you cannot be said to have chosen it—for there is nothing to choose it from; it would not make sense to say one chose it. Now this linguistic fact helps us to establish a logical connection between 'choosing' and 'alternatives'; i.e. it is a presupposition of choosing that there shall exist alternatives. Similarly in the case of the subject of this chapter: I want to say that education presupposes— is logically linked to—a moral view of society or man. And in making my point I make use of linguistic facts like these.

I said earlier that the concept of education was a normative concept, and I meant by this that it was concerned with standards and principles of a moral nature which enjoin what ought to be done. However, the word 'norm' has been stretched in recent years—it can for example refer to industrial targets—so it would be as well if I were briefly to show how moral principles differ from these other principles, which although clearly non-moral, are yet concerned with what ought to be done. I mean such non-moral principles about how we ought to work in order to fulfil certain output norms, and so forth; for there is a sense in which such principles are normative, insofar as they are concerned with what is considered desirable.

Now the differentia of moral principles is that they are self-justifying and categorical. That is to say they are ultimate, and no further principles are required for their support. Nor does their obligatory character depend upon the fulfilment of empirical conditions—other than an ability to fulfil those conditions, i.e. one has to be able to do what the principles enjoin, and not be physically prevented, and so on. I will explain what I mean by this:

We can divide reasons for performing a voluntary act into moral and non-moral reasons; i.e. those actions which we do on moral principle, and those we do because we want to. In each case we can say that we ought to do what we do, although only in one case is the 'ought' a moral one. Thus we might be told by a university senator that he ought to attend the meeting of senate (a) because it is his duty, and he feels morally obliged to attend, or (b) because he wants to know how the campaign for higher salaries is progressing. Now whereas the force of 'ought' in the latter case depends wholly on the desire for information about the salary position, the force of 'ought' in the former case depends upon no empirical condition at all, other than an ability to fulfil the obligation. Being non-conditional it is therefore categorical. Its obligatory character does not depend on what someone happens to want. So to say one ought to do so and so because one is morally obliged is to use 'ought' in a categorical sense. But to say one ought to do so and so in order to satisfy a desire—in this case for information—is to use it in a hypothetical sense; thus: one ought to go to the senate meeting if one wants to know about the salary position. But if one does not want to know then the 'ought' no longer has validity. The categorical 'ought', in contrast, depends upon no condition or further reason for its validity. It is self-sufficient. This is simply an application of Kant's Categorical Imperative.

Now if we apply this argument to fulfilling industrial norms, we can see that the justification of the principles about what we ought to do in order to fulfil the norms, depends wholly on whether the agent wants to fill them. The principles we ought to follow to hit the target are conditional upon our wanting to hit it. If you do not want to realize that particular end then the 'ought' is not binding. In other words it is conditional and non-moral. On the other hand the 'ought' in 'One ought to pay one's debts' does not depend on your happening to want to pay them. We all recognize this as a moral imperative which is unconditional. Of course I would not wish to deny that industrial norms can be adopted as a moral end—we can make a moral issue of anything—but this does not alter the distinction I have drawn.

To bring the discussion back to a practical issue in education, we can see that those who press their case for, say, sex instruction in primary schools do not rest their argument on what someone happens to want. Rather they would argue that such instruction is a moral imperative. It would make for happier and more balanced adults; and it is a moral requirement of the educational system that it should produce such people, and so forth. Obviously the obligation to give this instruction will derive from some ideal view of the person which embraces being happy and being balanced. So regardless of what people might happen to want, the moral obligation to give this instruction stands. Alternatively, those who are against sex instruction might argue that it could corrupt young minds and therefore ought not to be given. Again this notion of 'ought' would derive from a moral view and would not depend simply on what someone happens to desire.

The doctrine I am trying to establish, then, is that the justification of any educational system logically lies in some moral view of the human character or of society. And such a view is able to constitute a justification simply because of its logical tie-up with the concept of education itself. The clearest exposition of this kind of logical connection is in Plato's *Republic*. Here the justification of the education of each type of citizen whether a Guardian, Soldier, or Artisan has to be sought in the moral view which Plato took of society; a view which derives from a special metaphysical theory in which the Good plays an important part.

Now it may be asked why it is that I require both ideal man and ideal society in my analysis. Would not society do simply, for what is man outside society? To this I would reply that there is nothing in the definition of man, as we ordinarily understand the term, which entails that he is a social being: and therefore I would not want to preclude theories of education which imply the possibility of the existence of men as solitary beings, whose conduct yet conformed to some ideal. One could conceive, it seems to me, without self-contradiction, an education for Robinson Crusoe, where the aim was to inculcate certain desirable characteristics, which from time to time he could manifest adequately or inadequately, for example the virtues of fortitude and optimism of which presumably he would require a large measure. And it seems to me that a person could have these without supposing that other people are involved, as they would have to be in the case of characteristics such as truth-telling or honesty.

But to return to my main theme: one important consequence of my thesis is that it makes possible two sorts of educational dispute: technical arguments about whether or not a given end may be realized by this or that means, e.g. whether comprehensive schools will produce better examination results than grammar schools, where the desirability of better examination results is not in question; and moral arguments about the ends of education, e.g. where, say, a Marxist might disagree with a theocrat about a system of education, on the grounds that it fits the individual for a morally bad society. Quite clearly if you think someone has got the moral view wrong, it is rather more than likely that you will conclude that his educational system is wrong.

Having made the distinction between moral and technical argument in educational discussion, I should now like to consider the concept of education in its four categories of use and test my thesis that moral values are involved.

Category (1) is used with reference to training programmes, and these are mainly concerned with the teaching of particular skills, e.g. the educational programme for shop stewards, wireless operators, apprentices. Category (2) has a relation to trades or professions or practical activities, viz. technical education, legal, commercial, musical, art and medical education. Here the education is described in terms of the chief class of subjects studied; but, as I hope to show, it cannot simply be identified with training in a skill or set of skills. Category (3) examples are practical education, classical, academic; education appropriate to this or that sort of person, e.g. gentleman, artisan, etc. No particular profession or trade is mentioned. These examples are much more obviously near to the analysis I am suggesting, insofar as they seem to imply a way of life within a certain sort of society. Category (4) is concerned with the development of faculties, and this again is different from training for a particular skill: examples are intellectual education, and moral education.

Apart from (1), where we have nothing more than a synonym for 'training'—quite a different matter—I think there is no basic difference between these categories. However, this categorization is partly suggested by the article under 'education' in the *Oxford English Dictionary*, and therefore there is a *prima facie* case for using it as a framework for analysis. As far as I can tell these categories are exhaustive.

Now let me take each in turn:

(1) When we speak of education with reference to educational programmes of one kind or another, then it is my contention that 'training' is all that is implied. In other words 'education' in this context is simply a synonym for 'training'. Thus to speak of the

83

educational programme for, say, senior foremen is to speak of the training programme for senior foremen; and from this we can deduce that the people concerned are undergoing some kind of instruction designed to enable them to carry out a specific operation or pattern of operations. But we cannot deduce anything else. The point can be demonstrated by considering the inadmissibility of the claim, that because Mr X, a senior foreman, was taking part in the educational programme, it followed that he was being educated. Clearly we cannot make such a deduction, as 'being educated' implies education in a much wider sense. The fact is, when 'education' is used simply to refer to the teaching of certain skills, as 'educational programme' implies, then it is always used in the narrow sense of 'training'. And the fact that you are being trained for something does not imply that you are being educated.

In showing category (1) to be synonymous with training my aim was to discount this use for the purpose of my analysis. The implication being that the concept of training, unlike that of 'education' in its primary use, has no logical connection with values. However, this point has to be demonstrated, and the sense in which it has 'no logical connection with values' looked at rather carefully. For what I want to say is that although, as we have seen, sentences such as 'Smith is being trained for X' does not entail 'Smith is being educated', the reverse is not true, i.e. if Smith is being educated, it does follow that Smith is receiving some sort of training. However, the opportunity to explicate this point arises in the next section.

Examples of category (2) use are: medical education, legal, technical, commercial, musical and art education. Here the concept is employed in relation to a class of trades or professions, or practical activities, the name of the class giving a name to the type of education in question. At first glance it might be thought that here again we simply have another synonym for training as in category (1), but this would be wrong; and the error can be revealed easily by considering the fact that it is not self-contradictory nonsense to speak of someone's having had a commercial training but not a commercial education. He may, for example, have had a technical education. Now if commercial training and commerical education meant the same thing, then of course my example would amount to saying that someone who had a commercial training did not have a commercial training, and this is rubbish in any language.

If it is accepted, then, that they are not the same, what is the difference? The answer lies, I believe, in the difference between empirical facts and moral evaluations. When it is claimed that someone is being trained for a particular skill, the claim can be verified simply by making the appropriate empirical observations. If you are being trained to type or do calculus than I can assure myself this is so simply by observing and learning the facts. However, whether such training is to be called 'education' is not simply a matter of going and watching, for this will reveal nothing but further empirical facts. It would follow therefore that if I were to claim that the training was education, this would be going beyond the facts. This would be a matter, I contend, of committing myself to the view that it was aimed at some end considered valuable in and for itself, i.e. some moral end relating to an ideal person, or society in which the individual being educated has a part to play. It is this kind of purpose which constitutes the ultimate reason for the training, and gives us the logical licence to call it 'education'.

Now in any particular case it is an easy matter to discover whether the ultimate reason for the training is of a moral kind, simply by probing for an answer to the question, 'Why is the training being undertaken?' If the question is finally answered in terms of a moral end, then the educational nature of the training is established. Quite clearly, then, such a discovery is not based wholly and solely on empirical facts—moral facts have their part to play.

Let me try and illustrate this point. Suppose it were asserted that a certain society existed solely for the purpose of serving the interests of a tyrant. Now the training and schooling which the members of that society received could not, on my thesis, be called education, for its ultimate end would, *exhypothesi*, be the empirical one of serving the tyrant's interest. If he were to die or to be overthrown, and his interests no longer required serving, then the reason for the training would cease to exist. Now this is in direct contrast to the case in which the training has a moral purpose, i.e. is aimed at producing the good man or the good citizen. For in such cases the moral reason for the training, being non-empirical by definition, is not invalidated by changes of empirical circumstance. It may, of course, cease to have particular application if the empirical situation changed radically, e.g. if the society were wiped off the face of the earth by an avalanche; but this is simply making the point we have already noticed, that if the ability to fulfil the principles is lacking, the moral principles cannot apply. After all 'ought' implies 'can'. However, setting aside circumstances of this nature, it is clear that if something is intrinsically valuable, and ought to be realized, then the moral reasons for realizing it are unaffected by people's desires, wishes or requirements, or the state of the world. So we may say, then, that in my imaginary society the training ceases to have purpose once the tyrant's interests are no longer served, while in contrast, education proper retains its moral purpose whatever the changes in the world. This is another way of saying that the production of the good man or the good citizen does not require a reason—it is sufficient unto itself. To apply the Kantian principle once again, 'You ought to train people in this way if you want to serve the tyrant's interest—but if you don't want to there is no binding obligation' compared with, 'You ought to train people in this way because that is what you ought to do', i.e. it is a moral duty. In which case there is no 'if' about it.

Of course if it were considered a moral duty to serve the tyrant, then we have a different case altogether. In these circumstances the training would have a moral end, and not simply an empirical one. It would then be legitimate to describe it as education. But this change of circumstances only serves to strengthen the thesis I am propounding.

We are now in a position to see what I meant when I said at the end of the previous section that my claim 'Training has no logical connection with education' must be interpreted rather carefully. For although the concept of training does not logically embrace the concept of education, and consequently we cannot deduce from the description of a particular piece of training anything at all of an educational character; yet any particular piece of training can become educational if it is aimed at some educational end, i.e. some end involving an ideal of society or man. But it must be aimed in this way.

In category (3) the education in question, which refers to a way of life, is fairly obviously related to a view of society and does not require detailed analysis. In other words when we speak of practical education, classical, academic, or education appropriate to a gentleman, courtier, artisan, etc. there is presupposed an idea of society in which gentlemen, courtiers, etc. or people with the appropriate education (classical, academic) have a place.[1] But this fact does not imply that where, in a given society, such education is given, a place actually exists for people educated in this way. Such a belief would run contrary to the inertial law of educational systems. Some cynics would argue that educational administrations are always catering for a conception of society which disappeared the day before yesterday. (Compare this with 'education for a dropout, nihilist, recluse, anarchist'. The evident oddness probably relates to the fact that these have no place in any society, nor are they, conventionally speaking, moral exemplars.)

In category (4) with moral and intellectual education we have reference to the faculties. Even the most extreme sceptic is hardly likely to deny a moral connection to moral education, so we can go on to consider whether 'intellectual education', like other kinds, presupposes an underlying moral view of society or man. Now I think that I can most easily prove my thesis in this case by considering an objection. It goes like this: intellectual education is really no different from intellectual training. Each is concerned with the cultivation of the intellect. Now intellectual training is self-evidently education. Every civilized society takes this for granted. But you have already committed yourself to the view that training, whether of the intellect or anything else, is an empirical concept divorced from moral values; therefore intellectual education has no connection with morals. And this runs contrary to your thesis.

Now the force of this argument depends upon the erroneous identification of 'intellectual training' with 'intellectual education'. This may seem to some people a very fine logical point indeed, for although the distinction between education and training can conceivably be maintained in other instances, to try and draw it in the case of intellectual training may be to carry analysis too far. For surely, it could be argued, if anything is truly educational, it is the training of the intellect. But I contend that this is a mistake. And the mistake, I believe, is founded on the supposition that because our own society, and societies like ours, place so much emphasis on such training, as part of normal education, there must be a logical connection between the two concepts. However, I would maintain that intellectual training, insofar as it is simply concerned with the inculcation of certain habits of mind, or the teaching of certain skills however complicated, has really nothing at all to do with the concept of education, speaking logically—which is the only way you can speak when you are talking about concepts.

Let me illustrate this point: let us suppose that we are interested in examining the educational system of a remote civilized people whom we shall call Atlantans. Our interpreter and guide is an Atlantan who has recently learned the English language, and is apt occasionally to fall into error. We talk to him about education, and describe as best we can, with the aid of the *Oxford English Dictionary*, what 'education' means, and ask to be shown Atlantan education in action. He seems to understand, and takes us to a group of children who are being given instruction. From our observations we gather they are being taught a primitive geometry. This undoubted intellectual activity, we assume, is part of their intellectual education. However, when we come to question our Atlantan guide, we discover that geometry has no use in Atlantan society. It

87

is neither employed directly, nor valued as a mental exercise, nor do the qualities of mind it engenders form part of their conception of the ideal man, or the ideal Atlantan. In fact the whole purpose of the instruction is to keep the children out of the way while their parents engage in some ritualistic dance. Obviously our guide has misconstrued the concept; for he, from his point of view cannot call this activity 'education'. From our point of view—that is from the point of view of a member of Western civilization where intellectual training is the most important part of our system of education—we might be tempted to say that the children were being educated by accident. However this would only serve to underline the contingent (i.e. non-logical) relationship between intellectual training and the concept of education. For it is a contingent matter that a view of society should be entertained which includes in its ideal the notion of the intellectually cultivated citizen. If such a view happened not to be entertained we could not claim that the young Atlantans were being educated by accident. So here we have a case where it is possible to imagine a situation in which intellectual training takes place, yet the society which provides it manifestly regards it as non-educational. In fact one might go further and imagine a society where training the intellect could be regarded as sinful, and productive of an evil and corrupt character. It seems to me that there have been periods in history when society has come dangerously near to that position.

Just one brief and final point before I begin to apply my thesis to particular problems. This concerns whether in individual cases my analysis can be used as a criterion of application. I mean by this, can my analysis that education presupposes a moral view of society or man enable us to detect in a particular case, simply by inspection, whether this or that activity in which teaching and learning are involved, is to be called 'education'? Can it help us to decide whether case X is education but case Y is merely training, and so on, by observation? Clearly if this could be done, one would be in a position to wield a powerful instrument. One might be able to turn to certain institutions and claim that they were not really doing education at all, and perhaps should stop what it is they are doing, and hand it over to someone else. Now the answer is 'No', the analysis will not help in matters like this. For mere inspection of a learning/teaching situation cannot reveal whether or not there is a moral purpose behind it. One has to seek the reasons and intentions of those who have devised the teaching programme. From this it follows that any teaching programme, i.e. courses in judo, black magic, or tiddly-winks could be educational—for whether it is or no, has nothing to do with empirical or factual content of the teaching. Everything depends on the evaluative element which lies behind, i.e. on the moral reasons for the activity.

What my analysis can do, however, in a society where new techniques, methods and systems tend to spring in great profusion, is to inspire such questions as, what ideals do the new educational methods tend towards? Are they consistent with one another? Are they consonant with ideals already held? And at the philosophical level my analysis shows that judgments such as, 'This is education', are not at all like judgments such as, 'This is a horse'. For in the latter case our conclusion is based on certain empirical and observable marks of recognition; while in the former case, it consists in a divination or diagnosis that the activity in question has certain moral motives. Of course, when I speak of moral motives I do not necessarily mean that they are motives of which we, personally, approve. If this were the case we could not speak of education in societies of which we might disapprove, e.g. fascist societies. All that is required is that the educators themselves should see the training as leading to a morally desirable end, however much we, as spectators, abhor that end. We might be tempted to say that such education was not *really* education, because the ideals involved were base and repugnant.

But this would simply be a covert way of demonstrating our disapproval rather than making a comment about some objective feature of the subject under discussion. By saying it was really not education, we should not be denying the distinction between training in a practical skill which was not aimed at some ideal end, and that which was. This distinction would remain.

II

The second part of my chapter is devoted to characterizing educational argument, and demonstrating how the moral factor affects it. In other words, by hypothesizing the moral characteristic in the concept of education, certain features of educational argument can be explained. This is another way of giving some reinforcement to my main thesis.

Now if I am correct in supposing that to speak of education is to imply some criterion of value, some moral standard which gives purpose to the education, then one of the more obvious corollaries concerns the twofold division into which educational arguments fall. These, as I foreshadowed earlier, are technical and moral. Moral argument is about the ends or ideals the education is directed

T. F. Daveney

towards; technical argument is about the means by which a given
end is achieved. And it seems to me that all educational arguments
of a practical kind, whether they are about the provision of visual
aids for primary schools, or the purpose of a university, fall under
one or other of these heads.

On the technical side, theoretically, the room for dispute is
limited. For here we are arguing about matters of fact and probability, and these are, in principle, to be settled by observation,
experiment, and expert opinion. I mean such arguments as whether
a knowledge of elementary geometry will help a man to become a
better joiner, or whether a knowledge of Latin is helpful in studying
for an Arts degree, or whether discipline for the young will ultimately
make for more orderliness in civic conduct. It is to be supposed that
the ends are overtly agreed by the contesting parties, but what
requires resolution is how these ends are best achieved. We may
also include in this category quasi-moral disputes which seem on
the surface to be about matters of moral principle, but really
centre on disagreements about matters of fact, or the application of a
principle to a particular instance, e.g. X and Y may disagree on
the matter of state-aid for students. But on investigation it turns out
that X does not condemn state-aid on moral principle, but simply
because he believes the economy cannot stand it at the moment.
The argument then turns on this technical economic question.
Again X may disagree with Y, who advocates the use of violence by
students in order to gain access to their confidential files, which are
held in security by the college authorities. But further discussion
reveals that Y is arguing from the principle of justifiable violence,
with which X does not in the least disagree. The dispute then
becomes one about whether the present instance falls under the
principle of justifiable violence or not.

However, the real moral dispute, i.e. the dispute about things
valued for their own sake, is an entirely different matter: such
disputes basically are about matters of fundamental principle,
where the actual criteria employed by each of the disputants, in
maintaining his stand, are different. In these circumstances, and
where the criteria are quite clear and unambiguous, the argument
can consist only in contending that one's own standards should be
used in arriving at the final judgment, and not that of one's op-
ponent. This point is elucidated in an article by Professor W. B.
Gallie entitled 'Essentially contested concepts', published in the
Proceedings of the Aristotelian Society for March 1956. Imagine an
argument about the purpose of education taking place between a
Marxist, or some idealist theorist of the state, and a liberal democrat.

When all factual misunderstandings and inconsistencies have

been cleared up, there still remains what many would call a difference in attitude, but what in fact is a difference in the fundamental criteria by which the judgment 'this education rather than that' is to be made. This difference would show itself in the widely divergent views about what sort of society ought to exist, and the widely divergent theories which support these views. In the Marxist case we should have to be prepared to follow into the realms of Hegelian metaphysics, and in the other, perhaps into the theory of the nature of liberty as expounded by John Stuart Mill. But either way the net result would be an impasse: on the one hand the view that the state should provide the maximum freedom for the individual; while on the other, the view that people should be given what is good for them by those who know, and not merely what they want. Obviously since the purpose of education differs so radically in each case, so would the content; for it is the content of the education which would have to fit the citizens for these very disparate societies.

But having made the point that the moral argument consists in a basic conflict of criteria, I hasten to add that a bald confrontation of views which have nothing whatsoever in common is often postponed by unclear and shifting criteria. Now whereas educational disagreement in the case of clear criteria would be very well defined, in the case where this were not so, the disagreement would be amorphous and confused. Such confused disagreements are more likely to be found in societies where many views about the nature of the ideal prevail, than in societies where only one view prevails. I mean it is fairly obvious that if you have a very clear notion of the function of the state, as did Plato or Marx, you will have a pretty clear view of the education your citizen ought to have. The more detail you have about your ideal society, then the more clearly will you be able to define your educational system. Clarity can make disputes clear cut. But in open societies like ours, where roughly speaking there is no master plan, and only a broad conception that people ought to be able to do pretty much as they like, provided this does not inhibit the freedom, or affect the well-being, of others, the case is different. For not only are there many competing ideals, the ideals themselves are often vague and ill-articulated. This is to be expected in the kind of society which changes and develops as opinion changes and develops. Opinion does not shift uniformly and all at once, and there may exist concurrently many conflicting opinions about the ways in which society ought to move. The debate is varied, continuous, ever-changing and ceaseless. The logical consequence is that in conditions such as these the educational debate becomes very confused. For however much detail you put into your educational plan (that is, detail about curriculum and so forth) if the purpose of it is not too clear, then discussion and argument about it will not be too clear either.

So in circumstances such as these, attempts to answer the apparently practical questions, 'What is the best kind of system for secondary education?' or 'What is the real function of university education?' in our own current debate, are bound to run into difficulties. For terms such as 'best' and 'real' can only be meaningfully employed if there are clear criteria for their application; and if there are several sets of criteria then you are going to get several answers.

Let me try and illustrate these points by simply contrasting three answers to the question, 'What is the real function of university education?' Notice in particular the use of the word 'real', which typically introduces the philosopher's question. The implication is that the questioner knows all about the actual educational function, so he does not want to be fobbed off with an answer which refers him to the university statutes, or invites him to look round the departments to see what is going on. The question he is actually asking is, 'What ought the educational function of the university to be?' and this, I say, can only be answered in relation to some view of society or man which gives purpose to the activities being carried on under the general heading 'educational'. But let us look at the answers we are given and see in which sense they conflict:

(1) There is the opinion—perhaps a little *passé* now—that universities should be concerned with humane education. I do not mean by this simply teaching the humanities to the exclusion of science; in fact subjects as such do not necessarily enter into it. What is meant is that education should be concerned to ameliorate and improve by cultivating those attributes which distinguish man from the beast. These attributes are the moral and intellectual faculties in the widest sense of these terms, and the more they are developed, the argument runs, the more truly human and less beastly we become. This is a Greek notion which can be seen as deriving directly from Plato's classificatory metaphysics, in which man is regarded as a species cognate in some respects with animals, but different because of his ability to act virtuously and to think. In this view, knowledge and the ability to use the intelligence is an end in itself—something to be valued for its own sake. Now if someone were to hold such a view, then clearly his ideas about the content of education would be determined by it. They would take on a well-defined and recognizable shape. And naturally enough the arguments he conducted to convince people of the correctness of his educational programme would be determined by his moral outlook.

(2) Compare this view of university education with one which sees it simply in terms of training tomorrow's industrial managers and entrepreneurs. The kind of moral view of society which would give purpose to such education is hardly likely to be in harmony with that of the humanist, e.g. the pursuit of knowledge for its own sake, and the inculcation of virtue is not likely to loom large.

(3) Again, consider the proposition that it is the job of university education to launch the Constant Revolution which will lead to the destructuring and restructuring of society in endless cycles. Here, the desired, and presumably valued end, lacks clarity. Consequently one would be hard put to grasp how an educational system could fit a person for such a society. I mean one would be unable to comprehend how any system of training or instruction could be educational in this sense, because the question 'Education for what?' is virtually unanswerable. So a proponent of the Constant Revolution probably could not really begin to argue with the humanist.

It seems to me then, that these disputes and disagreements can be fully accounted for if we concede the moral element in the concept of education. And by 'accounted for', I do not mean that we can see how they can be resolved. They cannot. But we can see how they arise, and why they cannot be resolved.

But not only disagreements such as the ones already mentioned can be explained. The analysis can also be helpful in what appears at first sight to be the less fundamental area of teaching method. For the moral view which we take of society not only determines the particular content of our system of education, it can also determine the attitude which the teacher takes towards his pupil. This can conveniently be illustrated by reference to the current discussion on university teaching, which at first sight seems a technical discussion, but is, I believe one about values.

For example a university teacher who takes the humane Platonist, or Socratic view of education, would regard his job as one of amelioration of an individual who in certain aspects is deficient. To use Plato's metaphor, the pupil has yet to be brought into the light of the sun to see how things really are, rather than as they appear to be, down below in the cave. But the journey from the cave to the light of the sun is a very difficult one, and requires faculties which have been developed in a suitably rigorous environment. It is basically the teacher's job—on this Socratic view—to provide that environment; for ultimately the pupil must make the journey by his own unaided efforts. Therefore the teacher must constantly be testing his pupil, criticizing him and forcing him to make greater efforts; just as Socrates constantly tested and criticized the hypotheses of his students to help them give birth to fruitful ideas which led to real knowledge. Now three important conclusions follow from this conception of the teacher's task: first, he must stand in an avowedly paternalistic relationship to his pupil, and critics might argue that if not 'holier than thou', his attitude would certainly be 'wiser than thou', and even perhaps 'less like the beast than thou'! This would almost inevitably be the criticism if the pupil were an advocate of anarchy, in which authority is vested in no particular group or person. Assuming this were so, the conflict of moral outlook would be acute, for the very concepts of 'teacher' and 'pupil' carry with them a connotation of authority—leader and led—which the anarchist, by definition, objects to. One can imagine the absurdity of a situation in which a teacher in the humane tradition is doing his best to inculcate wisdom and virtue in a pupil who is resisting his efforts, and on the contrary is bent on some sort of equalitarian dialogue designed to break down the barriers of the traditional relationship. For Socratic teaching presupposes that the student comes willingly to be enlightened. An equalitarian dialogue just has no relevance at all.

The second point follows from the fact that Socratic teaching is a highly personal matter involving a unique pattern of responses at each encounter, and a basic sympathy between teacher and taught, which derives from their interest in a common moral objective, i.e. the affection—the improvement—of the student's mind and morals. There can be no methodology of such a relationship, any more than there can be a methodology of maintaining friendships—unless one is going to confer such a description on a few rule of thumb principles which are trivially obvious. The situation is rather like that of Professor John Wisdom's aspirant lion-tamer, who went to Ireland to learn the principles of lion-taming. But after a course of instruction he found, to his cost, that his principles never applied to any particular lion—for all lions are different. So if we were to send Socrates on a lecturers' training course, we should be wasting our time.

The third point also follows from the personal nature of Socratic teaching, and concerns the impossibility of replacing the teacher with machinery, however complex. (Needless to say this argument would have no force for a philosopher who believed the brain was no more than a computer.) If we do replace Socrates with a machine, something of great value might result, or it might not. But what is certain is that it would not do the same job. It is easy to see, then, how teaching methods utterly different from the Socratic would arise, if different ideals were embraced. Some proponents of the 'creativity' school, for example, would consider the Socratic method disastrous.

Let me sum up, then, all these points I have made about educational dispute: (1) The moral context is requisite in posing educational questions of a non-technical kind. (2) Where there is no moral context, or it is shadowy and ill-defined, there can be no satisfactory answers, and questions must be regarded as ill-informed or meaningless. (3) If questions are asked in the context of clear but conflicting views, there will be clear but conflicting answers. These answers will of course be just as more or less irreconcilable as the moral views themselves. (4) The only case in which a comprehensible and unchallengeable answer can be given, is where there is an unchallengeable and perspicuous set of values lying behind.

And perhaps these points of practical import may also be added: (1) Those who earnestly desire cut and dried answers to educational questions of a fundamental nature will only find them in a cut and dried society where the system of values is laid down and clear for all to see. (2) A society which admits of many and varied views about the way its educational system should develop, is by definition a society which admits of many and varied views about its own purpose and aims. The educational debate is therefore a debate about society. It is the moral debate which continues so long as people disagree about values and priorities. (3) If we are going to be clear about the sort of educational system we want, then we must be clear about our notion of the good society. Education inevitably is a moral concept, and educational discussions of a non-technical kind are, logically, moral discussions.

6 Moral autonomy as an aim of moral education

Kurt Baier

It is generally thought desirable, and as we shall see for good reason, that children should grow up into moral beings, and undesirable that they should not. Growing up in this desirable way means not only that they become moral rather than non-moral beings, but also that they become at least morally acceptable, if not actually morally good, rather than morally obnoxious or objectionable beings. Obviously such a desirable development is not accomplished in every case, nor is failure especially rare. Even if one is sceptical, as I am, about the current denunciations of the moral decline among the young (for when have not the old and middle-aged perceived the social changes around them as ominous signs of a weakening moral fiber or outright decadence?), one might agree that the task of furthering this desirable development could and should be promoted more effectively than this is now being done by those supposedly doing it, parents and the churches. But the moment this is said, one wonders who is better qualified than parents and ministers and how such qualifications could be acquired or conferred. What exactly could be the subject-matter of such teaching, instruction, or training? Is there a body of *moral knowledge*, or a reliable and easy *method* by which each individual can arrive at some solutions to his moral problems? Are learners to be taught more than 'moral information' and skills; are they also to be conditioned, induced, or frightened into conformity with some principles or rules? And what could these be but moral convictions of the dominant group in the society? We seem then to be confronted by at least two formidable problems. The first is that, since there is no agreed method for finding out what is right and what wrong, society must either leave it to chance, that is, to accidental environmental influences, what moral convictions, if any, will be held by the members of each new generation, or society must organize moral teaching in accordance with some preferred moral theory, which would surely amount to indoctrination. The second problem is that, since even conveying 'moral information' is not enough to bring about a satisfactory level of moral performance (as opposed to giving the learner the skill enabling him to turn in such a performance, *if he wants to*), society must either leave it to chance whether a person will turn in an acceptable moral performance or it must condition him to do things which he would not naturally or normally do or want to do, and which he will in the end do in the teeth of his real nature.

In this chapter, I want to examine a view, which appeals strongly to the *Zeitgeist* while at the same time seeming to offer a way around these difficulties. On this view, the aim of moral education must be to turn all children into morally autonomous adults. If society does that, this view maintains, then it neither indoctrinates nor conditions them, for when so educated, they will judge for themselves what is morally right and, having seen the importance of such judgments, will voluntarily act in accordance with them. This view is philosophical rather than pedagogical. It concerns itself with the aim of moral education, not with the factors that make for or against the attainment of this aim. However, it has in recent years received a good deal of attention and support from educational psychologists, above all from Piaget and his followers, and for this reason alone it merits extensive discussion.[1]

In this chapter, I can do little more than sort out a few of the most important things various thinkers have meant by 'moral autonomy' and eliminate some of the most popular ones as unsuitable candidates for the aim of moral education. Despite these limitations, I believe, however, that in the course of my discussion some of the central issues will be clarified and that the main *philosophical* difficulties which have clouded our thinking about moral education will disappear.

I

The theory that moral education should aim at turning youngsters into morally autonomous adults implies three radical theses which are often denied. The first is that we must sharply distinguish between a given coercive social order (including its law and custom) and a moral order. A given coercive social order contains the social rules by which some want a society to live, perhaps (though not necessarily) because they believe, whether rightly or wrongly, that if the society lives by such rules, it will result in a life for them or for the majority or the whole of the society, which they regard as a good life or the best possible life. By contrast, a moral order for a society is an order which actually accomplishes something (there are different views of what that is), irrespective of whether it also contains the rules which some or all the members of the society want to live by. Many types of theory explicitly or implicitly reject this distinction: traditionalists, populists, admirers of *Realpolitik*, believers in the will of the people, and so forth. Note that a 'given' coercive social order need not be an actually entrenched one; thus, populists attacking traditionalists wish to replace the entrenched coercive social order by one expressing the wants of another section of society.

The second implied thesis is that every (or at any rate every psychologically normal) human being is capable of achieving moral autonomy, that moral autonomy is not dependent on exceptional natural gifts or powers, such as a special moral sense or exceptional intelligence, or even on acquired skills beyond the reach of even the meanest endowment. Many philosophers deny this. I need merely mention Plato who held that only philosophers can acquire knowledge of the good and so become morally autonomous. The others can be at best heteronomous 'Auxiliaries,' men trained to follow the rules, laid down by the 'Guardian Philosophers,' whose rationale they have to take on trust from these authorities. The theory under review rejects such moral elitism.

The third implied thesis is that those who are morally autonomous, who know what is good and therefore what is right, will pursue the good and therefore do what is right, without having to be coerced into doing it, and that therefore there is, at least in moral matters, no need and no justification for authority and the use of force. On some radical versions of this theory there is, as we shall see, no need or justification for any authority or force. This thesis is, of course, also frequently rejected. Against the Socratic view that immorality is solely due to ignorance of the good, there is the Aristotelian view that it is sometimes due to weakness of will, or the view of some utilitarians (e.g. Sidgwick), that the morally right is to be defined in terms of the good of the greatest number, and that that good can and in all known social conditions often does conflict with the good of the individual, which latter good often has greater attraction for the individual than the former, and that therefore one cannot rely for moral conduct solely on the attraction of the good.

For a long time, the orthodox view was moral elitism of the Platonic kind combined with so-called 'pessimism about human nature,' the view that men do not by nature seek the good. If, then, the good is hard to see and if, moreover, people do not necessarily follow it even when they see it, it is desirable for men's own good that there should be recognized moral experts who determine the good and who, moreover, lay down those coercive rules for the guidance of the less clearsighted, which the latter must follow if they are to attain the good. In this way and only in this way, it was thought, was it possible to ensure that they would not do themselves and others irreparable harm. And what was more natural in the circumstances than to ascribe to the learned churchmen and their most learned princes the theoretical expertise required to formulate these rules? What's more, if they were such experts, then they were best qualified to perform not only the role of rule-maker, but also that of rule-applier, casuist, advisor, and judge, guiding the less well-trained individuals in what they ought to do.

The earliest 'autonomist' attacks on this view took the form of pitting some new authority, the authority of individual conscience, against the old established (religious and moral) authority of the priests, bishops, and the Pope. Against the backdrop of the prevailing Christian theory of conscience such an attack was not a very radical departure, because it left intact the view that the voice of conscience was a God-implanted voice, a private inner mouthpiece of God Himself, the little man's own personal pope, more accessible and more reliable than the Pope in Rome.

This traditional view of conscience does, however, conceal an ambivalence on the important question of the nature of its authority: is it natural or conventional (*ex officio*)? Is it authoritative the way an authority on marsupials is or the way a ticket inspector is? Do we recognize a certain distinctive inner voice as authoritative because following it in the past has always turned out to be right, or because we believe it to be the voice of someone or something occupying a certain office or position with that competence, the competence of telling us what we ought to do. Bishop Butler[2] embraces both these views. He thinks of conscience as having natural authority when he speaks of human nature as 'an economy.' He thinks of it as having conventional authority when, in the same sentence, he speaks of human nature as having 'a constitution.' He thinks of it (Sermon III) as having natural authority when he likens the principle of conscience to that of self-love in calling each a 'principle of reflection' (though not necessarily reflection according to the same method) and both operating within the economy of human nature, as when a man, foreseeing his utter ruin if he followed present satisfaction, unlike an animal, resists that temptation, and so acts in conformity *with the economy of* his nature. He thinks of conscience as having conventional authority when he calls it: (Sermon III):

> a faculty, placed within, to be our proper governor; to direct
> and regulate all under principles, passions, and motives of
> actions. This is its right and office: thus sacred is its authority.
> And how often soever men violate and rebelliously refuse to
> submit to it, for supposed interest which they cannot otherwise
> obtain, or for the sake of passion which they cannot otherwise
> gratify: this makes no alteration as to the *natural right* and
> *office* of conscience.

The problem of how the economy of human nature gives *greater* (natural) authority to the principles of conscience than those of self-love and the passions is brushed aside by simply ascribing to conscience *higher* (conventional) authority, whose credentials are not thought to need investigation because conscience is regarded as the voice of God in us.

The rise of individualism, with its rejection of moral expertise and its advocacy of universal individual moral autonomy, tends to support the conventional, *ex officio* interpretation of the authority of conscience. For if everyone is equally qualified to make moral judgments, and if making moral judgments amounts to consulting one's conscience, then such consultation cannot be reflection in the sense of reasoning, for that might yield results of unequal soundness, depending on the individual's powers of ratiocination, but must be merely listening to a voice identifiable as that of conscience by its timbre rather than by the content of its deliverances.

That the psychological phenomena of what we call 'conscience,' the pangs, qualms, hesitations, and fears, the promptings, urgings, and impulses, the guilt and remorse and shame we experience in certain situations, are now typically interpreted in this Protestant fashion, as an inner oracle telling each of us what *he* ought or ought not to do, can be seen by an examination of our very way of speaking. As Ryle put it:[3]

> if asked to advise *someone else* on a moral point, I could not without absurdity say that I must consult my conscience. Nor, if someone else misbehaves, can my conscience be said to disapprove. . . . (Nor if you plan to misbehave could I say that) *my* conscience won't be clear if *you* do it.

The *conscientious objector* claims, not that his conscience tells him that it is wrong to kill, but only that it is wrong *for him* to kill. Like the orthodox Jew who employs a 'sabbath goy' to answer the telephone for him or the Catholic gynaecologist who sends his wealthy patients to a Protestant abortionist, the conscientious objector (as traditionally understood) primarily wants to avoid dirtying his hands.[4]

But if this is what moral autonomy comes to, if it is universal individual (*ex officio*) autonomy of conscience, then it cannot be the aim of moral education. For such an interpretation turns morality into a wholly private affair, an affair between each individual and *his* personal guide. But such a view of morality leaves out the most important part of a morality, public morality. Such a view has no room for what is morally right and morally wrong, as opposed to what someone with conventional authority has forbidden or commanded some particular individuals to do.

Kant, developing an idea of Rousseau's, gives a new account of the authority of conscience, by assigning to every individual a new moral function, namely, moral legislation. This is the origin of the contemporary idea of moral autonomy, i.e. universal individual moral self-legislation. The Protestant individualist revolt against expert authorities interposing themselves between the ingeniously inferred or revealed will of the Divine Legislator and the human subject eager to obey, had left unchallenged the individual's obligation to obey *the will of another.* Kant took the further step of replacing the Divinity by Reason, thus transferring the role of moral legislator from the Divinity to the individual. The individual is thus no longer seen merely as a moral subject. He is construed as a moral legislator, and though still obligated, still subject to a will, it is his own will, or rather the will of his rational, i.e. higher self.

Conscience is construed as the name for an 'inner moral court,' and the various roles played in it, the individual himself apparently appearing simultaneously in the roles of accuser, accused, judge, sentencer, and punisher. This multiplicity of roles creates an appearance of absurdity:[5]

> conscience has the peculiarity that though this whole matter is
> an affair of man with himself, man sees himself, nevertheless,
> compelled to conduct this affair as though at the bidding of
> another person. For the business here is the conduct of a lawsuit
> (cause) before a tribunal. But if the man accused by his conscience
> is represented as one and the same with the judge, then such a
> mode of representation is absurd in a court of justice; for in
> that event, the accuser would certainly lose every time.
> Therefore, as far as all man's duties are concerned, his
> conscience will have to suppose someone other than himself
> to be the judge of his actions, if his conscience is not to
> contradict itself. This other may be a real person or merely an
> ideal one which reason creates for itself.

Kant solves this problem, as he solves many other similar ones, by his distinction between the phenomenal and the noumenal self:[6]

> man as subject ['Subjekt,' i.e. command*er*] of moral legislation
> proceeding from the concept of freedom, in which he is subject
> to ['untertan,' i.e. command*ed* by] a law he gives to himself
> (*homo noumenon*), is to be regarded as different from the
> sensible man endowed with reason (*specie diversus*). . . . This
> specific difference is that of the faculties of man (the higher

and the lower) which characterize him. The former [*homo noumenon*] is the accuser, against whom the accused is granted a counsel (legal adviser). At the conclusion of the reports the internal judge, as a person with authority, makes his decision about happiness or misery, taken as moral consequences of the deed in question.

The distinction between the noumenal and the phenomenal self which is used to explain the variety of roles played by a person in the court of conscience, is also used to explain how a person can be both a moral legislator and a moral subject; how he can both bind and be bound; free and obligated.

Of the many problems to which this theory gives rise, we can attend to only one which is, however, fatal to the conception of moral autonomy as an aim of moral education. For if it were to be such an aim, it would have to be possible to aim at turning every child into a morally autonomous adult. But this is impossible, for the idea of universal individual autonomy, i.e. self-legislation (moral or non-moral) is an absurdity.

In its literal sense, 'autonomy' normally applies to societies rather than individuals. A colony becomes autonomous when it throws off the legislature of the mother country. We may want to say that it becomes 'more autonomous still' when its first dictator is replaced by an elected legislature, that is, when a larger section of its members are assigned a share in the making of the laws that regulate their behavior. But such a democratic legislature does not make the members of the society autonomous in the sense in which the society itself is, namely, subject only to laws which it alone has made. It is logically impossible for each of the members of a society to be subject only to laws which he alone has made, subject only to his own will and no one else's. If no member of a society were subject to the will of any other, then there would simply be no law and so no legislation including self-legislation. Such independent individuals would be subject not to laws, but only to rules or maxims which each imposes solely on himself *and on no other*. The necessary consequence of no one being subject to rules made by anyone but himself is that no one makes rules for anyone but himself, so no one makes laws, so no one makes laws for himself either.

It is of course possible that in a given society the laws should be made by one single person, in which case he is literally autonomous, but then no one else is. But if the society is 'autonomous in a high degree', that is, democratic, and many members have a share in determining what the law shall be, then each member is subject to laws largely determined by the will of others. Even if each member has a share in making the law, he can have no more than a share; and if an equal share, then necessarily a small share only. This must remain true even in the highly unlikely event that all the members of a society want to have exactly the same laws for a significant period of time. For even then, each individual will be subject to laws made largely by others, although then the laws he will be subject to will be the same as if he alone had made them. Moral autonomy is thus impossible if, as some have thought, it means not being subject to the will of another.[7] The best one can hope for is being subject to other people's wills which are not in conflict with one's own. Moral autonomy, meaning universal individual moral self-legislation would thus be possible only if one happened to live in a society in which all the legislative wills of the society coincided.

It might be thought that producing such mutual co-ordination of legislative wills might be a worthy aim of moral education. Kant at any rate seems to have thought that there was a possibility of producing it, although his universalization procedure was a method not so much for securing uniformity as for determining correctness. In his view, every person who, when proposing to adopt a maxim of action, asks himself whether he could at the same time will that that maxim should become a universal law of nature and wills it in accordance with the answer, imposes moral legislation on himself, precisely because he so regulates his legislative will that everyone comes up with the same answer; or, failing that, at any rate thinks that further examination would eventually yield an agreed answer and that one of the parties now disagreeing would concede that he had made a mistake.

We need not here go into the much-debated question of whether or not Kant's test really is a practically usable test of correctness because, practical or not, its applicability importantly transforms the nature of the 'legislative' activity. Conceived as an activity to which this correctness test applies, it is no longer a way of combining individual wills into a collective will, as in a voting procedure, but a way of determining the correctness or incorrectness of an answer to a question. It no longer attempts to formulate a collective command telling a class of people *to do certain things* under certain conditions, but a judgment which has been checked by a certain group of people telling a specified class of people *what they ought to do* in certain circumstances. In the former case (at any rate when the popular majority principle is adopted), the number of individual votes for and against a proposed law determines the eventual content of the law. In the latter case, the correct performance of the test determines the judgment: the majority may well be in the wrong. In the former case, when voters change their minds, the

law changes. In the latter case, when an error in the test is discovered, everyone has to admit that the earlier judgment had
always been in the wrong. Apologies, corrections, repairs may well
be in order. In the former case, the procedure determines what
is law, whether or not it ought to be. In the latter case, the procedure
determines what people *believe* is the (moral) law, though it may turn
out that the majority was mistaken.[8]

If this is moral self-legislation, then it is very different indeed
from the kind of democratic political arrangement whose presence
in a society entitles us to call it self-governing or (highly) autonomous. It is moreover important to bear in mind the different roles
these two types of legislation must have in the rational determination of the conduct of members of a society. In particular, it is
important not to think that each individual when searching his
conscience or morally deliberating about what to do can arrive at an
answer to that question by an act of moral self-legislation. When one
deliberates morally about what to do, one proceeds somewhat like a
legal adviser to a client, though of course with morality taking the
place of the law. In both cases, one attempts to find the navigable
passage between the legal or moral prohibitions and requirements
which are already in existence and which restrict one's legal or
moral freedom of action. These one has to discover, one does not
there and then create them by the appropriate legislative acts.

It may now be thought that collective acts of 'moral legislation',
just like those of collective 'legal legislation', could take place at
regular intervals. For obviously one may have doubts about the
soundness of currently recognized moral rules and principles. And
one may try to set one's doubts at rest by applying Kant's universalization test; by asking whether any legislator could will to make
these rules or principles into universal laws of nature. But now the
differences and their importance should be obvious. In the case of
ordinary laws, such a test, even if favorable, would be merely *a
preliminary to a change* of the law, and the General Assembly may or
may not act on the results of the test: they may change the law or
leave it as it is. But in the case of moral rules or principles, as far as
the individual performing the test is concerned, the supposed moral
rule or principle would *ipso facto* be shown to have been unsound:
there is no need nor scope for a further legislative act of deliberately
changing a moral rule or principle. It would be highly misleading to
call even general formal applications of the universalization test, or
other types of examination of generally accepted moral rules and
principles, preliminaries to, or actual, acts of moral legislation.

More importantly, even if we accept Kant's test as conclusive for
general moral propositions, such as 'killing is wrong,' it is still not

conclusive as far as the answer to any particular moral question is concerned. Perhaps the universalization test shows that there never should have been a law authorizing the payment of abortion costs to welfare recipients, perhaps that badly-qualified black students should never have been admitted to graduate schools. But that does not show that welfare officials should not make such legally prescribed payments, that admissions officers should rescind their admissions or that graduate schools should cease to take these differences into account. Conversely, the fact that I believe—and even if my belief were obviously true—that a legislator could not but will to require, on pain of severe sanction, the installation of anti-pollution equipment in industries which would otherwise cause serious pollution, does not show that, even *before* such a law is passed, it is wrong for me not to install such equipment, though it may show that it is wrong for me to put pressure on legislators not to pass such a law.

My judgment that certain general rules or principles pass the universalization test, does not suffice to show that I am morally bound to obey them. Conversely, the judgment that certain valid laws and recognized moral principles do not pass that test, does not show that I have no obligation to obey them. Performing these tests on specific laws, rules, and principles is not therefore comparable to making or abolishing laws.

My role as deliberator (before I act) and as accuser, accused, or judge (after someone has acted) is to apply prospectively or retrospectively to a specific course of action the already existing laws and acknowledged moral principles made available by my society to its members for this very purpose. Of course, a moral being is not confined to these specifically judicial roles: he may also play the role of moral reformer, that is, the role of rational critic of these laws and principles which constitute part of the conventional practical wisdom of a society. But this role need not be played at the time when he deliberates or judges. In fact, if it is played at that time, it should arouse the suspicion of special pleading. But whenever it is appropriate to play it, it is in any case not the role of moral legislator.

Kant is therefore guilty of a double-barreled error. He seems to have jumped from the fact that a society which grants its members democratic rights of participation in the making of laws, is autonomous, to the conclusion that the individual members of such a society are also literally autonomous. And he seems to have confused the important role of a moral critic or reformer of the morality of his group with the non-existing role of a moral self-legislator.

The conclusion I wish to draw is that there is no such thing as moral autonomy if that means universal individual self-legislation in moral matters, and that therefore moral autonomy so interpreted cannot be the proper aim of moral education.

II

More promising than the Rousseau-Kant ideal of moral self-legislation are three other related conceptions of moral autonomy: moral self-mastery, independence of moral judgment, and moral self-determination. The main similarities and differences between the Rousseau-Kant conception and this group can perhaps be put in this way. Both think of morality as being concerned with the determination of every person's conduct in accordance with some ideal (morality) and both recognize the danger of the occurrence of deflections of this process from its proper course. The former attempts to characterize this process as a kind of legal system, except that the legislator is that element in each individual which is best and moreover, therefore, legislates the same thing in all individuals. The latter give no general account of what that process is like, but each of them focuses on a different point in the process at which there is acute danger of breakdown or deflection from the proper course, and offers its interpretation of autonomy as a safeguard against such breakdown or deflection.

In the examination of these three conceptions of autonomy I want to keep before our mind the question of whether in adopting any or all of these as aims of a program of moral education, the educator would be fostering something indispensable to any moral being or would instead be pushing a contentious moral position (say, anti-authoritarian individualism); whether other educators objecting to any of these interpretations of autonomy as aims of moral education would be opposing an essential feature of moral maturity, or merely a possibly false moral precept? Would such opposition be comparable to an astronomy teacher arguing that confirmation of astronomical theories by observation through telescopes was a mistake, or would it be like arguing against the steady-state theory? I hope my examination can make some contribution towards an answer to this question, even though actually presenting a case for an answer is beyond the scope of this paper.

If autonomy is interpreted as self-mastery, then autonomy is a person's propensity to conform his behavior to his decision about what to do. As I use the term (which is rather indeterminate in ordinary usage), it includes self-control (resistance to urges, such as laughing or sneezing; to the show of emotions, such as crying or screaming; to the impulses tied to the emotions, such as blurting out

secrets or running), strength of will (resistance to threats and temptations), will power (resistance to fatigue and pain), tenacity
(resistance to the desire to change one's mind caused by adversity,
low prospects of success, and the like), and resoluteness (resistance to
feelings of doubt and uncertainty). *Moral* autonomy then is naturally
construed as *moral* self-mastery. But how does 'moral' qualify
self-mastery? When we speak of sexual self-mastery, this is more
naturally interpreted as a person's propensity to conform his
behavior to his decisions about what to do despite sexual impulses in
conflict with his decision, than as the propensity to conform his
behavior to his decisions in sexual matters despite other kinds of
impulses in conflict with his decision. But since it would be most
implausible to think of moral self-mastery as a person's propensity
to keep his moral impulses in check when they conflict with his
goals, I shall take moral self-mastery to mean a person's propensity
to keep other impulses in check when they conflict with his decisions
not to do what, as he thinks, it is morally wrong to do.

On this view, the teaching of moral self-mastery is therefore
closely related to the teaching of virtue. It includes the inculcation
of a good will. It is, in an important respect, like teaching a seal to
perform, and unlike teaching a pupil sewing, the principles of a
healthy diet, or even personal hygiene. Like the seal, the learner of
moral self-mastery is taught not only *how* to perform but *to* perform.
The training of the seal has not accomplished its end if the seal has
learned how to balance the ball on his nose and now does it when
he feels like it, but will not do it when the trainer cracks the whip or
holds up the fish. Instruction in sewing has succeeded if the learner
can sew when she decides to, even if she hardly ever or never
decides to sew. Teaching moral self-mastery has not been successful
if the learner never decides to do what he judges morally right to
do, or never bothers to make such judgments, even supposing that
if he made such a decision, he would manage to resist conflicting
urges, impulses, threats, temptations, and so on. Of course, the
teaching of moral self-mastery is also in an important respect like
teaching the principles of a healthy diet and unlike training a seal
to perform, in that it involves teaching the learner not to do what he
judges morally wrong and not to do it *because* it is wrong. The seal
need not learn to judge what to do nor to acquire something
analogous to a good will: the will to do whatever he judges the
thing to do. Teaching the seal to perform no doubt involves a certain
amount of intelligence on his part, but it does not involve reason
and reasoning. There is therefore no such thing as teaching the seal
self-mastery.

Moral autonomy in this sense would seem to be a suitable candidate for an aim of moral education, for adults without moral self-mastery are not moral beings. Note, however, that inclusion of moral self-mastery among the aims of moral education is perfectly compatible with elitism concerning moral knowledge. One may believe in training people in moral self-mastery, even in teaching them to be virtuous, yet not believe that everybody is capable of *judging* for himself what is right and wrong. One may hold, as Plato does, that the institution of morality presupposes that moral knowledge is in principle attainable, that some can and do attain it, but that it is beyond the reach of most, and that the latter cannot properly judge what is right and wrong but must acquire their moral beliefs from those who have this ability.

Acceptance of moral autonomy, in the second of the interpretations now under discussion, is tantamount to a rejection of this moral elitism. On this conception of moral autonomy, a person is morally autonomous if he has *independence of moral judgment*; if his moral beliefs are not simply taken from those he had been taught blindly to revere. But exactly what would one have to teach a person if one wished to teach him independence of moral judgment and what would success consist in?

The first thing to notice is that there are different standards of independence, some so high that no one can reach them, some so low that everyone does, and some in between. Some writers, especially those influenced by Rousseau, tend to be so extreme that only complete isolation of the learner, preventing him entirely from being influenced by his elders and peers, can protect him from losing his independence, or rather can enable him to acquire it.[9] Others do not forbid consultation but insist that when consulting others, the autonomous man will make their advice his own by determining for himself whether it is good advice. In Wolff's words:[10]

> He (the autonomous man) may learn from others about his moral obligations, but only in the sense that a mathematician learns from other mathematicians—namely by hearing from them arguments whose validity he recognizes even though he did not think of them himself. He does not learn in the sense that one learns from an explorer, by accepting as true his accounts of things one cannot see for himself.

I call such interpretations of autonomy or independence 'extreme' because they make it impossible for anyone, or for anyone without exceptional qualification or not in exceptional conditions, to be autonomous or independent.

At the opposite extreme are interpretations such as those one encounters not infrequently in Existentialist writings when the aim is to show that everyone is rightly held responsible for what he did even when he did nothing, or did not deliberate, or in any ordinary sense decide, before acting. These make it impossible for anyone not to have independence of moral judgment. On such an interpretation whatever one does is one's decision and all one's decisions are based on one's judgment and so, whether one likes it or not, it is necessarily one's own independent judgment which has determined one's conduct. I call such an interpretation 'trivial.'

In between these two interpretations, the extreme and the trivial is the 'moderate,' which attempts to draw a distinction between dependence and independence of judgment, for ordinary persons in ordinary circumstances. On the moderate interpretation, independence of moral judgment is not ascribed independently of what the person does, nor is it withheld simply because the person accepts an opinion on some issue without having given it adequate examination himself or without himself evaluating someone else's judgment of the issue. He has independence of judgment if he does these things wherever he has the necessary qualifications. He does not have independence of judgment if he does not do these things, even though he has the qualifications, but accepts instead someone else's opinion because he is afraid of arriving at opinions in conflict with those of the other.

Consider the case of an Irish peasant who asks for and accepts the advice of his priest in matters of divorce and birth control even though he does not understand the arguments by which the priest arrives at his recommendations—but assume that the peasant would not ask nor in this manner accept the priest's advice on insecticides. Now, on a trivial interpretation, the peasant has independence of judgment, and would have it even if he sought the priest's advice on insecticides—because it is his decision and so his judgment to accept what the priest tells him. On an extreme interpretation, the peasant does not have independence of judgment, because he does not subject the priest's argument to his own evaluation. On a moderate interpretation, the peasant has independence of judgment so long as he accepts the priest's judgment only because he believes he lacks the necessary expertise in these matters himself, believes (perhaps on good grounds) that the priest has it, and trusts the priest as well as his judgment.

Plainly on neither the trivial nor the extreme interpretation can independence of judgment be a suitable aim for moral education. For if everyone necessarily is autonomous or if only exceptional people, and only in exceptional circumstances at that, can be autonomous in this sense, then there is no point in aiming at autonomy through moral education. But autonomy in the moderate interpretation would seem to be a suitable aim for moral education. It would seem to be important that people use whatever knowledge they have in the determination of what it would be right and what wrong for them to do, without fear of thereby displeasing their neighbors. It would moreover seem to be desirable that they use their skill in judging these issues themselves, for usually they will be in the best position to consider all the relevant matters and they will not in such matters often have good reason to put greater trust in someone else and his judgment than in themselves and their own judgment.

There is, however, a second dimension along which the standard of independence may vary: determination of what it is wrong for a given person to do on a particular occasion involves a reasoning process of great complexity involving the use of various types of proposition as 'premises' from which to move to (I hesitate to say 'infer') the judgment of what to do, and also various procedures for 'testing' the soundness of these premises. There is only little space left to me, but perhaps it will be helpful if I use it to distinguish, in the next paragraph, the four main types of proposition used in this form of reasoning, and if I mention that the procedure for arriving at a judgment of what to do is most like, though not quite like, the procedure a lawyer may use in advising a client (possibly himself) on whether a proposed course of action is lawful or unlawful. There are of course other types of moral judgment, such as whether someone in doing something he has already done has done the right thing, whether he deserves commendation or condemnation for doing it, whether he should be punished or compensated, and so on, but we cannot and need not deal with such judgments here. The reason for introducing even this amount of complexity is to show that the question of whether someone has independent moral judgment can be seriously misleading, since one may confuse it with the question of whether he has attained a certain level or standard of the mastery of moral judgment. Insistence (especially of the 'extreme' kind) that everybody must make his own judgment or evaluation of what he ought to do morally speaking, is more plausible if one does not notice that it is different from and presupposes a certain level of mastery of moral judgment. The moment one notices the difference, it is not nearly so obvious that everybody, *whatever his level of mastery of moral judgment*, should, or should be encouraged to, make his own. And once we are aware of this, we must then ask the question of whether in our design of moral education we should devote more time and energy to raising the learner's level of the mastery of judgment or the level of his independence of moral judgment, if we cannot (as would seem inevitable) in all cases bring both to the highest level.

We can now describe briefly the four types of moral proposition and the way in which those we make at one level require for their substantiation others from the next higher level. Propositions of type (i) are those employed in answers to questions of whether or not it would be morally wrong for a given person to do a certain thing here and now. They are analogous to those used by someone's legal adviser in telling him whether or not it would be unlawful for him to do a certain thing here and now. Propositions of type (ii) are those employed in answers to the more general question whether certain types of act, such as killing someone or not supporting someone, are morally wrong for anyone, or for certain classes of people (soldiers, husbands, mothers), and that always, or in certain circumstances (war, when penniless, etc.). In arriving at judgments of type (i) one has to use judgments of type (ii). Their function is thus analogous to claims made by someone's legal adviser to the effect that, say, refusal to pay alimony is unlawful for anyone in any circumstances in such and such a state. Propositions of type (iii) are used to state what he takes to be the most general moral principles, such as justice or benevolence, or what he takes to be the supreme principle of morality, such as the Golden Rule, or the Principle of Utility, or the Categorical Imperative. They are employed in testing the soundness of judgments of type (ii). Their function is roughly analogous to that of a legal adviser's claim that a given statute is or is not constitutional. Lastly, propositions of type (iv) are statements about the nature, function, and rationale of the institution of morality. They are used to explain and justify a person's reliance on the general moral principles or the supreme principle of morality he in fact relies on. There is nothing analogous to this in the case of a legal system: from statements about the nature, function, and rationale of such a system we can at best argue to what a constitution *ought* to contain, not to what it does contain.

It would seem that a moral education should produce in every adult at least mastery of moral argumentation involving propositions of types (i) and (ii). Without such mastery they would perhaps not have reached the level even of Plato's auxiliaries. Plato's auxiliaries presumably took from the philosopher guardians not so much directions and commands for each particular occasion of moral decision, but a set of propositions of type (ii), the analogue of the Ten Commandments, which then enabled them to determine the morally appropriate course of action on each occasion. A good case can also be made out for the desirability of inculcating mastery at levels (iii) and (iv), only there is little agreement among philosophers, or for that matter any other group of experts, on what that expertise might consist in. It is in this field that moral philosophers can make their most important, their Newtonian contribution.

The last conception of autonomy to be examined is that of individual moral self-determination. This conception focuses on the will of others, especially of course in the form of the law, as one of the danger points where an individual's efforts to behave in accordance with the requirements of morality might be thwarted. We can deal briefly with an obvious 'trivial' and 'extreme' interpretation. The former maintains, of course, that everybody necessarily determines himself (morally) because what he does must count as his decision since he could always have done something else instead. The latter maintains that an individual has (moral) self-determination only if he has freedom to do what he decides to do. Plainly neither interpretation yields a suitable aim for moral education, since on the first there is nothing for moral education to aim at and on the second, the aim (freedom) would have to be an aim, not for moral education, but for political reform or revolution involving the abolition of any form of coercive order.

There is, however, a more sensible moderate interpretation. It allows that a person's achievement of moral self-determination is neither necessary, nor impossible in a society with a coercive order. Moral autonomy as the freedom to do whatever it would not be wrong for one to do and which therefore no one could have a moral right to prevent or forbid one from doing, is such a moderate interpretation of moral self-determination. Clearly 'moral' here means 'not immoral', not 'not non-moral': self-determination within the limits set by morality, not self-determination in moral matters, i.e. of what these limits are. The enemy of moral self-determination is every form of social oppression, whether by the government and the legal order, by powerful social groups or individuals, or by public opinion. Such social oppression is often thought to include paternalistic forms of coercion, that is, coercion to do what is for the coerced person's own good, but which it would not be morally wrong for him not to do.

Whatever the merits of moral autonomy in this sense, it is clear, however, that it cannot be a suitable aim of moral education, for success in this would not consist in the acquisition by the individual of some ability or some propensity. Success depends on the appropriate organization of society. If moral self-determination is included in moral education, it cannot be included as one of its aims, but only as one of the values or ideals to be recommended to the learners. A defense of such inclusion awaits a clearer understanding than we now have of the argumentation capable of establishing any values or precepts, i.e. propositions of types (ii) and (iii).

There is, it seems to me, a lesson for moral education in all this. If, as I am inclined to think, moral autonomy is a desirable element of moral education and if it is to be construed as moral self-mastery, independence of moral judgment, moral self-determination, or a combination of these, then any program of moral education must include instruction in moral reasoning. Now, this suggests that philosophers of moral education give a high priority to the task of constructing methods of moral reasoning which would enable the individual without too much difficulty to answer for himself what it is right and what wrong for him to do. For it is hardly deniable that most people do not now know how to do this, if indeed anybody knows. And until such a method is perfected, perhaps it would not be a bad idea to include in a curriculum of moral education courses in legal reasoning since, although there are important differences (which should be stressed), there are also very great similarities, and there is not, in any case, as far as I can see, anything more like moral reasoning than legal reasoning.

Notes

1 Cf., e.g. Jean Piaget, *Six Psychological Studies*, New York, 1967. See also Jean Piaget, *The Moral Judgment of the Child*, London, 1932; Millie Almy, Edward Chittenden and Paula Miller, *Young Children's Thinking*, New York, 1966; L. Kohlberg and E. Turiel, *Moralization Research, the Cognitive Developmental Approach*, New York, 1971; L. Kohlberg, 'Education for justice: a modern statement of the Platonic view' in N. F. and T. R. Sizer (eds), *Moral Education*, Cambridge, Mass., 1970; L. Kohlberg, 'Stages of moral development as a basis for moral education' in C. M. Beck, B. S. Crittenden and E. V. Sullivan (eds), *Moral Education: Interdisciplinary Approaches*, Toronto, 1971.

2 Bishop Butler, Preface, *Fifteen Sermons upon Human Nature*.

3 Gilbert Ryle, 'Conscience and moral convictions', *Analysis*, 1940. Reprinted in G. Ryle, *Collected Papers*, London, 1971, p. 185.

4 Cf., e.g. the excellent discussion of these questions by Michael Walzer, 'Conscientious objection', *Obligations*, Cambridge, Mass., 1970.

5 I. Kant, *The Metaphysical Principles of Virtue*, New York, 1964, p. 101 [438–9].

6 *Ibid.*, pp. 101–2 [439], footnote 19. I have made a few minor changes in the translation.

7 Cf., e.g. R. P. Wolff, *In Defense of Anarchism*, New York, 1970. 'As Kant argued, moral autonomy is a ... submission to laws which one has made for oneself. The autonomous man, insofar as he is autonomous, is not subject to the will of another.' See also J. J. Rousseau,

The Social Contract, London, p. 14: 'a form of association . . . in which each while uniting himself with all, may still obey himself alone . . .' Also, p. 28: 'they obey no one but their own will.'

8 For a good discussion of this difference, see B. Barry, *Political Argument*, London, 1965, pp. 58–66, 292–5.

9 For an excellent discussion of Rousseau's developmental theory as expounded in *Emile* and elsewhere, see Judith N. Shklar, *Men and Citizens*, London, 1969, especially chs 2, 3; for a briefer discussion, see Robert S. Brumbaugh and Nathaniel Lawrence, *Philosophers on Education*, Boston, 1963, especially pp. 77–9; cf. also A. S. Neill, *Summerhill*, New York, 1960, and *Summerhill: For and Against*, New York, 1970.

10 R. P. Wolff, *op. cit.*, p. 13.

Values in education (1)   7

Glenn Langford

My subject in this chapter is values in education. This is a topic which is raised, in an interesting way, by Professor Peters's well-known account of the concept of education and which receives detailed consideration in his book *Ethics and Education*.[1] I will begin, therefore, with the account of education given there, or that part of it which is relevant to my purpose (*ibid.*, p. 24):

> Not all terms have meaning on the model of names by being
> associated with some typical referent. And surely 'education'
> is a term of this sort. 'Education' is not a term like 'instruction'
> which picks out a particular type of activity. Something, of
> course, must be going on if education is taking place. . . . But
> no specific type of activity is required. . . . In this respect
> 'education' is like 'reform'. It picks out no particular activity
> or process. Rather it lays down criteria to which activities
> or processes must conform.

The first criterion, the one with which I will be concerned, is that 'education' 'implies that something worthwhile is being or has been intentionally transmitted in a morally acceptable manner' (*ibid.*, p. 25). I will confine myself to the first part of this requirement, i.e. the requirement that something worthwhile is being or has been intentionally transmitted. The second criterion, which is concerned with knowledge, understanding and cognitive perspective, lies outside the scope of my present concern.

It seems obvious to me that the word 'education' is typically used as a referring expression, i.e. as the name of a sort or type of practical activity. I find the view that education is not an activity puzzling therefore. It complicates the account to no advantage and may be a source of considerable difficulty later. The view that education is not an activity is, indeed, expressed only in a qualified way in the passage just quoted. What is said there is that 'education' does not pick out a 'particular type of activity' or 'particular activity or process'; and that 'no specific type of activity is required'. Looking at these phrases in turn, I am not clear what work the word 'par-

[1] R. S. Peters, *Ethics and Education*, London, 1966, p. 25

ticular' does in the phrase 'particular type of activity'; since 'particular things' are normally contrasted with 'sorts or types of things'. Turning to the second phrase, I agree that 'education' does not pick out a 'particular activity or process'. It is more like the word 'chair' than the words 'the Speaker's chair in the Palace of Westminster', though either 'chair' or 'education' may on occasion be used to refer to particular things, as in 'Sit in the chair' (in the dentist's surgery) or 'Education is going to the dogs' (in this town). Finally, I agree that 'no specific type of activity is required'; but this is true also of 'instruction', with which 'education' is contrasted here and which is later (*ibid.*, p. 79) described as 'a polymorphous concept including all sorts of things like asking leading questions, dropping hints, making suggestions, converting interests into tasks and processes, and so on'. It is agreed, therefore, that 'education' is not the name of either a particular activity or of a specific type of activity; but this leaves open the question whether it is the name of an activity of a non-specific type or sort. This does not, however, seem to be Professor Peters's view. Later in *Ethics and Education* (p. 40), he says: 'teaching is an activity, though a complex one; educating is not'. Elsewhere[2] he is even more explicit. Why, he asks, should talk about aims 'be so peculiarly apposite in the case of education? A quick answer might be that education is a highly diffuse and difficult activity in which many earnest people engage with great seriousness without being altogether clear what they are trying to do.' But, he goes on to say, this 'is not quite right'; since 'education is not an activity. We do not say, "Go along, go and get on with your educating" as we would say, "Go along, go and get on with your teaching". Educating is no more an activity than reforming or improving are.'

Disagreement about whether education is an activity could, of course, spring from disagreement about what an activity is; but I do not think that that is the case here (*Ethics and Education*, pp. 151–2):

> An activity implies first of all an agent who is active rather
> than passive. . . . Sneezing and coughing, for instance, are not
> activities unless they are done with some sort of skill or effort,
> or according to certain conventions. . . Activities . . . involve
> rules and standards and they usually have some kind of
> point. . . . Some activities are absorbing because of their
> palpable and pleasurable point, such as eating, sexual activity,
> and fighting. But erected on this solid foundation of want is
> often an elaborate superstructure of rules and conventions,

[2] R. S. Peters, 'Aims of education—a conceptual inquiry' in *Philosophy and Education*, Ontario Institute for Studies in Education Monograph Series No. 3, p. 34.

which make it possible to indulge in these activities with more or less skill, sensitivity, and manners.

In 'Aims of education' (p. 2) he points out that ' "aim" belongs to the same family of concepts as does "purpose"; so also do "intention" and "motive". They are all conceptually connected with actions and activities. . . . Actions and activities are identified, in the main, by reference to how the agent conceives of what he is doing.' We may be unable to identify an action, therefore, simply by observing the bodily movements made in performing it; it may be necessary to ask the agent what his purpose 'in performing the action was'. And (p. 3) in 'raising questions about the aims of actions or activities . . . we are saying, as it were, "What precisely are you trying to do?" ' To this I will add a sentence from *The Concept of Motivation*: 'The paradigm of a human action is when something is done in order to bring about an end.' Actions are therefore to be explained 'in terms of a man's reason for doing something'.[3]

It is assumed here that the analysis of 'activity' follows that of 'action' and this, I think, is roughly correct. Basic to 'action' is the idea of bringing about change. In human action, the change is brought about by the agency of a person who has some conception of the situation in which and on which he is acting; and who acts in order to bring about changes which he wishes, or wants, to bring about. He does what he does, therefore, with the intention of bringing about certain changes; and if asked will normally be able to say what his intentions, that is the intentions with which he acted, were. In doing so he will be saying why he did what he did, that is giving the reason for his action. I agree, then, that the means-end model applies to actions and activities and that social constraints operate on choice of both means and ends.

I think it is important, however, to make a distinction between actions and activities. Actions are undertaken with the intention of achieving a more or less immediate end; and may or may not form part of some more temporally extended, complex pattern of activity in which the person is engaged. Activities themselves have an overall purpose which provides the principle of their identity and to which the individual actions which are their parts contribute. They may be divided into theoretical activities, the overall purpose of which is the achievement of truth and in which observation plays a more independent role; and practical activities, the overall purpose of which is to bring about change, in which the role of observation is relatively subordinate. Examples of the former, taken from *Ethics and Education*, p. 144, include 'science, mathematics

[3] R. S. Peters, *The Concept of Motivation*, London, 1958, p. 4.

(and) history', and of the latter, 'cooking and carpentry'. A further distinction can be made between activities in which a number of persons join together to co-operate in the achievement of a common or shared purpose, which I will call social activities; and those in which only one person is involved. 'Combing one's hair, hunting for a stud, eating one's dinner ... writing a book, and watching a play', if these are accepted as activities, need involve only one person; whereas 'making love' requires a minimum of two (*ibid.*, p. 151). Science, mathematics and history are theoretical social activities; education, on my view, is a practical social activity.

My first point of disagreement with Professor Peters, then, is that on his view education is not an activity, whereas on mine it is. I want now to consider the relationship between the criteria which, on Professor Peters's view, are laid down by the word 'education', and the activities or processes to which they are applied. His view seems to be that one looks at a purported example of an educational activity or process, such as instruction or teaching, and applies to it the criteria laid down by the word 'education'. If the activity or process conforms to the criteria then it is an educational activity or process; otherwise it is not. If the relevant criteria are applied and mistakenly taken to be met, then someone who describes the activity or process as educational is using the word 'education' correctly, but what he says will be false. If this interpretation is correct the activity or process must be identified as an activity or process of a certain sort before, and independently of, the application to it of the relevant criteria. The criteria, therefore, are external to the activity or process thought of as an activity or process of a certain sort. This may seem unfair to Professor Peters; he does, after all, say (*ibid.*, p. 27) 'it is only too easy to conceive of education as a neutral process that is instrumental to something worthwhile which is extrinsic to it'. But I am not saying that, on his account, the criteria are external to the meaning of the word 'education'; to think of a process as educational is, of course, to think of it as involving the transmission of what is worthwhile. What I am saying is that the criteria are external to the meanings of the words used to describe the activities or processes to which they are applied. This, indeed, is a consequence of the view that education is not an activity. The position is different if, as in my own view, education is thought of as an activity. The overall purpose of an activity can be thought of as a set of criteria to which subsidiary actions and activities must conform if they are to count as parts of that activity. The criteria are then internal to the activity, since an activity is identified by reference to its overall purpose, and the criteria *are* the overall purpose looked out from a perspective internal to the activity. If education is not an activity, however, the criteria laid down by the word 'education' cannot be thought of in this way.

A further related consequence of the view that education is not an activity is that Ryle's task/achievement analysis does not, at least in its most interesting form, apply to the word 'education', despite the claim in *Ethics and Education* (p. 26) that ' "education" is a special case of what Ryle calls an achievement word'. It has clear application only to processes—for example, perceptual processes like seeing and cognitive processes such as remembering—and to activities—for example, running in a race, teaching, or doing science or history—the notions of which have certain standard intentions built into them. It has application, therefore, only to words which are used ambiguously to refer either to the tasks which people set themselves—that is, to their purposive strivings, their attempts to achieve the goals which they set themselves, in short to the processes or activities in which they engage; or to their achievement of success in those processes or activities, or to the products of those activities. It draws attention to the fact that the same word, for example 'seeing' or 'teaching', may be used either with or without the claim that the relevant intention has been achieved. Winning a race is not an activity, therefore, but the aim of winning a race is internally related to the corresponding task of running in a race. To understand what a race is is to understand that the standard intention of those who run in races is to win the races in which they run. In talking about worthwhile activities, Peters himself says that (*ibid.*, p. 146), 'the activities in question all have some general point which must be sensed by their participants and they all have standards of correctness and style built into them which give rise to characteristic appraisals.' But this is true of all activities; it is because activities 'all have some general point . . .' and 'standards of correctness . . . built into them' that the task/achievement analysis has application to them.

If education is an activity it follows that a separate account cannot be given of that activity and the end towards which it is directed, since the activity is identified by its overall purpose. Being an educated man, for example, is not an activity; but it is to be the successful product of the educational activities which were directed to that end. One cannot, therefore, say what an educated man is without referring to those activities; one cannot, that is, give a separate account of 'education' and 'the educated man'. On Professor Peters's view this is possible; indeed, he provides such an account in his article 'Education and the educated man'.[4] He says,

[4] R. S. Peters, 'Education and the educated man', *Proceedings of the Philosophy of Education Society of Great Britain*, vol. 4, no. 1, January 1970, pp. 16–17.

for example, 'that we talk quite naturally about Spartan education. (But) . . . it would be almost a contradiction to speak of an educated Spartan; for "educated" as qualifying a person, keeps its association with "an educated man", and one of the things which we know about most of the Spartans is that they were not educated men.' On my view, the words 'Spartan education' would normally be used to refer to a particular activity identified by the end towards which it was directed, that is, the production of educated Spartans.

It is of course true that, just as the overall purpose of an activity may or may not be achieved, so also the criteria laid down by the word 'education' may or may not be satisfied. If they are not, however, there are no grounds for describing the processes or activities to which they are applied as educational, since education is neither a process nor an activity. 'Education' is therefore an achievement word in the sense that it is used to claim an achievement, the achievement involved in the satisfaction of the criteria which it lays down. It is not, however, an achievement word in the sense that it is a word which can be used ambiguously either to claim an achievement or to refer to a corresponding task, i.e. to a process or activity directed to that end.

The criteria laid down by the use of the word 'education', then, are external to the meanings of the words used to describe the activities or processes to which they are applied. I will now turn to the particular criterion in which I am interested, expressed in a key sentence in *Ethics and Education* (p. 25) quoted earlier: the word 'education' 'implies that something worthwhile is being or has been transmitted in a morally acceptable manner'.[5] As stated earlier, I will concern myself only with the requirement that something worthwhile be transmitted, leaving out of consideration the requirement that the manner of transmission be morally acceptable. The word 'implies' has, I take it, the strict meaning given to it in logic; it is not used in the psychological sense prevalent in ordinary speech, where it often means no more than 'suggests'. Indeed, in *The Logic of Education*[5] the discussion takes the form of a search for 'logically necessary conditions . . . for the use of the term "education" '. The sorts of things which logically imply, or entail, one another are statements rather than either words or sentences. What we need to know is what can be asserted by the same person in the same context without inconsistency, since the conjoint assertion of inconsistent statements is self-stultifying and defeats the primary purpose of language, which is communication. The claim, then, is that the statement 'This activity or process is an educational

[5] P. H. Hirst and R. S. Peters, *The Logic of Education*, London, 1970, p. 20.

activity or process' entails the statement 'This activity or process involves the transmission of something worthwhile'. Consequently anyone who asserted the first statement and denied the second would contradict himself; what he said could not possibly be true. We would not know, therefore, whether he thought that the activity or process was or was not educational, or whether it was or was not worthwhile.

This seems straightforward; but there are, of course, complications. Professor Peters points out, for example, that 'a sociologist or anthropologist might speak of the education system ... of a community without implying that he thought it desirable. But,' he points out (*Ethics and Education*, p. 25), 'in such cases the implication is that those whose system or code it is consider that it involves what is desirable.' We have, therefore, the following alternatives:

(1) 'This is an educational process, activity or system' implies 'This process, activity or system involves the transmission of what is worthwhile'.

(2) 'This is an educational process, activity or system' implies 'Those engaged in this process, activity or system consider that it involves the transmission of what is worthwhile'.

In both cases it is the person who asserts the implicans who is committed to the assertion of the implicandum if he is to avoid inconsistency. In the first case, however, the person using the word 'education' makes a value judgment; in the second he merely reports the fact that one has been made.

These alternatives need not be regarded as mutually exclusive; and I take it that the suggestion is that we use the word 'education' in both ways on different occasions, and that the context provides a sufficient guarantee against misunderstanding. This may be so; in trying to clarify the concept of education, however, it is important, as Professor Peters points out (*ibid.*, p. 24) 'to distinguish between central and peripheral usages of the term'. Elsewhere he says ('Education and the educated man', p. 9): 'Once we understand from our own case how terms such as "educate" and "moral" function we can use them in an external descriptive sort of way as do anthropologists, economists and the like.' The use of 'education' in sense (2) need not be external since it may be used in a first person way by one who is himself actively engaged in the activity concerned; but it is descriptive. I think it is clear, therefore, that Professor Peters's view is that (1) provides the central case.

If, following Professor Peters, (1) is taken as central, i.e. 'This is an educational process, activity or system' implies 'This process, activity or system involves the transmission of what is worthwhile', further questions may be asked. As Professor Peters says: 'It is a further question what the particular standards are in virtue of which activities are thought to be of value and what grounds there might be for claiming that they are the correct ones.' But it seems to be his view that it is not necessary to answer these questions in order to complete the analysis of the concept of education, since he goes on to say (in *Ethics and Education*, p. 25) 'that all that is implied is a commitment to what is thought valuable'. This, however, is only partly correct; there is, as he says later (*ibid.*, p. 91), 'no logical necessity about the particular values ascribed in particular societies to the variable of being "worthwhile" '. Indeed, in my view there is no necessity of any kind; it is a contingent matter. But it is a philosophical matter how the phrase 'is worthwhile' is to be interpreted; and until we know this the analysis is incomplete. Is the person who says 'This process, activity or system involves the transmission of what is worthwhile' to be understood as saying either:

(1a) 'and anyone who disagrees with me is wrong' or

(1b) 'though others may disagree with me, without my being prepared to say that they are wrong'.

I do not think a philosophical analysis of the concept of education can be neutral on this point, even if it can, and should, be neutral on the question of content, i.e. as to what is to be held worthwhile.

It should be noted, in passing, that even if (2), in its first person use, is taken as central, i.e. 'This is an educational process, activity or system' implies 'Those (including myself) engaged in this process, activity or system consider that it involves the transmission of what is worthwhile', a similar question arises about how the phrase 'is worthwhile' is to be interpreted. It could be interpreted either on the lines of (1a) or (1b), to produce (2a) and (2b).

The position arrived at so far is as follows. 'Education' does not name an activity; rather it lays down criteria to which activities and processes, such as instruction or teaching, must conform if they are to be accepted as educational activities or processes. The criteria are, therefore, external to the activity or process thought of as an activity or process of a certain sort. The criterion I have been considering is that what is being transmitted by the activity or process must be worthwhile. In deciding whether examples of instruction or teaching are educational, therefore, we look at what is being transmitted by them and decide whether it is worthwhile; worthwhile, that is, according to the person using the word 'education', not those engaged in the instruction or teaching. The question which I am now considering is how the words 'is worthwhile' are to be interpreted. I suggest that Professor Peters's view is represented more accurately by (1a) rather than by (1b), i.e. that 'is worthwhile' is to be interpreted as subject to the rider 'and anyone who disagrees with me is wrong'.

There are some indications that this is so even in Part One of *Ethics and Education*. Professor Peters says (p. 26) that ' "education" is a special case of what Ryle calls an achievement word'. As I pointed out earlier, 'education' is an achievement word only in the limited sense that it is used to claim an achievement. What, then, is special about 'education' as an achievement word? 'To educate someone', Professor Peters says (*ibid.*, p. 26), 'implies not only some sort of achievement, but also that it is worthwhile.' Later he says that the reason why you cannot ask for an extrinsic end to education is that ' "education" implies the transmission of what is of ultimate value'; and in the same paragraph (p. 29) he adds:

> Things like science and carpentry can be practised and passed on both for their own intrinsic value and because of the contribution which they make to extrinsic ends such as productivity, housing, and health. But in so far as they are regarded as part of someone's *education* they are regarded *ipso facto* as having value, and therefore as having reasons for doing them built into them . . .

In considering the distinctions suggested in these quotations, it is worth remembering that what is to be assessed for its worth is what is being transmitted by those engaged in the activity or process, such as instruction or teaching, to which the criteria laid down by the word 'education' are being applied. What is being passed on are 'worthwhile states of mind' (p. 26); and what this amounts to is 'the initiation of others into worthwhile activities' (p. 144), the activities concerned being those which form the content of the curriculum of an educational institution. In other words, those engaged in the practical social activities of instruction and teaching are concerned to introduce others to theoretical and practical social activities such as science and carpentry; and it is the latter activities which are being assessed for their worth.

First, then, 'to educate someone implies . . . some sort of achievement'. Instruction and teaching are activities which can be carried on with or without success; 'education' implies that they have been or are being carried on successfully. Second, 'education' implies 'not only some sort of achievement, but also that it is worthwhile', in the opinion, that is, of the person using the word 'education', not the person engaged in the instruction or teaching. What is being assessed now is the activity being passed on, the science or carpentry; the activity of passing it on, the instruction or teaching, being assessed only indirectly. In itself the distinction between achievements which are worthwhile, or of value, as it is alternatively expressed[6] and those which are not worthwhile, or lack value, does no more than draw attention to the fact that people differ in the things which they value and, therefore, in the activities in which they choose to engage. For those who set themselves the tasks they attempt the relevant achievement is always worthwhile; otherwise why should they attempt to achieve it? Third, the activities concerned, such as science or carpentry, must be 'passed on . . . for their own intrinsic value'. This suggests that intrinsic value is something which activities possess, i.e. that intrinsic value is a property of activities; and that people engage in such activities, and introduce others to them, because they possess that property. But the same social activity may have intrinsic value for one person taking part in it and instrumental value for another; given that education is an activity it provides an obvious example. The distinction between intrinsic and instrumental value makes a distinction between two sorts of reasons why people engage in activities; they engage in them either for their own sake or because they hope thereby to achieve some further end. Indeed, since intrinsic and instrumental value, though contrasted, are not mutually exclusive, they may engage in them for both reasons. For example, people may play chess or do logic exercises either because they enjoy doing them or because they hope thereby to improve the quality of their thinking or philosophizing or for both reasons. Intrinsic and instrumental value therefore are not in any sense properties of activities but a function of the way in which individuals view activities and, consequently, the way in which particular activities fit into the more general pattern of activity which makes up the individual's life. The distinction between intrinsic and instrumental value draws attention to two sorts of reasons why people engage in activities not to two sorts of activities or to two sorts of properties of activities which provide reasons for engaging in them. People differ in the activities in which they engage for their own sake and, therefore, in the activities which they regard as having intrinsic value. Activities and processes such as instruction and teaching, insofar as regarded as educational, are regarded as having instrumental value, i.e. are valued for the sake of the activities into which they initiate others.

A further distinction can be made between values which are internal to an activity and those which are external to it. As pointed out earlier, all activities have an overall purpose by means of which they are identified. The individual actions and observations

[6] See, e.g. R. S. Peters, 'What is an educational process', *The Concept of Education*, London, 1967, p. 4.

which are their parts are performed with the intention of contributing to that purpose; it is in this way that they are identified as parts. The overall purpose of an activity, therefore, not only provides a principle of identity of the activity and its parts but also a standard by means of which moves within the activity are assessed. They possess or lack instrumental value insofar as they contribute to the achievement of the overall purpose of the activity. Looked at from a perspective internal to the activity, therefore, the overall purpose of an activity may be thought of as a set of values internal to that activity. All activities have internal values which are accepted by those who take part in them. The values internal to an activity, therefore, provide reasons for or against particular moves within the activity; and insofar as the activity is a social activity those who take part in it will have values in common and will tend to agree about the details of what ought to be done within that activity. In other words in consequence of their shared purpose they will tend to agree about what count as reasons for doing things within the context of that activity. Internal assessment of moves in an activity may be contrasted with evaluation from a point of view external to the activity; for example, regarding a piece of scientific equipment as of aesthetic value.

Finally, to ask about the instrumental value of education ('for an extrinsic end') (*Ethics and Education*, p. 29) is to fail to understand that ' "education" implies the transmission of what is of ultimate value'. If something is regarded as of ultimate value, therefore, it cannot, logically, be regarded as of instrumental value. Since to regard something as of intrinsic value does not prevent questions being asked about its instrumental value, 'having ultimate value' cannot be equated with 'having intrinsic value'. The introduction of ultimate value and, therefore, the refusal to allow a clear sense to the question 'what use is education?' is, I think, a mistake. The subject of the judgment of ultimate value is the activity or activities, such as science or carpentry, into which people are initiated by means of educational activities and processes such as instruction and teaching. And it is obviously false, as Professor Peters realizes, to say that we cannot raise questions about the usefulness of such things as science and carpentry. The requirement that 'education' implies the transmission of what is of ultimate value, therefore, has the consequence that the concept of education lacks application; and this is obviously unacceptable.

What I think Professor Peters wishes to say is that 'education' implies the transmission of what is, necessarily, of intrinsic value; that is, of what must be regarded as of intrinsic value (though it may also be regarded as of instrumental value) or, to put it the other way around, of what cannot be regarded as of only instrumental value. The expression 'necessarily having intrinsic value' is clumsy and Professor Peters does not use it; but he does rely on the idea expressed by it. It is this, I think, which leads him not merely to deny that education is an activity but also to point to 'the impossibility of conceiving of educational processes in accordance with a means-ends model . . .', in 'Aims of education', p. 12. 'Means' and 'ends' are correlative terms, each defined in terms of the other. Ends are identified as ends because means are adopted to bring them about; they have intrinsic value, therefore, insofar as they are adopted as ends. Professor Peters's view, however, is that some activities possess intrinsic value independently of their adoption as ends by any individual or group of individuals. Intrinsic value is therefore more like a property than a relation; though, in view of the criticism of naturalism in *Ethics and Education*, presumably a non-natural property. It is an objective matter, or question of fact, that some activities possess intrinsic value. I have expressed this by saying that they necessarily possess intrinsic value.

'By "objectivity",' says Professor Peters in *Ethics and Education*, p. 99, 'is meant the assumption that error is possible . . . and that whether or not a person is in error depends on facts independent of the opinions or attitudes of any particular person or group of persons.' Anyone, therefore, who does not agree that the relevant activities have intrinsic value is mistaken, since there are objective reasons for regarding them as having intrinsic value. I may watch television because I enjoy it, whereas you crochet shawls. I therefore have a reason for watching television just as you have a reason for crocheting shawls; but there is no reason why I should crochet shawls or why you should watch television. The suggestion is, however, that there are objective reasons or, as Professor Peters puts it, 'good reasons', why we should both do some things such as, perhaps, science and carpentry; to fail to accept such reasons is to make some sort of mistake.

Facts are often contrasted with values because, Professor Peters suggests, 'what is valuable is thought to be a matter of opinion'; but, he points out (*ibid.*, p. 96), 'what is a matter of fact' cannot be equated with 'what can be observed'. Though, therefore, what is, necessarily, of intrinsic value cannot be decided by observation, it may still be a question of fact. 'What is a matter of fact' in this extended sense, however, means 'what there is an agreed decision procedure about', by reference to which disagreements may be resolved. In this sense there are mathematical facts, facts of logic and facts of law. What has to be shown is that there are facts about which things are, necessarily, of intrinsic value. I will now turn to

Part Two of *Ethics and Education* in which Professor Peters claims to do this.

In chapter 5 of *Ethics and Education* (p. 144), 'Worthwhile activities', Professor Peters points out that 'science, mathematics, history, art, cooking and carpentry feature on the curriculum, not bingo, bridge and billiards'. And he goes on to say that his purpose in the chapter is to show 'that there must be good reasons for pursuing these sorts of activities rather than others', though 'this does not imply that there are equally good reasons for saying that some activities included on a curriculum are more worthwhile than others which are also on a curriculum'.

'It cannot', he says (*ibid.*, p. 146), 'be argued in general that if people on the whole want something and continue to pursue it, this is sufficient to show that it is worth-while.' As I have pointed out, however, the phrase 'is worthwhile' is ambiguous. The fact that people engage in an activity because they want to do so does show that, for them, it has intrinsic value, since this is precisely what it means to say an activity has intrinsic rather than instrumental value; but it does not, of course, show that it necessarily has intrinsic value. Professor Peters goes on to argue (p. 146) that in the case of curriculum activities such as 'science, art, and history', 'a strong case can be made out for Socrates's view that if a man does not pursue or at least feel drawn towards what is good then he does not really understand it; for the activities in question all have some general point which must be sensed by their participants and they all have standards of correctness and style built into them which give rise to characteristic appraisals'. 'The sort of knowledge that is required in these pursuits is not merely a matter of intellectual understanding. It has a "feeling" side to it, which is exhibited in appraisals which are related both to the point of the activity and to the standards of skill, efficiency and style which characterise it.' And he concludes (p. 147) that 'to understand such an activity is to be committed in some way to its pursuit'. But what is said here of curriculum activities is true of all activities, whether pursued for their own sake or for the sake of some further end. All activities possess internal values which are related instrumentally to their point; to engage in an activity, for whatever reason, is to accept the standards which are internal to it. One who was not concerned to distinguish between true and false statements on the basis of the evidence for or against them, for example, would not be doing science at all. On the other hand those who are doing science may be doing it either for its instrumental or its intrinsic value. One cannot therefore argue that whatever possesses internal value *ipso facto* possesses intrinsic value, since all activities have values which are internal to them and some activities may be regarded as of only instrumental value. This is not to deny, of course, that insofar as a reference to intrinsic value is part of the meaning of 'education' (and in that sense internal to 'education') to regard science and carpentry as part of someone's education is *ipso facto* to regard them as having intrinsic value. The most that can be said, then, is that the 'feeling' side may be absent in activities regarded as of only instrumental value. The claim that to understand an activity is to be committed to its pursuit, therefore, must be made of all activities or of none; and, unless what we are being offered is an implausible definition of 'understanding', the claim has been substantiated of none. In any case if what is claimed is true of all activities it could hardly provide a principle of discrimination.

This is, in effect, admitted in the following section (section 2, 'Pleasure and pain'). Indeed the only conclusion finally claimed for section 1 is 'that what is crucial is not the fact of wanting but the character of what is wanted. The question then is whether anything general can be said about the character of such activities and whether any good reason can be given why they should be regarded as more worthwhile than others.' This question is taken up again in section 3, 'Activities and their justification'. 'What has to be shown . . . is why a person who asks the question "Why do this rather than that?" must pick out activities having certain characteristics rather than others.' And the preceding paragraph (p. 154) makes it clear that this question is not 'concerned with . . . instrumental or technical judgements but with judgements about the activities or states of affairs which are intrinsically good, from which instrumental or technical judgements derive their normative force. That there must be such judgements about ends is obvious. Otherwise giving reasons for actions would be an endless paper-chase.'

Professor Peters begins by asking 'what seriously asking this question presupposes' (p. 154) or, as it is expressed on the previous page, 'what a person is committed to who makes use of his reason in attempting to answer the question "What ought I to do?" ' First, (p. 153) 'asking this question seriously presupposes that the questioner is capable . . . of a non-instrumental and disinterested attitude' (p. 154). But from the argument of the previous paragraph, 'instrumental or technical judgements derive their normative force' from 'judgements about activities or states of affairs which are intrinsically good'. Anyone, therefore, who engages in any activity whatsoever is capable of 'a non-instrumental and disinterested attitude'. Such an attitude, therefore, cannot be peculiar to those who engage in activities only after asking 'why do this rather than that?' It is difficult to see, therefore, how there can be 'many people [who] are strangers to this attitude' (p. 154).

Anyone who has 'a non-instrumental and disinterested attitude', however, 'can see . . . that there are considerations intrinsic to activities themselves which constitute reasons for pursuing them . . .' (p. 154) and these 'considerations must derive from the nature of the activities concerned . . .' (p. 155). This, however, does not get us very far; if I choose to watch television rather than to crochet shawls, then, necessarily, there must be a difference between television and crochet; since to choose is to choose between alternatives which differ from one another in some way. I may choose a bull's eye from a bag of bull's eyes on the basis of its colour, since bull's eyes come in assorted colours; but I cannot intelligibly be said to choose an aniseed ball from a bag of aniseed balls, since one aniseed ball is indistinguishable from another. If I am told I can have whatever I like for breakfast provided it is baked beans, then I do not have much choice; nor is the situation much improved if I am offered a 'choice' between two identical plates of beans. Is there anything more to be said? Professor Peters says (p. 155) that 'particular activities can be appraised because of the standards immanent in them rather than because of what they lead to'; and that activities have 'their own built-in standards of excellence'. To say that activities can be appraised because of the standards immanent in them is to say only that activities can be appraised in respect of their intrinsic value, i.e. that we choose to engage in some activities for their own sake; while to say that activities have their own built-in standard of excellence is to say what is true of all activities, i.e. that they have values which are internal to them. To understand valuations which are internal to an activity 'from the inside is, in a sense, to be positively inclined towards doing things in some ways rather than others', as Professor Peters points out (p. 155). But this is to say no more than that to engage in an activity is to accept the values which are internal to it.

So far, then, no grounds have been produced to show that there are certain activities which must be regarded as having intrinsic value, and, therefore, that what is of intrinsic value is, in some cases at least, a question of fact. The final section of chapter 5 'The case for curriculum activities', begins (p. 157) by pointing out that theoretical activities could be justified by reference to their point, the pursuit of truth; or by pointing to 'the unending opportunities for skill and discrimination which they provide'. So far as the first point is concerned, those who happen to want to find out about the octopus brain have a reason for studying it, while those who do not have not; and so on generally. Similarly, those who like to exercise skill and make discriminations have a reason for engaging in activities which afford them the opportunity to do so; the rest of mankind, who display a marked preference for the simple life, have no such reason. Again (p. 158), 'scratch golfers . . . (may) get bored with the game because they have mastered it'. It is equally true that students of philosophy get bored with philosophy because they show no signs of mastering it.

'The strongest arguments for . . . science or philosophy or history however, derive from the character which they share over and above what they have in common with games and pastimes. The first is the nature of their cognitive concern' (p. 158). 'Some games . . . such as bridge or chess, have considerable cognitive content; but this is largely internal to them.' 'Curriculum activities, on the other hand, such as science, history, literary appreciation, and poetry are "serious" in that they illuminate other areas of life and contribute much to the quality of living' (p. 159). This, however, looks like one step forward and two steps backwards; for the object of the exercise is to show that curriculum activities *must* be regarded as having intrinsic value. And it is difficult to see how this can be done by claiming that they have instrumental value in that they 'contribute to the quality of life'. Indeed whether they have even instrumental value because of their contribution to the quality of life will depend both on the nature of that contribution and on the view taken of how life should be lived. The prevalence of materialist values in Western Europe and America, for example, may indeed be a consequence of the rise of science and technology; but it is surely a matter of opinion whether this counts as an improvement. On the other hand, though a person engaged in research in the more esoteric branches of mathematics, for example, 'develops conceptual schemes and forms of appraisal', it is difficult to see they could be said to 'transform everything else that he does' (p. 160).

Finally, Professor Peters asks, 'Why . . . must a person who asks seriously the question "Why do this rather than that?" be committed to those sorts of activities which have this special sort of cognitive concern and content built into them? The answer is obvious enough, namely that these sorts of enquiries are all, in their different ways, relevant to answering the sort of question that he is asking' (p. 161). It is not obvious to me, however, that this answer is correct or even what it amounts to. Anyone having a choice to make will, if the choice is an important one and he is sensible, first make sure that he is aware of the full range of alternatives between which he is free to choose. He will therefore need to know that there are such activities as doing science or carpentry, as well as watching television, crocheting shawls and playing tiddly-winks. 'The description of

disinterested activities, and hence the discussion of their value . . .'
will, it is true, 'depend on how he has learnt to conceive them; . . .
he has to see what he is doing in a certain way.' But, once again, this
is true of all actions and activities, however trivial, including,
indeed, raising one's arm as contrasted with a mere movement of
one's arm. Consequently a man playing tiddly-winks is 'thinking
about what he is doing in various ways which are inseparable from
the doing of it' (p. 162). Insofar as it is true, therefore, that the
only way to answer the question 'Why do this rather than that?' is
'Try and see' it is true whatever 'this' and 'that' are. Moreover, it
follows that it is impossible to *choose* to do philosophy, for example,
rather than merely to plump for it; since you cannot choose to do
philosophy unless you know what philosophy is and you cannot
know what philosophy is without doing it. It is also true that many
of those who plump for philosophy choose to spend their time
gossiping in the coffee bar once they find out what they let themselves in for without, apparently, any sense of falling into error.

The last few pages of chapter 5 provide a definition of the word
'seriously'. Games are not serious in that they 'are hived off from
man's curiosity about the world and his awe and concern about his
own peculiar predicament' (p. 164). 'To ask the question "Why do
this rather than that?" seriously is therefore . . . to be committed to
those enquiries which are defined by their serious concern with
those aspects of reality which give context to the question which he
is asking' (p. 164). In other words, the answer to the question, asked
seriously, is 'Do this, because this is serious, rather than that, which
is not serious.' If the question is not asked seriously in the sense
defined but simply in the sense that an answer is genuinely sought,
it will always be possible to ask: 'But why do what is serious?'; and
this question is not self-answering.

Professor Peters, then, has not shown that there are any activities
which must be regarded as having intrinsic value; that is, which
necessarily possess intrinsic value. Even if there are activities which
necessarily possess intrinsic value we have been offered no way of
distinguishing them from activities which are, simply as a matter of
fact, regarded as possessing intrinsic value; at best, therefore, we do
not know when to use the word 'education'.

Finally I want to consider the possibility that Professor Peters was
not merely unsuccessful in what he tried to do but that the attempt
itself was misconceived. I will therefore consider arguments presented in chapter 4 of *Ethics and Education* to show that this is not so.
There he tries (p. 121) 'to establish that the general principle of no
distinction without differences is a presupposition of practical
discourse, or that it is presupposed in any attempt to determine

what ought to be done'. To use practical discourse is, as a matter of definition, to ask the question 'What ought I to do?' And since the notion of 'ought' is taken as 'more or less equivalent to the notion of there being reasons for something', one who asks 'What ought I to do?' 'is asking for reasons for adopting one alternative . . . course of action . . . rather than another.' And 'a reason for [action] A rather than [action] B is some aspect under which A is viewed which makes it *different* as a course of action from B.' He concludes that 'to use practical discourse seriously is to be committed to the search for such reasons'. This, clearly, is a definition of practical discourse arrived at by defining practical discourse in terms of asking the question 'What ought I to do?' and 'ought' in terms of asking for reasons.

Immediately, however, he goes beyond this definition (p. 122).

> The search for features of a situation which would justify one course of action rather than another presupposes that a reason for doing something cannot be constituted simply by the fiat of an individual. For if he is deliberating about the characteristics of A rather than B in order to choose, he must presuppose that there might be features possessed by either A or B which would make his choice correct or wise.

And he adds 'choice cannot be a matter of individual fiat if there is to be a possibility of its being shrewd, wise, correct, intelligent, or far-sighted'. I will consider here only the applicability of the term 'correct'. Different considerations might arise if 'shrewd', 'wise', 'intelligent' and 'foresighted' were considered; they appear to relate primarily to either prudential judgments or judgments about choice of means. Answers to the question 'What ought I to do?' then may be correct or incorrect, depending on whether they can be justified by pointing to a reason for making that choice rather than some other. What counts as a reason is not determined 'simply by fiat of an individual'; not everything offered as a reason, therefore, is acceptable as such. Reasons, in other words, come in two sorts, good and bad; and we know this much even if we do not know how to tell the difference between them.

It is far from obvious, however, that this is so. It does not follow from the definition of practical discourse that reasons may be described as good or bad. The only account of 'reason' given there was 'some aspect under which A (i.e. one action) is viewed which makes it *different* as a course of action from B (i.e. some other action)'. If A is different from B, however, then B is different from A; the mere fact of difference points neither one way nor the other. We are left, therefore, with the unsupported claim that what counts as a reason may properly be described as good or bad.

The temptation to make such a claim springs in part from the ambiguity of the words 'reasoning' and 'reason'. Inferences from premises to conclusion are valid if made in accordance with the rules of inference; there is then good reason to accept the conclusion as following from the premises. Beliefs about what is the case may be based on evidence or directly on the evidence of the senses; there is then good reason for holding them. There may also be grounds for believing that the adoption of certain means will lead to the achievement of a desired end; it is then rational, or reasonable, to adopt those means. But the word 'reason' is also used as, in effect, a synonym for 'want'; I have a reason for trying to get what I want. If I want A (say, a cup of tea) rather than B (say, a cup of coffee) it is true that there must be 'some aspect under which A is viewed which makes it different . . . from B'; and I have a reason for adopting whatever course of action will lead to a cup of tea. But it cannot be assumed, without argument, that reasons in this sense may properly be described as correct or incorrect.

Perhaps, however, the claim that reasons for action may be correct or incorrect is part of a more extended definition of practical discourse. In that case one can say that 'to use practical discourse seriously is to be committed to the search for reasons, which can be shown to be correct reasons, for following one course of action rather than another', since this is true by definition. But to offer a definition is not to show that anything corresponds to that definition, even though many people think that it does. This is illustrated very clearly by the failure of the ontological argument to move from a definition of God to the statement that God exists.

The same point can be made using Professor Peters's preferred terminology of presupposition. Talk of presupposition is appropriate when the *use* of certain expressions presupposes, or takes for granted, the *truth* of certain statements. For example, the use of the referring expression 'all John's children' in the statement 'All John's children are asleep' presupposes the truth of 'John has some children', though it does not say that John has some children.[7] The claim being considered is that the use of practical discourse—for example, asking 'What ought I to do?'—understood in the defined way— presupposes that there are reasons which can be shown to be good reasons for following one course of action rather than another. But it does not follow from the fact that someone who says 'All John's children are asleep' presupposes that John has some children that

[7] This example is taken from Professor P. F. Strawson's *Introduction to Logical Theory*, London, 1967, p. 175.

John really does have some children. Similarly it does not follow from the fact that the use of the word 'ought' in the question 'what ought I to do?', understood in the defined way, presupposes that there are reasons which can be shown to be good reasons for following one course of action rather than another, that there are good reasons for following one course of action rather than another. Anyone who offers prayers to God presupposes that there is a God to whom prayers may be offered; one who prays to God, therefore, cannot consistently deny that God exists, though he may refrain from asserting it; but this does not prove that God exists. If there are no grounds for believing that what is presupposed by a form of discourse is so then the obvious thing to do is to abandon that way of talking. What requires to be shown, therefore, is that reasons for choosing one course of action rather than another may properly be described as good or bad; and this, I concluded earlier, has not been done.

Values in education (2) 8
Reply to Glenn Langford
R. S. Peters

Introduction

Ethics and Education, as I admitted in the Introduction, was completed about two years too soon. It had structural defects and, though I would still stand by the basic positions put forward, some of the analysis and argumentation was unclear and lacking in cogency. In this category I would place the analysis of 'education' and the deployment of the arguments for worthwhile activities.[1] But though I was uneasy and perhaps unguarded at times in suggesting that education is not an activity, it never occurred to me, until I read Glenn Langford's paper, that this is a major issue about which it is of much moment whether one is mistaken or not. I propose, therefore, to examine first of all what there is to be said for or against the claim that education is an activity. I shall then ask whether anything much depends on what one says about this issue. I shall finally make one or two comments about the issues connected with 'worthwhile activities' and objectivity.

1. Educating as an activity

Langford gives no positive reasons for supposing that education *is* an activity. He seems just to assert it. He points out that activities differ from actions in having an overall purpose; he distinguishes theoretical activities (e.g. maths) from practical ones (e.g. cooking) and individual from social activities and claims that education is a practical social activity. He comes to this conclusion presumably because education involves activities of some sort which have a principle of unity in that they contribute to some overall end. He therefore assumes that this overall end is an end in view for those taking part in the activities, making these sub-activities within the super-activity of 'educating'.

This transition is, of course, quite illegitimate. There are many cases of activities which contribute to an end or outcome without there being a corresponding super-activity whose overall intention is to bring about this outcome. I have usually given the parallel of 'reform' in this context; that of 'corrupt' would do quite well. But perhaps even clearer cases are 'achievements' such as 'bore' or 'interest'.[2] To bore people one usually has to engage in some activity or activities such as telling a story, giving a lecture, etc. But, if by doing so, one bores people, one does not have to have this outcome in mind. Indeed most bores emphatically do not. Similarly one can educate someone without having the remotest intention of so doing. A knowledgeable young man, for instance, may take his ignorant girlfriend with him on trips to the country because he enjoys her company. The outcome is that the girl's understanding of geography is vastly improved. His company and communications are highly educative for her, as well as the country scenery, but not intended to be so by either party concerned. As Rousseau put it, 'Education comes from nature, men, and things.'

These cases might be admitted but it might be claimed that they are peripheral ones which we understand because of the central cases in which the outcome is arrived at by the agent concerned in the activity of educating. But difficulties then break out about regarding 'educating' as an obvious case of an activity. The difficulties are many. Activities begin at a time, go on for a time and stop when the agent so decides. But does educating? Langford nowhere comments on the quaintness, to which I draw attention, in saying things like 'Go and start your educating', 'Stop educating at 3 p.m.', 'Educate for half an hour and then take a rest'. There are some people, such as Helen Freeman, who even claim that teaching is not an activity, let alone 'educating'. But, whatever the merits of this more extreme type of thesis, it certainly does not sound strange to substitute 'teaching' for 'educating' in these sentences. Still less does it sound strange to talk about obvious activities such as fishing and gambling in this way. And how can a great educator *stop* educating people unless he or she becomes a recluse? For, like George Eliot's heroine in *Middlemarch* 'the effect of her being on those around her' may be 'incalculably diffusive'. Many of the most important outcomes in education are not those which are consciously planned or intended.

One of the differences underlying the inappropriateness of talking about educating in this way is surely that activities are usually discharged in a range of fairly specific acts. Teaching involves a range of acts by means of which some kind of content is communicated to learners. Scientists perform a range of manipulative and perceptual acts. Cooking is inseparable from doing specific things with utensils, ingredients, ovens, and so on. But what does educating involve? Librarians, administrators, publishers, film-makers, poets and musicians may all be described as educating their fellow-men. But the types of acts to which they have recourse are so varied that it is somewhat forced to regard them as engaged in a common activity. And, of course, all such people can in fact be educating people without intending to do so. Indeed, someone might draw the attention of a film-maker to the extent to which he is either educating or corrupting the public. This might surprise him; for he might just think of himself as entertaining them. But it is surely a characteristic of an activity that the agent knows that he is engaged in it without having to be informed of it by others. There is an inappropriateness in telling a person that he is cooking, gardening, or playing the violin.

Activities of some sort are, of course, usually involved in educating people. They have a principle of unity in that they contribute to the state of mind of an educated person with its criteria of exhibiting knowledge and understanding and being valuable. But people who contribute to this end may or may not have it in view. And even if they do have it as an end in view, there are respects in which even this most favourable case seems forced as an example of an activity. To take a parallel: suppose people become more conscious of the effects of their activities on the environment so that they increasingly bear this in mind in a vast range of activities. Is there now some new super-activity of conservation? Similarly, with the increase in sensivity to suffering in the last hundred years, we talk about people as humanitarians and of humanitarian activities. But is there now a super-activity of minimizing human suffering? 'Education', as I have pointed out, used to refer to any process of bringing up, rearing, and so on. But from the nineteenth century onwards it has gradually been tightened up to pick out activities and processes which contribute to the state of mind of an educated man. Educators, like humanitarians, are people who conduct and assess activities with an explicit awareness of criteria which the outcomes of these activities may or may not satisfy. They *may* consciously plan a range of activities with these criteria conceived of as ends in view. But this does not entail that they are now engaged in a super-activity.

It follows from these points that I agree with Mr Langford when he says that, in my view, the activities involved in educating people can be identified independently of the application to them of the criteria laid down by 'education'. For if I do not think that educating is an activity I cannot claim that its overall purpose can be thought of as a set of criteria to which subsidiary actions and activities must conform if they are to count as parts of that activity. In a similar way one can identify the activities involved in corrupting people independently of any reference to thoughts in the minds of corrupters of corruption as an end in view.

Education, as I have previously put it, is a chancy business. This is in part due to the fact that the achievement of the criteria definitive of being educated *necessarily* depends on people other than the educator, namely the learners. Success in education, as in corrupting, boring, or interesting people, necessarily depends on how others respond to the educator's efforts or lack of them. A person can work away instructing people, perhaps very mindful of the criteria involved in his pupils' becoming educated, perhaps not; but what is crucial is how they take what he says. They may feel so insecure that they just learn what he says more or less by rote. If this is the outcome then he is not educating them, however he conceives what he is doing.

This point is particularly pertinent with regard to the state of mind of an educated man; for this involves a certain kind of knowledge and understanding that is not just narrowly specialized, as I have previously argued. Now understanding, above all states of mind, involves attention and effort on the part of the learner. He has, as it were, to be 'ready' before the penny drops, as Piagetians are never tired of insisting with regard to the grasp of concepts basic to making sense of our experience. This end cannot be brought about just by planned instruction and the appropriate use of incentives. Given that most of the outcomes of being educated are states of mind of this sort rather than merely a well-stocked memory, the unpredictability of success is not difficult to explain.

It does not follow from this, however, that an entirely 'separate account' can be given of the activities involved in education and of the outcome of being an educated man. The reason for this is nothing to do with education being an overall *activity*. It is because education necessarily involves learning, and the various achievements involved in learning logically require antecedent activities or processes of a certain type. A person, for instance, could not understand Euclid unless he had encountered mathematics in his prior experiences of learning. Thus if an educated man is one who has some depth and breadth of understanding, he must have had prior experiences which are logically appropriate to the development of these general outcomes. There is a sense, therefore, in which one cannot give a separate account of 'education' and 'the educated man'. But this is not because education is an activity; it is because of certain logical features of human learning. And, incidentally, in criticizing what I say about Spartan education not leading to educated men, Mr Langford fails to notice that I am here contrasting the general sense of 'education', which means just any process of rearing, with the specific sense in which processes of learning are thought of as having some unity because they contribute to the outcome of an educated man.

2. What depends on insisting that educating is an activity?

Other arguments could be advanced for casting doubt on the
thesis than educating is an activity. But it seems rather pointless to
do so unless anything of great moment depends on whether we call
educating an activity or not. So let us consider what might depend
on this.

Mr Langford seems anxious to establish that education is an
activity because of some thesis which he wants to defend about the
subjectivity of value judgments inherent in education. He claims
that if education means the transmission of what is worthwhile, and
if the worthwhileness of its overall end is envisaged as such by
those engaged in the activity of educating, then it is obvious that the
valuation is from the point of view of those engaged in the activity.
For they do all sorts of things for the sake of achieving their overall
purpose. This purpose provides reasons for or against particular
moves within this overall activity. So those who take part in this
social activity will have values in common and will tend to agree
about the details of what ought to be done within that activity.

This is true enough. But surely the question can be raised whether
what they value really is valuable. In a similar way, as Mr Langford
points out, if the end of an educated man is, as I have argued, an
outcome which may or may not be envisaged as an overall aim, and
if it is one that is thought of as worthwhile, either by external
assessors or by those who are engaged in teaching, instructing, etc.
the question can be raised whether it really is worthwhile or not. It
does not matter whether the agents involved in an activity, or
external assessors of it, or the learners themselves are doing the
valuing. The question of their being mistaken can still be raised.
And what one thinks of the answer to this general question or,
indeed, of its legitimacy, depends on one's general views on ethics.
For whatever the status of judgments of worthwhileness there must
obviously be people who think things worthwhile. It could not, of
course, be a property of activities or states of mind apart from
people. But the issue of objectivity is not this. It is rather whether
such judgments must necessarily be related to the desires, aspirations,
etc. of the *particular* people who are making the value judgments. I
do not see how Mr Langford's insistence that education is an
activity advances the discussion of this fundamental issue in ethics.

The point presumably of emphasizing that education is *not* an
activity is to make those engaged in it rather more conscious than
they are of the unintended outcomes of their endeavours. Most
teachers, when they go into schools, just learn to work the system.
They grade and examine children relentlessly, they reward and

punish them, they make decisions without consulting them at all, and perhaps they teach in a way which tends to stifle criticism and enquiry. Other teachers achieve amazing results almost in spite of the methods which they employ and the curriculum to which they are chained. Asking questions about the educational value of many of their activities is a way of drawing attention to what actually happens and to its value as distinct from what they conceive of themselves as bringing about. If they become more aware of what their activities may contribute to the development of educated men and women they will not necessarily produce such people. But at least they may think twice about continuing with practices that are obviously counter-productive in relation to such an outcome. Insisting that education is an activity, for all its impropriety, may make them more mindful of their aims; but it may do so in a way which draws a veil over the nuances. It may lead them to think of the transactions involved in a way which makes them too rationalistic, too confident in their capacity to bring about results which depend in part only on their own agency. It may make them too oblivious of the fact that such results depend equally on the agency of learners.

3. The status of judgments about what is worthwhile

The latter part of Mr Langford's paper is concerned with a critique of my account in *Ethics and Education* of the grounds for thinking that being educated is a worthwhile state to be in. This account was confused because it does not clearly distinguish between grounds for what is worthwhile in general and grounds for what is worthwhile in being educated in particular. There are various states of mind which are valuable but which are not the prerogative of the educated—e.g. being compassionate and courageous. The values of being educated are connected specifically with the possession of knowledge and understanding. It is, therefore, for these values that a justification has to be given. In *Ethics and Education* two types of justification were in fact given for knowledge and understanding. But it was not made sufficiently clear that they were given for these specific states of mind rather than for valuable states of mind in general.

Similarly, the two different types of justification were not clearly enough associated with different interpretations of 'worthwhile'. The first hedonistic type of justification, which was not thought to be convincing, was for 'worthwhile' activities as interpreted as a desirable way of spending one's time. The claims of practical activities, involving skill and understanding, together with the claims of theoretical activities, were considered in respect of their potentiality for absorbing participants and mitigating boredom. Mr Langford, however, does not really consider the case for arguments of this type. He dismisses them by pointing out that some people prefer the simple life rather than studying octopus brains— an obvious point that is, of course, the *starting point* of those like Mill who have been concerned about the 'quality' of pleasures. He also thinks that the fact that some students get bored with philosophy because they cannot master it is sufficient to counter the point that some pursuits, such as games, lack the open-endedness of pursuits such as science and philosophy which provide endless opportunities for novelty, mastery and stimulation. But this shows nothing at all; for people can equally well get bored with golf because they cannot master it. The comparison must surely be between different types of pursuit in respect of their potentiality for providing continuous satisfaction, not between the competent and the incompetent. These arguments, however, are admitted to be inconclusive, though not for Mr Langford's reasons, and a transition is then made to another type of argument and to another sense of 'worthwhile'.

The other sense of 'worthwhile' can be illustrated by the case of a man like Socrates who regarded discussing fundamental problems with young men as 'worthwhile' even though he may have found it boring at times. The 'worth' of such activities derives from the demand that reasons should be given for belief or courses of action and the refusal to take things on trust and from authorities. This demand has little to do with values of a hedonistic sort; for being concerned about truth has a worth which is independent of its benefit. Indeed the state of mind of one who is determined to find out what is true, and who is not obviously deluded or mistaken about how things are, or about what he really wants as distinct from what he thinks he wants, can be regarded as an ultimate value which provides one of the criteria of benefit. This was the central point of Socrates's answer to Callicles. And there are a group of virtues which are inseparable from any attempt to decide questions in this way. These are virtues such as clarity, non-arbitrariness, impartiality, a sense of relevance, consistency, respect for evidence, sincerity and truth-telling.

How then are values of this sort relevant to the attempt to justify the knowledge and understanding of an educated man? Surely because the activity of justification itself would be unintelligible without them. If a justification is sought for doing X rather than Y, then X and Y have to be distinguished in some way. To distinguish them we have to rely on the forms of discrimination which are available, to locate them within some kind of conceptual scheme.

For instance, if the choice is between going into medicine or going into business some understanding of these activities is a prerequisite. Understanding such activities is not just a matter of trying them; it is a matter also of conceiving of them in various ways and this is an open-ended business. So an open-ended employment of various forms of understanding is demanded. And such probing must be conducted at least on the presupposition that obvious misconceptions of what is involved in these activities are to be removed. There is a presumption, in other words, that it is undesirable to believe what is false and desirable to believe what is true.

Furthermore if a reason is to be given for choosing X rather than Y, X has to be shown to have some feature which Y lacks which is relevant to its worth and desirability. If smoking is a threat to health and chewing gum is not, these are relevant considerations, given that health is desirable. And this, in its turn, presupposes two types of belief, one about the effects of smoking as distinct from chewing gum, and the other about the desirability of health. Further questions can, of course, be raised about the desirability of health, which may lead to fundamental questions in ethics. But whatever the status of such explorations they too are part of the quest for further clarity and understanding. Maybe the enquirer will be chary of saying that what he ends up with is 'knowledge', but at least he may claim to have eliminated some errors and to have obtained more clarity and understanding of the issues involved. Arbitrary assertions will have been rejected, irrelevant considerations avoided, and generalizations queried for their evidential basis. These procedures, which are constitutive of the search for truth, are not those for which some individual might have a private preference; they are those which he must observe in rational discussion, in any attempt at justification. This would be unintelligible as a public practice without 'worth' being ascribed at least to the elimination of muddle and error.

Mr Langford rather pours cold water on this type of argument by saying that 'Anyone having a choice to make will, if the choice is an important one and he is sensible, first make sure that he is aware of the full range of alternatives between which he is free to choose.' But he gives the game away by introducing the notion of the 'sensible' man. The point is that, though all men live under the demands of reason, they acknowledge these demands to varying degrees. Those who acknowledge them fully are called 'sensible' or 'reasonable'. He thus accepts the type of point that I am making in putting forward what he takes to be a refutation of it. He then goes on to misunderstand my point about the role of human conception in choice. Of course doing anything involves conceiving of it in some way. This is a conceptual necessity. But my point is that there is great variability both in conception and in account taken of relevant facts. In choosing between alternatives, in addition to trying them, one can be more or less conscious of what they may involve. How, for instance, is one to conceive of smoking if one is deliberating about whether to give it up or not? Do the danger to health and its expense feature, as well as its aesthetic and sensory properties? Reason demands at least that one does not ignore relevant facts.

Mr Langford, in spite of his introduction of the notion of the 'sensible' man, objects to my introduction of 'seriousness' at the end. This is a shorthand for acceptance of the demands made by reason on us. What do I mean by this? Very briefly that men do not just have expectations of their environment; they have beliefs and sometimes claim knowledge. No sense can be made of such notions without value being placed on truth. Belief, for instance, is the attitude appropriate to what is true. Similarly in the sphere of actions men are not just programmed by an instinctive equipment. They conceive of ends, deliberate about them and about the means to them. They follow rules and revise them. Assessment has a toe-hold in every feature of this form of life. This constant scrutiny and monitoring of human actions would be unintelligible without the presupposition that there may be better or worse ways of conducting one's life. 'Seriousness' is the attitude of mind that is appropriate to the acceptance of such demands of reason.[3]

Mr Langford might admit all this but say that, in the end, especially in the sphere of action, the demands of reason are only instrumentally valuable because people need to know in order to satisfy their wants, including their desire for knowledge itself. Value must always fall into the first hedonistic category of 'worthwhile'. I do not think that this view is ultimately either coherent or defensible unless 'want' is used in a very general sense which makes it a conceptual truth that anything that people can value must be, in some sense, what they want. For, first, to want is always to want under some description that involves belief; hence wants can be more or less examined. Reason demands examination. Second, one of the most perplexing questions of conduct is whether, in any ordinary sense of 'want', people ought always to do what they want to do. Third, the very notion of 'instrumentality' presupposes a demand of reason. For, as Kant put it, taking a means to an end presupposes the axiom of reason that to will the end is to will the means. Thus the demands of reason are presupposed in the form of thought that might lead us to think of its value as being instrumental only.

There is, however, another intermediate type of argument with which I had a rather half-hearted flirtation in *Ethics and Education* which, in a sense, tries to connect my two different senses of 'worthwhile'. It is an attempt to make something of the Socratic connexion between knowledge of the good and being disposed to pursue it. Mr Langford is probably right in pointing in several places to the lack of cogency in the suggestion, for instance, that if people really understand what there is in, e.g. philosophy or science, they will be disposed to pursue it, and their failure to pursue it indicates a lack of proper understanding. But I am still rather unhappy about giving up the attempt to make *any* such connexion. To explain my un-happiness I will have to set out more systematically the connexion between the state of mind of being educated and 'worthwhile activities'. Indeed I shall be pleased to do this; for I am constantly irritated by having my view of education represented baldly as just involving 'initiation' into worthwhile activities.

Two types of value have been distinguished, which underpin the life of an educated person, leaving aside moral values such as justice and the minimization of suffering, which structure the interpersonal realm of conduct. These are (i) hedonistic values connected with the avoidance of boredom, in relation to which activities involving knowledge and understanding might be accorded a high place; (ii) values implicit in the demands of reason which give rise to virtues such as clarity, consistency, hatred of arbitrariness and so on. Insofar as a reasonable or 'sensible' person examines his beliefs or conduct these virtues govern his enquiry; but he does not necessarily find this kind of examination enjoyable or absorbing. It *may* not, in other words, be thought of as worthwhile in the first sense.

Now, for reasons connected with the notion of human learning, a man can only develop a state of mind characterized by knowledge and understanding by pursuing, to some extent, theoretical *activities* such as science or literature and/or practical activities requiring some degree of understanding. But why, having become educated, should he devote himself at all to activities of this sort? Why should he choose to spend some of his time in reading, taking part in discussions or in demanding practical activities such as engineering? On occasions, of course, in acknowledgment of the demands of reason, he may feel obliged to enlighten himself on some issue, to seek information relevant to his beliefs and actions. And whilst so doing he submits to the standards of such a disinterested pursuit. But why should he seek out any such pursuits? To take a parallel in the moral sphere: why should a person who accepts the principle of justice, who acknowledges its demands on his life by relevant actions and enquiries when occasions arise, pursue the promotion of justice as a worthwhile activity, e.g. by working as a judge or as social reformer? Similarly, in this sphere of worthwhile pursuits, why should not an educated man settle for a job which is un-demanding and which allows him plenty of time for playing golf, which is the one activity which he really enjoys apart from eating, sun-bathing and occasionally making love to his wife? He is, of course, capable of seeing point in a more Dewey type of life of expanding experience and understanding. He is not a philistine; but he just loves his game of golf more than any of the more in-tellectually taxing types of pursuit. Golf is to him what he presumes that science is to the other fellow. Is this way of life credible?

To summarize:

(a) There are activities such as science, engineering, the study of literature, etc. by engaging in which a person becomes an educated man—one who has breadth and depth of understanding and who is prepared to examine his beliefs and conduct.

(b) As an educated person he may, later on, see reason to pursue such activities on occasions, if he sees their *relevance* to some issue of belief and conduct, though he may not find them particularly absorbing. Such exercises will be manifestations of his acceptance of the demands of reason.

(c) But, as an educated person, he will do *some* things for their own sake. Whatever he does will be, to some extent, transformed by his level of understanding, but will he necessarily pursue, for their own sake, some activities of the sort that he pursues or has pursued in contexts (a) and (b)? Is it intelligible that he should both be educated and find *all* such activities too frustrating and boring to pursue them for their own sake? Would such a man be any more intelligible than Kant's moral being who is virtuous only out of respect for law? Socrates may have sometimes regarded his pursuit of truth with others as a boring duty, though we know that he did not always find it so. But does it not seem inconceivable that he could *always* have found it boring? And is this *simply* because of the empirical fact that he spent a lot of time that way?

This is, I think, a more precise explication of the underlying considerations which led me to attempt some kind of connexion between being educated and spending some of one's time on 'worthwhile activities'. Mr Langford exposes some of the weaknesses in my half-hearted gestures towards making some kind of connexion. But I am still unhappy about making the connexion completely contingent.

Mr Langford ends his paper with general points about objectivity and the presupposition of practical discourse in general. This raises too many issues to deal with in this reply, which is already too long.

Notes

1 I have subsequently had another shot at trying to formulate better what I was trying to say on both these issues. See R. S. Peters, 'Education and the educated man', *Proceedings of the Philosophy of Education Society of Great Britain*, vol. 4, January 1970; and 'The justification of education' in R. S. Peters (ed.), *The Philosophy of Education*, London, 1973.

2 I owe these examples to Mrs Helen Freeman, who has invented a new category of what she calls 'perficient verbs'. She claims that 'teach' is such a verb. See H. S. Freeman, 'The concept of teaching' in *Proceedings of the Philosophy of Education Society of Great Britain*, January 1973.

3 For a fuller exposition of this argument see 'The justification of education', mentioned above.

Aspects of education

part 3

Language and moral education[1]

R. M. Hare

9

In this lecture I am going to try to bring philosophy to bear on a practical problem. But before I start, I had better try to explain to you what I think philosophy is, and what reason I have for supposing that it could possibly have any bearing on any practical problem. I have to explain what it is, because people have used the word 'philosophy' in so many different ways that you will not understand, without an explanation, the precise sense in which I am using it. And I have to say why I think philosophy has a bearing on practical problems, because many people do not think so, and because once you understand how I am using the word 'philosophy' you may well ask yourselves how such an abstract subject could possibly have any practical bearing.

It is certainly possible to use the word 'philosophy' in such a way that it is only too obvious that it has a bearing on practice. People sometimes talk, for example, of 'the philosophy of dry fly fishing', and mean no more by this than 'the general principles of dry fly fishing'. If I were using the word 'philosophy' in that way, I could talk for one hour or several hours about the philosophy of moral education, and of course my talk would be relevant to the practice of moral education, just as a lecture on the philosophy of dry fly fishing could hardly help being relevant to the practice of dry fly fishing. But that is not how I going to use the word 'philosophy'. The discussion of the general principles of dry fly fishing is a job for dry fly fishermen; and the discussion of the general principles of moral education is primarily a job for schoolmasters and educationists. As a philosopher I have, I think, a contribution to make, but it is of a different kind.

What then is philosophy, as I am using the term? It is the art or science which does for words what mathematics does for numbers. We all spend quite a lot of time talking; and some of this we spend arguing with one another, using words for this purpose. It is no

[1] This is a revised and shortened version of two public lectures given in the autumn of 1968 in Toronto under the auspices of the Ontario Institute for Studies in Education. I am grateful to the faculty of the Institute for many kindnesses. Most of the matter omitted appeared as part of my paper 'The practical relevance of philosophy' in my collection *Essays on Philosophical Method*, London, 1971.

accident that philosophy started in Greece, because the ancient Greeks were perhaps the most argumentative people the world has ever known. It was one of them, Socrates, who made for the first time the move which started philosophy in the sense in which I am using the word. He found some people arguing about some substantial question; and instead of joining in the argument on one side or the other, he insisted on having some key term in it explained to him. He did not put his questions as questions about the meanings of words; but they *were* that. To know what rightness is, is to know what we mean by 'right'.[2] In the same sort of way, you could imagine a father and his son having an argument today about whether something is right or wrong (it could be about something important or about something unimportant—about whether it is right to fight for one's country, or about whether it is right to grow one's hair long); and you could imagine some modern Socrates coming along and saying to them 'How can you possibly settle your argument if you don't know what you mean by "right"?' And this advice would be sound. For until we understand the questions we are asking, how can we possibly set about answering them?

Although this kind of demand for the explanation of the meaning of a word could come up in many fields (and there are, correspondingly, many branches of philosophy), moral philosophy, which tries to elucidate the meanings of the moral words like 'right' and 'wrong', has always been one of the most important branches, simply because questions about right and wrong are both very important and, often, very baffling. Certainly, if philosophers could help us to answer questions about what is right and wrong by explaining the meanings of these words, they would be doing us all a service.

Can they help? It might be thought, and has been thought by many people, that mere verbal elucidations can never help us decide substantial questions. These are the people who urge philosophers not to waste their time—or at any rate not to waste other people's time—by engaging in these 'verbal trivialities'. Socrates in his day was subject to the same sort of attack. However, I do not think that anybody will join in this attack who has spent much time discussing serious and difficult moral problems. For you do not need to be a philosopher to see that what often leads to a complete impasse in such discussions is that the disputants are utterly at a loss to know what would settle the argument; and this, if one looks a little deeper, turns out to be because they do not fully understand the meaning of the moral question they are asking. The rules of valid argument about any question are determined by the

[2] See my introduction to *The Dialogues of Plato*, tr. Jowett (London, 1970).

meanings of the words used in discussing the question; if you do not know these meanings and these rules, you cannot distinguish for sure between valid and invalid reasoning.

There is certainly one way in which we might hope quite easily to settle moral arguments by establishing the meanings of the moral words. Unfortunately the hope turns out to be illusory; it is too short a cut, and it was, historically, the realization that it was too short a cut that led people to say, as so many people have said recently, that philosophy can do nothing for moral argument. This is the way advocated by the kind of moral philosophers I am going to call descriptivists—of whom the largest party are those called naturalists. This is hardly the place to explain these terms. But, briefly, a descriptivist is a person who thinks that it is a matter of fact whether an action is right or wrong—a question to be established simply by a more or less protracted factual enquiry. According to the naturalists, the most influential school, it is possible to give an account of the meaning of, for example, 'wrong', which has the following effect: once we know that this is its meaning, and know the non-moral facts of a situation, there is nothing more that we need to do in order to 'read off', as it were, whether a certain act in that situation would be wrong. It is just like knowing the meaning of the word 'triangular'. If we know the meaning of that word, then we can look at a certain figure in front of us, satisfy ourselves that it is bounded by just three straight lines, and say, accordingly, that it is triangular.

Philosophers have argued that this programme is in principle misconceived—that 'wrong' is not the same sort of word at all as 'triangular', and that it is not possible to give the sort of account of its meaning that would enable us to settle moral arguments in this easy way. I agree with these philosophers, and have done my best in my writings to show why they are right.[3] Here I shall only say that nobody has in fact produced any account of the meanings of the moral words which settles, in this easy way, moral disputes like the ones we have been considering. And in my view this is not just bad luck.

As I said, it was the rejection of this short cut that led people to think that there was no way at all, even a longer way, of bringing philosophy to bear on practical moral problems. This has led in recent times into a division of moral philosophers, in many people's minds, into the good guys and the bad guys. The good guys are the ones who think that the short cut I have mentioned really after all exists; the bad guys are those who think that it does not. I am one of

[3] See especially my *The Language of Morals*, Oxford, 1952, ch. 5; *Freedom and Reason*, Oxford, 1963, chs 2, 10; and *Essays on the Moral Concepts*, London, 1972, chs 3–6.

the bad guys. But, unlike the rest of the bad guys, I do think that there is another way of reaching the same objective—that is, of making philosophy relevant to practical questions.

Let me try to explain how I think this can be done. I said earlier that philosophy is the art or science which does for words what mathematics does for numbers. What then is this? What mathematics does for numbers is to reveal the logical properties which are implicit in the very meanings of the number-words, and the other words that we use in mathematics like 'plus' and 'equals', and thus show us that we cannot consistently say certain things—for example, 'Two plus two equals five'. In short, it establishes the *logical properties* of numbers. Ethics or moral philosophy does the same for words like 'right' and 'wrong'. It thus shows us that there are certain things that we cannot consistently say, using these words. What both mathematics and ethics do is something absolutely and purely formal. They explain to us the logical properties of the words in question, which are implicit in their meanings, and thus show us how to avoid inconsistencies in their use. And the way this helps to settle arguments in both fields is the same. Just as, once you know the formal properties of the numbers, you know that there are certain things you cannot consistently say, so, once you know the formal properties of the words 'ought', 'right', 'wrong' and the like, you know that there are certain things in morals that you cannot say.

I shall be explaining and illustrating later what I think are the two main formal properties of moral language. These are what we have to understand, if we are to make anything of the moral education of our successors. They have to be taught this language, because knowing and using it is an essential condition for taking one's part in a civilized and peaceful or even a viable society. The language of morality is as essential a requirement for the building of societies as is the language of mathematics for the building of space-craft. Both are relatively recent inventions (one can trace the development of our moral language in recorded history, just as one can trace the development of mathematics and its language; the ancient Greeks did not have either mathematical or moral languages which are as developed as ours). And both could get forgotten. The effect of failing to pass on the language of morality would be as disastrous in its own way (indeed more disastrous) as it would be if we never taught our children to count.

Having said how, in theory, moral philosophy can be relevant to the problems of moral education, I am now going to be much more rash, and give my opinions about some practical problems in moral education, on which I can make no claim to be an expert. These are problems on which empirical work is needed, and is being done, by psychologists and sociologists in particular. Philosophy can do nothing to render superfluous, or anticipate the results of, such empirical work. I am not trying to do any armchair psychology or sociology. But all the same, I have been struck, during the time my own children have been growing up, and in the course of many conversations with other parents and children, with how often what was happening seemed to illustrate particular points in moral philosophy.

This was, when you come to think of it, no accident. For moral education is, at least in part, education in the use of a language— that is to say, in the use of the moral language. Thinking morally— which is one of the things that a morally educated man has to do— is only the mental correlate of speaking morally. Indeed, for obvious reasons, the speaking has to come first. We are taught to speak morally by hearing other people do it (for example our parents). When we have learnt to use the moral words out loud, we must have learnt also to use these concepts in our thought. If we had not, we should not be using the words in our speech to others with an understanding of their meaning. Learning to use a word for communication with others, and learning to employ the same concept in one's thought, cannot be two separate and independent processes. Therefore, what we are learning when we learn to think morally (and this, as I say, is involved in becoming a morally educated man), is determined by the nature of the moral language in which we do our thinking. And this is the province of the conceptual study called moral philosophy.

The moral philosopher, therefore, has some right to give his opinions about the practical problems of moral education—because he has studied the nature and structure of the language, learning which is part of getting morally educated. Just as a person who was going to do research into mathematical education would do well to study the logical character of the mathematical concepts, so a moral educator would be well advised to know something about the logical character of the moral concepts. For if he does not, he may not really be educating people in the right subject at all. And this is what has actually happened in some cases—indeed, I think, in a great many. Some parents and schoolmasters and other moral educators are like people who try to teach mathematics without knowing the difference between, say, mathematics and an empirical science. And the relation between language and education is much more general than this; it is now realized that if a child has a family background which hampers the acquisition of a rich and articulate language, his whole education will be handicapped, because he will simply lack the linguistic vehicle for the thoughts which otherwise he might have had.

I want to take each of the two main features of moral language in turn and ask what practical implications for moral education there are in the fact that moral language has those features. First I shall have to explain, in a crude way, what each of these features is. I am not going to try to justify my assertion that moral language possesses these features; I have done this to the best of my ability in my writings.[4] The first of these features is what has been called 'prescriptivity'; this is the one that is most neglected by moral educators. It can be described roughly by saying that moral judgments are things that you are supposed to act on. To see this, just consider how strange we should think it if somebody came to us and said 'I'm very bothered about what I ought to do; can you advise me?' and then it turned out that he did not think that whatever answer he gave to the question had the slightest bearing upon his actions—on what he actually decided to do. We ask what we ought to do because we have to decide what to do, and think that the two questions, though not identical, are connected. Exactly what the connexion is I am not going to discuss; it is a difficult matter. For my argument in this lecture it will suffice to say that it is a very intimate one.

One of the practical consequences of this feature of moral judgments will be immediately obvious. This is that nobody is likely to be much of a success as a moral educator if he is not himself trying sincerely to live up to the principles which he is advocating. If he is not trying to live by them himself, this at once gives rise to the suspicion that he does not really and sincerely hold them. This has always been realized by anybody who thinks about moral education; but the reason for it has not always been understood. The reason is that since the *raison d'être* of moral principles is to guide our actions, the person whose actions are not guided by his (alleged) moral principles may well be only paying lip-service to them. I am excluding the case, of course, of the man who succumbs to temptations, as we all frequently do. The man who succumbs to temptation and breaks one of the moral principles which he says he holds may not incur the charge of insincerity if he is obviously upset about what he has done. But if he plainly regards his own transgression with equanimity, he is not likely to be very successful in teaching either his own children or anybody else that principle.

But there is another consequence of the prescriptivity of moral judgments which is even more important. This is that if moral judgments are prescriptive, it is no use treating them as if they were

[4] See footnote 3, p. 151.

just like ordinary statements of fact. Teaching children morality is not going to be like teaching them the names of the Great Lakes or the properties of the potassium salts. For if they adopt a certain set of moral principles as a result of the moral education they get, this will be the adoption of a way of living; and you are not going to get them to adopt an entire way of living just by *informing* them that that is, as a matter of fact, how they ought to live. Adopting a set of moral principles—which is what, at the end of the process of moral education (if it ever ends) they will have done—is (however inarticulate or even unconscious it may be) a *choice* of a way of life; and choosing a way of life is obviously a very different thing from learning the names and dates of the Roman emperors. The better educated they are in general—the more they have learnt to be alive to, and to enquire into, what is going on around them—the less likely they are to accept what you tell them about morality as if it were a piece of information. And even if they did do that—even if they did take your word for it that those were the facts about morals, namely that they ought to do such and such and refrain from such and such, the result would not be a moral education. For if that were the sort of thing they had learnt, they would be unlikely to think of it as something that had a bearing on their actions. They would be more likely to turn into what may be called 'So what?' moralists. These are the people who say 'Yes, I know I ought— so what?'.

There is another even more insidious danger in thinking that moral education is the teaching of a lot of moral facts. One sees it happen so often. Children are brought up by their families or their schools with the idea that moral principles are matters of objective fact. Then, later, they get wise to the impossibility of ever establishing what these alleged moral facts are. Some people say you ought not to practise birth control; other people say it is quite all right and even in some circumstances laudable. There is no way of telling which of these parties is right. So, after engaging in these discussions for a bit, they come to the conclusion that there are no moral facts to be ascertained. And since they have been brought up to believe that morality, if there is such a thing, is a body of objective facts, they at once, having decided that there are no moral facts, come to the conclusion that there are no such things as moral principles—that it is just not the case that one ought to do or to refrain from anything in particular. So, as I said, the effect of a descriptivist moral education is often complete moral nihilism.

If only these people had had it explained to them, much earlier on, that that is not the sort of thing that morality is. If only somebody had said to them 'You have got to live some way or other—you can't get out of that; so you had better start thinking before you get much older what way it ought to be. We older people can perhaps help you by suggesting possible ways of living which we have found satisfactory; you may decide in the end to live a different way, and that's up to you; but perhaps if you look at how other people live and what they say about it and what results it has, it may help you to reach a firm conclusion about how you ought to live yourself.' Of course we may not actually say this to our children; but if it is clear to them that this is our attitude to their moral education, one of the essential conditions of moral education may be achieved—namely communication. Our children will go on talking to us about their problems. Even when they are away from home, they will write us letters raising questions that have struck them; we shall learn from the way they put these questions, and they may learn from the way we answer them, if we can answer them. If, on the other hand, they think that we have a ready-made set of answers which is not open to discussion, they probably will not write or talk to us at all.

At this point I want to say something about two catchwords that are all too current in discussions of this subject, and are often used as a substitute for thought. One is 'permissiveness' and the other is 'rebellion'. People talk nowadays about 'the permissive society'. The use of expressions like this has done enormous harm by giving the impression that the choice that faces us in moral education is one between prohibiting things and permitting them. The 'permissive society' is, presumably, one in which a great many things which used to be prohibited are now permitted. But it cannot be emphasized too often that morality is not primarily a matter of prohibiting or permitting things; it is a matter of deciding what one ought to make of one's life in society and one's relations with other people. The principles one adopts for determining this life and these relations will, of course, prohibit some things (for example killing people just for kicks) and permit other things. But the picture evoked in my mind when people talk about 'the permissive society' is one of some curious creature called 'society' which used to go about prohibiting things but now goes about permitting the same things, with the suggestion that this creature (whatever it is) had no reasons for prohibiting the things it prohibited, and has no reasons now for permitting the things it permits. In the mouth of somebody like Malcolm Muggeridge, the phrase 'the permissive society' makes me think that its user considers it a good thing, for its own sake, to prohibit things, and a bad thing to permit things. In the mouths of people on the other side, it gives me the impression that they think that to permit *anything* is to strike a blow for liberty. But is not it really more important, not to have arguments about whether it is a good thing to prohibit or a good thing to permit, but to discuss, as we try to form for ourselves and help our children form for themselves a viable morality—to discuss *what* things, in this morality, ought to be permitted and *what* things ought to be prohibited? If we had that sort of discussion with our children, we might get somewhere.

The same sort of thing happens with the word 'rebellion'. You get one lot of people going round shaking their heads about the rebelliousness of the young; and another lot of people going round talking as if rebellion was in itself a good thing. You even hear parents saying something which I think they must have got from popular psychologists who write in the newspapers—for they would never have thought up anything so silly for themselves; they say that their object in bringing up their children is to give them something to rebel against. But surely the point is that rebellion is in itself neither a good thing nor a bad thing. It depends on *what* you are rebelling against, and *what* you are trying to put in its place. If parents are trying to force on their children moral rules which have no basis in rational thought, then it is perhaps a good thing for the children to rebel. If, on the other hand, the rebellion is just the result of impatience or of a desire to have a good time regardless of the sufferings imposed on others, then it is a bad thing. Perhaps in general it is more likely to be a bad thing than a good thing, because it is, after all, one of the most wonderful things in family life if parents and children can, after the children have grown up, go on loving and respecting one another, and rebellion often puts an end to this. But as a parent I neither want my children to rebel against me nor want to crush the rebellion if it occurs; what I want is that we should be able to go on talking to each other about moral questions —because I know that I shall learn a lot from these discussions, and I hope that my children will.

Now I think I ought to say something to correct a false impression which may have been received from what I have said so far. I have been talking as if it was all a matter of rational discussion with one's children about the moral principles which they are adopting. But of course neither parents nor children are entirely rational; and children start off by being almost completely irrational. You can hardly have rational discussions with a two-year-old about whether he ought to pour his food on the dining-room carpet. Children are bound to go through what Piaget called the heteronomous stage in the development of their moral ideas—the stage in which they take them as given, or as a question of what their parents and schoolmasters as a matter of fact permit or prohibit. What I am saying is: try to help them to pass on from this to the autonomous stage, in which they do their own moral thinking. For this is what they have in the end to do if they are going to be morally educated. The most common cause of failure in moral education is that children get stuck in the heteronomous stage. Parents sometimes behave as if this were what they wanted; but the results are usually disastrous. Either the children never learn to think for themselves or they learn to think, but not morally.

What I have been calling the heteronomous stage in moral education is not merely a regrettable necessity. It is also a useful part of the preparation for moral autonomy. For what has to be learnt is moral thought; and this means thought directed towards the formation and adoption of moral principles. Nobody can learn to do this kind of thinking unless he knows what sort of thing a moral principle is. So it is a real advantage to be brought up, even heteronomously, in a system of moral principles which is a working example of the sort of thing that morality is. The child may later reject some of these moral principles and adopt others with a different *content*; but at least he will have learnt the *form* of a moral principle. If the child has been brought up to think that one ought to fight for one's country and kill its enemies, but then becomes a pacifist and thinks that one ought not to kill people in wars, at least he will be still meaning the same thing by 'ought'; he will still be using the same moral language that he learnt earlier. And it would be difficult to learn this moral language without learning it in the context of *some* given set of moral principles, even if those principles are going to be later abandoned or modified. So it is no help to one's children to keep them insulated from one's own moral principles, such as they are. The child may later reject these principles; but he may at least have learnt what a moral principle is. Perhaps, even, the principles of the parent will be a useful foundation for building on; the child may modify a lot, but he will not be in the bewildering position of having to start from nothing.

What I have said is actually not quite right. If the child had learnt the moral language in a merely heteronomous way, and meant by 'wrong', for example, no more than 'forbidden by my parents', he would not have learnt even the form of a moral principle. He would have learnt the wrong language altogether. But what I mean is this: if the child can see that the *parent* is using the word in an autonomous way, and understand what this involves, in terms of the content which the parent gives to his moral principles, the child may learn, through observing and copying his parent, what it *is* to think morally. Then, even if the child later, in thinking morally himself, comes to reject the *content* of the parent's moral principles, he will still retain a knowledge of their form; he will still be thinking morally, which is the essential thing that moral education has to achieve. For this process to be successful, it is necessary that the parent should himself be thinking morally, and thus autonomously, and should make it plainer than some parents do just what this involves. We have to start sharing with our children, quite early on, the secrets of our moral thought. This means letting them know about the processes of thought that we are going through, as well as about their conclusions. If parents could become more articulate and clear-headed and honest in their own moral thinking, their children would pick up the art a lot more easily.

I now want to try to sum up the lessons that are to be drawn from the fact that moral principles are prescriptive. The first is that parents and other older people are trying, if they are setting about the moral education of their children in the right way, to help them choose for themselves a morality or way of life. They will do this most successfully if they are facing the same way as their children, towards the future, difficult and uncertain as it is. They are then doing the same kind of moral thinking about the same kind of problems—problems which the parents may, but very likely may not, have themselves faced in the past. For though some of the problems are old, some of them are new. Nuclear weapons have been invented, and so have more or less reliable methods of contraception; boys and girls behave quite differently from the way they used to, and expect others to behave differently. Parents and children face the same future, though they will play different roles in it, and the children probably have more of it to face than the parents have. The parents have, correspondingly, more past, and in it have played roles not altogether unlike those which the children are playing now—they have faced, if not the same, at least similar questions. If, when facing these questions, or even in retrospect, they have thought coherently and sincerely about them, they can help their children—but on one condition, that the relation between them is such that the children are interested in what the parents have to say. Their past is not going to help the parents if all it has given them is a morality of 'What will the neighbours think?' Only insofar as their children think that the parents are themselves thinking sincerely and prescriptively about what people ought to do in various situations, will the children pay much attention to the parents' moral opinions. This means that the parents have to be genuinely trying to live by the moral judgments which they make about their own (i.e. the parents') problems, and it also means that when they make moral judgments about their children's problems, they must make them as if they were their own problems —as if they themselves had to live with the results of accepting those moral opinions. It has to be understood on both sides that what one decides one ought to do is what one does. And that is what I mean by the prescriptivity of moral judgments; if one has not learnt that they have that feature, one has not really learnt to think or speak morally.

I now come to the other feature which I think moral language has. This is known in philosophical circles by the formidable name of 'universalizability'. The idea is not new (it goes back in essence at least to Christ's teaching, and was elaborated by Kant[5]); but it is far from being well enough understood. The simplest way I can think of to put this point is the following. When I say that I ought (or even that it is all right) to do a certain thing in my own situation, I thereby commit myself to the view that if the situation remained exactly similar, except that my own role in it was different (for example, I might play in the new situation the role of some other person whom I am contemplating hurting or robbing or killing), then the person, who in the new situation occupies the role which I now occupy, ought to act (or it would be all right for him to act) in the same way. In short, moral judgments are not tied to individual people as agents; they are tied to *features* of individuals and of their situations. I am not saying that what is sauce for the goose is sauce for the gander; for it might conceivably make a difference to the morality of the act that it was done by a gander, not a goose; but at least, what is sauce for the goose must be sauce for any precisely similar goose in any precisely similar situation. So if I, a gander, am thinking of maltreating my goose, before I can say that it is all right to do so, I have to agree that it would be all right for me, were I to turn into a goose just like this one, with the same desires and aversions, and in the same situation, to be maltreated in the same manner. I stress that in putting oneself in this way into other people's shoes, one has to put oneself completely into their shoes, including the places where the shoes pinch *them*; one is not allowed to say, for example, 'I don't mind this sort of treatment as much as she does'. The point is that, if you were in her situation exactly, you would mind it as much as she does, because the minding is part of the situation.

If this really is, as I think it is (though I shall not try to prove it in this lecture), a feature of the logic of moral language, then it is obviously of crucial importance for the practice of moral education.

[5] Luke 6: 31; I. Kant, *Groundwork of the Metaphysic of Morals.*

You may have been feeling, as I discussed the other main feature, prescriptivity, that this by itself left us free to prescribe or to adopt absolutely any way of life we pleased. That is true. But when it is combined with the second feature, universalizability, the two together give us all that is essential to hold us in the path of a morality which is sufficient to make life liveable with others in society.

What I want to do now is to try and draw out some of the practical consequences for moral education of the fact that moral language has this second feature, just as I did in the case of prescriptivity. And the first consequence it has is really a very obvious one. Since one of the moves which has to be made in moral thought about almost any moral question is to put oneself in the shoes of the other people affected by one's actions, it is an essential part of moral education to become able to do this. And this involves two abilities or skills which, though they have the same function in the logic of moral thinking, are psychologically such different things that they can conveniently be listed separately.

The first of these skills is the ability to discern and discover what the effects of our actions are going to be. The question 'What should I be doing if I did that?' is really the first question that has to be asked when we face any moral problem. And it is perhaps necessary to point out, because some philosophers have denied it, that what I should be doing includes the consequences that I should be bringing about. If the consequence of my pulling the trigger will be that a man dies, then in pulling it, I am bringing about his death. I said that to be able to discern and discover the effects of our actions is something that the morally educated man has to have learnt. If anybody wants to object that this has nothing specifically to do with *moral* education, I am not going to quarrel about words. All I wish to insist on is that all our moral education will be wasted if the products of it are so ignorant or so imperceptive that they do the most terrible things with the best of motives.

There is, however, an ability which falls into this general class, which is so intimately a concern of moral education that, as I said, I am going to list it separately. This is the ability to discern the feelings of others and how our actions will impinge upon them. If someone cannot do that, at any rate to some extent, then his moral education really has been unsuccessful. If for example a boy is unaware that a girl—this particular girl—is unable to enter into and slip out of love affairs with the nonchalance which he himself can command, but is really being deeply hurt by his behaviour, then I would not call him a morally educated person.

If any of you have read a book on this subject called *Introduction to*

Moral Education, by Wilson, Williams and Sugarman, you will recognize my debt to these writers. The two abilities which I have just listed correspond to those which they call GIG and EMP. I think that there is no special problem about incorporating the production of GIG (general ability to know the consequences of our actions) into moral education. Educators are already doing it with greater or less success by the ordinary methods of general education. I have, however, just one suggestion to make about this. If, while seeking to improve their pupils' knowledge of the world, school-masters were to try—as some do—to relate this information to choices that they will have actually to make in situations which raise difficult moral problems, they would both make the lessons more interesting and do something for moral education on the side. To take an obvious example, lessons on current affairs take on an added importance if they are related to the questions 'How ought I to vote?' or 'Ought I to allow myself to be drafted to fight in my country's wars?'

However, when we come to EMP (the understanding of people's feelings) there is here, perhaps, a special lesson for educators. It is commonly said, and with truth, that imaginative literature and drama and art in general can help people to learn to understand other people's feelings. So we have here a justification (a very important though not the only one) for the inclusion in the curriculum of both schools and families the study of works of the imagination. But this is said so often that I do not need to stress it. Instead, since fiction has so many supporters (in some philosophical circles you lose caste if you fail to read a novel a week)—since fiction is in need of no advocacy, I should like to put in a word for fact. The writer of fiction has other motives (often excellent aesthetic motives) than the desire to portray the world as we are actually likely to find it. If young people get all their knowledge (so-called) of the world out of novels, they may not be fitting themselves in the best way for coping with the general run of human situations. This is especially so in matters concerning sex. For obvious reasons, and mainly because it makes their books more interesting, novelists tend to concentrate on the more unusual sexual situations. If these occurred constantly in everybody's life— which thank goodness they do not, or our moral education really would have failed—then there might be a lot to be said for getting people as they grow up to form for themselves moral principles primarily designed to cope with these extraordinary situations. But as it is, one hopes (and it should surely be an object of moral education to secure this) that most of our boys and girls will have the usual sort of happy family life; and to this end (as in other fields of morality) what they most need is a body of sound working moral principles which will do for ordinary situations. It would be a pity if they abandoned these because they might not do in situations which, we hope, they are never likely to meet. Indeed, if they do abandon them, it will make such situations much more likely, and thus, I am convinced, decrease the prospect of human happiness (for it is an almost universal truth that people in the best novels are never happy).

So really, I think, it is even more important to learn to sound the feelings of actual people in one's family and school than it is to explore the doubtless aesthetically more exciting feelings of people in novels. How is this to come about? Well, I have one small suggestion among many that could be made. This is that parents, especially, should not try as hard as some of them now do to keep their children in the dark about their feelings. Many parents who have read or heard about the writings of popular psychologists have got hold of the idea that at all costs they must not be cross with their children. They have adopted a saint-like ideal of parenthood, which it is humanly impossible to realize, and perhaps not even desirable; according to this ideal, the parent loves his children constantly and never even feels anger with them—let alone shows it. The result in practice, with human parents, is that when their children do things which annoy them, they at first give no sign of this. Gradually, as time goes on and the offences—or perhaps other far more trivial offences—are repeated, the strain gets intolerable, and the parent comes out with some wild irrational outburst of rage over some incident which may be quite trivial and quite unrelated to the real cause of the annoyance. How much better it would have been if the parent, when he felt mildly annoyed by something the child did, had mildly shown it! Then, at least, the child would get to know how its actions affect other people's feelings in this kind of situation— whatever it is—and not be, as so many children are, utterly per- plexed and at sea.

I could say a great deal more about this and kindred subjects; but space forbids. I want now to come to another quality that the morally educated man has to have, which, like the last two, is required directly by the nature of morality itself. Knowledge of the effects of our actions, even the most intimate and sensitive under- standing of the feelings of other people, is not enough. The skilled torturer has a very thorough knowledge of just how his actions are affecting the feelings of those whom he is tormenting. To this knowledge has to be added *love* of our fellow men, or what Wilson calls PHIL. This requirement has received so many classical statements in Christian and other literature (I have already referred to two) that I will not dwell on it, beyond pointing out again that it arises directly from the nature of morality itself. To love men is to treat their interests as of equal weight with our own (as one might put it, to treat their good, and indeed their very existence, as of equal importance to our own good and our own existence[6]). And this is required by the very logic of the moral words if we are thinking morally; for this logic forbids us to include in our moral principles any reference to individual persons as such; we cannot therefore, if we are thinking morally, prefer our own interests to those of other people. I emphasize that it is not that we *ought* not to do this; it is that, if we are using the word 'ought' correctly to make a moral judgment, we *cannot say* that we ought to do this—it would be an abuse of the word.

How is this love to be taught? This is what the psychologists ought to be, and to some extent are, working on. I have only one small lay suggestion to make, and that is, that it is most likely to be taught in actual situations in which people are in close contact with each other, i.e. not in the conventional classroom. I think that this question really is beyond my scope as a philosopher. But I know of a great many families in which it is taught; so these are what we should study. The most important thing of all in moral education is to have parents who love one another.

The picture of moral education which emerges from all this is that of children, first of all, learning to find their *own* moral principles to guide their *own* lives, with, of course, what assistance older people can give them; and secondly, of these principles being truly moral principles, which involves them being applicable whether you are the agent or the victim in the action which they enjoin. I am convinced that if parents first, and then children, understood better the *formal* character of morality and of the moral concepts, there would be little need to bother, ultimately, about the content of our children's moral principles; for if the form is really and clearly understood, the content will look after itself. So I would say to parents: 'Try to get your children to understand what morality is, which means first understanding this yourself; if they understand that, and you understand it too, you will not be displeased with the content of the morality which they adopt.'

I have not said anything about some virtues and other good qualities which have figured very largely in the classical discussions of moral education. I mean those qualities which one has to have if one is

[6] See Aristotle, *Eth. Nic.*, 1170 a 25–b 8.

successfully and consistently to *act* on the principles which one has formed for oneself. This class includes, first, the intellectual and other skills needed to get done what we think ought to be done—such as prudence, foresight, and even gamesmanship. And it includes, secondly, what have always been thought of as peculiarly moral virtues (they figure prominently in Aristotle's list[7]): the virtues which give us the strength to do what we think we ought to do even when it is very very difficult. These are the virtues of courage, endurance, self-control and the like. They are obviously a very important part of moral education; and if I do not say more about them, it is only because I have not the space, and because, *for this generation*, what I have actually talked about seems to me to require more emphasis.

It is no easier in practice to impart these good qualities than the ones I spoke of earlier. In fact it is probably much harder, because they are so much matters, either of temperament, which we cannot do much about, or of experience, for which we have to wait. For example, it is not typical of the young to be prudent; they will often, in the pursuit of laudable ideals, do things which later (if they survive) they will perhaps acknowledge to have been just silly. Parents and others can offer advice, but it may or may not be taken, and if it is not, there is often not much that the parent can do about it after the child has reached independence. The only thing he can do is to keep in communication, and hope. I do not think that parents should blame themselves very much if their children do things which seem to indicate a lack of circumspection; sometimes it is the parents who fuss too much. They should blame themselves more if they have not produced children who are able to think and act for themselves.

The present time is a very hazardous one for the young, because they are at the mercy of a great many dangers which most previous generations were spared. Most of these dangers are there in consequence of the activities of those in older generations who, seeking excitement in preference to rigorous thought, have filled the world with every kind of emotive rhetoric and propaganda, some of which is very skilfully presented and commands a huge audience through the media. The 'permissivists' have no monopoly of rhetoric and propaganda; but they *have* a near-monopoly of the attention of a great many of the young who, as a result, get a pretty unbalanced diet of rhetoric. It is no use thinking that any kind of censorship could remedy this state of affairs; and it would not be desirable even if it could. The only remedy is for as many

[1] *Ibid.*, II–IV.

as possible of the young, and the old for that matter, to learn to sift this mass of rubbish which is poured out on both sides of these questions for the grains of truth which it may contain; and this is a thing which, if they can hang on to a common language in which they can communicate, and understand all the time what both of them are saying, young and old can do together.

Is religious education possible? I O

W. D. Hudson

Before attempting to answer the above question, I must try to make
clear what I take it to mean. In a book on the philosophy of
education, it hardly needs saying that I take the question in a
philosophical sense, viz. 'Is religious education philosophically
possible?'; but because the word 'philosophical' can mean different
things to different people, I need to explain what I have in mind
when I speak of *philosophical* possibility. The best way to do this, I
think, is to contrast such possibility with possibility of another kind
and so I will first say what this other kind of possibility is and
then bring out the difference between it and what I have called
'philosophical possibility'.

The question 'Is religious education possible?' could be taken to
mean 'Can religious education actually occur?' Baldly stated thus,
this form of the question is uninteresting because everyone knows
that something called religious education not only can, but actually
does, occur in schools and elsewhere. However, there are some
particular contexts in which this form of the question becomes more
interesting and in which the answer to it is not immediately obvious
to the questioner. For example, a parent who wants his child to
receive a special sort of religious education—Roman Catholicism,
Seventh Day Adventism, or whatever—might go to the school and
ask 'Can this be arranged?' Or, to take another example, an
education committee, which is deeply concerned to see religious
education of a high quality given within its schools might ask
itself 'Can this be done?', where what it wants to know is how much
expense or reorganization would be needed to import enough
religious education specialists to do the job properly. Or, as yet
another example, an educationist who believes that the abstract
language in which religion is traditionally expressed means nothing
to young children might ask himself, 'Can other language be found
which will make religious ideas intelligible to young children?'

All such questions are concerned with what I will call '*practical
possibility*' to differentiate it from what I mean by 'philosophical
possibility'. They are questions as to whether or not something
which somebody wants to do can, in practice, be done. Very many
questions of this sort arise in connexion with religious education.

When authorities, parents or teachers have cleared their heads as to precisely what they mean by religious education, then they have to solve all kinds of practical problems in their efforts to make it possible. But in this chapter I am not concerned with questions of that kind.

What I am concerned with is questions about the *concept* of religious education and in particular with this question: *does the expression 'religious education' make sense?* Can there be such a thing— where the 'can' is, so to speak, a logical 'can'? There is, we all know, something—perhaps many different things—*called* religious education. But does this description itself make sense? When one considers carefully what 'religious' means and what 'education' means, is the concept of religious education an intelligible one? Such questions concern what I have called philosophical possibility and what it would be more precise to call *logical* possibility. The only way to determine whether or not religious education is possible in this sense will be by a linguistic analysis of the expression 'religious education'. Such an analysis, I think, should take us along three closely related lines of enquiry as follows:

(i) We shall have to ask what are the correct definitions of the words 'religious' and 'education' in order to arrive at any understanding of what the expression 'religious education' must mean, if the words within it bear their normal meanings.

(ii) Then we shall have to consider whether or not the expression 'religious education' is a contradiction in terms. Conceivably, for instance, the meaning of 'religious' could turn out to be such that anything so described must necessarily involve indoctrination: whereas the meaning of 'education' could turn out to be such that anything so called must necessarily eschew indoctrination. If this were the conclusion to which our analysis led, then we should have to decide that religious education is a self-contradictory notion. Alternatively, however, we may find that, given a correct definition of its terms, the expression 'religious education' is not self-contradictory.

(iii) In the light of our enquiries thus far we shall have to appraise the extent to which the expression 'religious education' is, in practice, misused. If this expression is a contradiction in terms, then its misuse is, of course, total, in the sense that it is absurd so to describe anything because the description itself does not make sense. But if, given correct definitions of 'religious' and 'education', it is logically possible to conceive of religious education, then the misuse of the expression may not be total, in the sense that there may be something which it would not be absurd to describe as religious education. In that case, we shall be able to say whether what is in fact called religious education in schools etc. can properly be so described or not. If we come to the conclusion that it cannot, then we may want to urge that it be replaced with something which can, though of course this step will take us beyond mere philosophical analysis.

These, then, are the three lines of enquiry which I shall pursue respectively in the remaining three sections of this chapter. But I make no secret of the fact that I am vastly more confident of having asked the right questions than of being able to provide the right answers. What I shall offer by way of answers will certainly be tentative and incomplete; no doubt they will be at some points debatable if not mistaken; but I venture to hope that they will constitute a case for the possibility of religious education which is not entirely unconvincing.

I. The definition of 'religious' and of 'education'

'Religious'

I take 'religious' to mean 'having to do with religious belief'. There are two philosophical points which I wish to make about the religious universe of discourse, viz. (i) that it is logically constituted by the concept of god; and (ii) that the language in which religious belief is expressed has a certain complex character. Both of them, I think need to be understood before we can have any clear notion of religious education. I will take these points in turn and try to explain them as simply as possible.

(i) By religious discourse I mean talk about god. The concept of god (and I will explain the small 'g' in a moment) *constitutes* religious discourse in the same sense that the concept of a physical object constitutes physical science, or the concept of moral value constitutes moral discourse. Universes of discourse are logically constituted by concepts or sets of concepts which determine the presuppositions and the ways of reasoning in accordance with which the relevant kind of discourse proceeds. Anything thought or said within the discourse concerned *must* (logically) be thought or said in terms of its constitutive concept (or concepts). It may be helpful if I illustrate what I have in mind from the cases of physical science and morality respectively. This will take a little time but it will, I hope, help to make clearer what *mutatis mutandis* I want to say about the concept of god and religious discourse.

Physical science is a universe of discourse constituted by the concept of a physical object, i.e. a spatio-temporally identifiable particular which can be observed by physical sense. For physical science, the world consists of such objects and can be explained and experienced only in terms of them and their inter-relations. True, the physical objects which form science's subject-matter may be large or small in size and of long or short duration. True again, they may be observable easily or observable only by means of highly sophisticated aids to sense, such as cloud chambers or radio telescopes. But the fact remains that unless any X is a physical object it cannot (logically) form part of the explanations which a physical scientist, as such, offers, or of the experiences which, as such, he has.

Morality is similarly a universe of discourse logically constituted by a concept (or set of concepts), namely moral vlaue. If anything is explained within morality—e.g. what ought to be done—it must (logically) be in terms of this concept; and if anything is said to be a moral experience—e.g. a sense of guilt or a feeling of responsibility—it must (logically) be one which is available only to those who conceive of moral value.

The so-called 'open question argument' supports the former contention.[1] Whatever has been said about an action or state of affairs in non-moral (i.e. in naturalistic or super-naturalistic) terms—e.g. that X will maximize happiness—it still *makes sense* to question the moral value of such an act or state of affairs—e.g. to ask 'But is it right to do what will maximize happiness?' Some moralists have tried to by-pass this hard logical fact. They have been so committed to some moral belief (e.g. the utilitarian view that it is right to maximize happiness) that they have claimed this belief to be true by definition (e.g. that 'right' *means* 'maximizing happiness'). Then they have argued that their opponents, in questioning this moral belief, are asking a question which does not make sense because it is self-answering. To take our example, opponents of utilitarianism as such raise the question, 'But is it right to do what will maximize happiness?' Its defenders, to whom I have just referred, reply that if 'right' means 'maximizing happiness', all the question just posed amounts to is 'Is right right?', or alternatively 'Does what maximizes happiness maximize happiness?' and there is no sense or point in asking such questions because the answer could not (logically) be other than 'yes'. If 'right' could be defined as 'maximizing happiness', then utilitarians would have here a knock-down argument against their opponents and that is why this manoeuvre has seemed so attractive to some of them. But other utilitarians have realized the price which has to be paid for it, namely that it would not only render their opponents' position impossible but their own belief vacuous. Utilitarians, as such, believe that it is right to maximize happiness. But if 'right' did mean 'maximizing happiness', then what they as utilitarians would stand for is the insignificant tautology that what maximizes happiness maximizes happiness, or what is right is right. This would render their position vacuous because it empties their belief of any moral content and reduces it to the recognition of a trivial point about language with which nobody who understood the meaning of words would quarrel. It will be seen from all this that moral terms cannot be replaced without loss or change of meaning by any non-moral terms, and so if anything is explained within morality, it must (logically) be in terms of moral value.

As for my other claim, that if anything is said to be a moral experience, e.g. feelings of guilt or a sense of duty, it must (logically) be available only to those who conceive of moral value, I think this is easy to show. Would it make sense to say, for example, that someone felt remorse—as distinct from regret—without implying that it was felt about something which ought morally to have been done? I may regret that it was a rainy day yesterday but I can hardly be said to feel remorse that it was because it cannot be said that there was anything which I ought to have done to prevent rain. On the other hand, if I forced you to go for a walk with me in the rain yesterday and you are now in bed with a cold, I could certainly be said to feel remorse about that, just because it could be said that I ought not to have made you come out in the rain. Words like 'remorse' which are used to describe moral experiences can always be shown to carry such 'ought' implications. In other words they cannot be conceived of unless moral value is conceived of also.

I hope that this rather long digression about physical science and morality has served its purpose of making clearer what I mean when I speak of a universe of discourse being constituted by a concept (or set of concepts) in the sense that anything which is thought or said within it must (logically) be thought or said in terms of that concept. Now let us return to our main concern, religion, and consider the question: what concept (or set of concepts) constitutes it?

I want to say that it is the concept of god. By 'god' here I mean: transcendent consciousness and agency with which the believer as such has to do. Deliberately I write 'god' here and throughout this paper with a small 'g' to make it evident that I do not have monotheism alone in mind. Animism, polytheism, or monolatry, besides monotheism, are constituted by the concept of god. Within all such systems of belief, that is to say, explanations and experiences are available only to those who conceive of god. I hope that my use of the small 'g' will not worry any reader. The logic of the word 'god' or 'God' is a complicated matter[2] and I cannot here engage in a long discussion of it. But I have made it clear how I define 'god' for our purposes in this paper.

Religious discourse is constituted by the concept of god, then, in the sense that everything which is said within it must (logically) be said in terms of god. This applies to both affirmations and negations— talk of what god is or does and of what god is not or does not do. All religious discourse presupposes god in this sense, just as all that is said within physical science presupposes physical objects, and all within morality, moral value. The concepts of a physical object or of moral value are *sui generis* in the sense that one cannot (logically) substitute for talk of them talk of anything else without loss or change of meaning. Talk of god is likewise *sui generis*. It cannot be reduced to anything else. Unless one is thinking or speaking in terms of transcendent consciousness or agency in some form, one is not engaging in religious discourse.

When people have religious experiences or arrive at religious explanations, it is because they have, so to speak, brought to the interpretation of what has occurred the concept of god. Experiences can always conceivably be described in non-religious ways (e.g. this prophet who thinks god has called him can be said to be suffering from paranoia etc., etc.) and religious explanations, replaced by non-religious ones (e.g. god did not really save the ship at sea, it was just that the storm abated at a fortunate moment etc., etc.). But insofar as experiences or explanations are conceived to be religious, they must (logically) be conceived of in terms of god. When you drop the concept of god, you replace religious discourse with something else. Just as it is logically impossible for a scientist *as such* to explain or experience anything except as a physical object, or for a moralist *as such*, to do so except in terms of moral value, so it is logically impossible for a religious believer *as such* to explain or experience anything except in terms of god.

It might be useful to add here that disbelief is of two logically distinct kinds where religion is concerned: we may call them disbelief *within* religion and *about* religion respectively. Within religion, for example, a Jew may not believe what a Christian says about god (e.g. that god sent his son to save sinners). This is simply disagreement within religion, i.e. in terms of god. But an atheist does not believe different things *about god* from a theist. He does not believe in god at all. His unbelief is about religion as a whole—the latter's constitutive concept, god, he says, corresponds to nothing which in fact exists. I shall return to this distinction below when I come to discuss whether or not religious education is education *in* religion or *about* it.

I appreciate that the definition which I have, in effect, given here to religious discourse raises some complex questions. Let me note two.

Is this definition sufficiently comprehensive? What, for instance of Buddhism in its more mystical forms? It dispenses altogether with the concept of god as I have defined it, but surely it is a form of religious belief! I recognize the force of such an objection to my analysis. In reply, I may have to concede that 'religious belief' is a composite term for a whole family of varied phenomena and cannot be conceived as one universe of discourse in the way that physical science can. If this is so, then I shall have to concede further that all I have been saying about the meaning of the word 'religious' applies only to certain uses of that expression, namely those where it applies to some form of god-talk. But this concession need not worry me because the expression 'religious education', if it has any significance for most of my readers, will mean education in some form of theism; and so it does not matter if all I have defined is a universe of discourse which includes theism, rather than religious belief as a whole.

Another question which the definition of religious discourse as constituted by the concept of god, i.e. transcendent consciousness and agency, raises is: what does 'transcendent' mean here? It means at least two things: (a) that this consciousness and agency surpasses human consciousness and agency in some respect— e.g. divine consciousness is more acute, divine agency more powerful, etc.; (b) that divine consciousness and agency are conceived to subsist in the absence of some conditions which are necessary to the subsistence of human consciousness or agency—for instance, god is conceived as consciousness or agency which does not need a physical body in order to be conscious or active, as human consciousness and agency evidently do. There is a problem as to whether or not this latter notion of transcendent consciousness or agency makes sense. Are consciousness and agency conceivable without a body? Some philosophers think not. I have tried to argue elsewhere that they are.[3] But this complex philosophical problem need not delay us at the moment because the only point I want to bring out is that in order to understand the concept of god, we must recognize the ways in which talk of god's consciousness or agency differs from talk of man's.

Drawing together in summary what I have said so far about the meaning of 'religious' in the expression 'religious education' it comes to this. Such education will be education in the concept of god: that is, it will mean learning to think and speak in terms of transcendent consciousness and agency, and understanding how the meaning of words may have to be extended or modified in their application to god.

(ii) The other philosophical point which I said I want to make is that the language in which religious belief is expressed has a certain complex character. It is only when we understand this complex character that we can see what it is to be, or not to be, religious. I have just been speaking about the complexity of the notion of transcendence but it is a different sort of complexity to which I now turn. What I have in mind is complexity in what is being *done* with words within religion, i.e. when religious belief is expressed. A believer is someone who does these things with religious language: an unbeliever, someone who does not. This sort of unbelief is not unbelief within religion but about it. To refuse to use language as it is definitively used within religion is, of course, to reject religion.

Different things can be done with words. They can, for example, be used to make statements, ask questions, issue commands, utter exclamations, etc. There are normally indicators in written language (e.g. word order, mood of the verb, punctuation, etc.) corresponding to each of these activities so that a given sentence can be identified as statement, question, or whatever. Sometimes, though, what looks superficially like one kind of utterance may in fact serve the purpose of another. Take for example, the sentence, 'You are going to the station'. This has the grammatical form of a statement but it is easy to imagine contexts in which it could function as a question, a command or an exclamation. So far as spoken language is concerned, the mere inflexion with which it is uttered can make it one thing or another. Try saying 'You are going to the station' out loud, whilst intending it as statement, command, question or exclamation in turn and you will find that it is possible to make it sound like any of them.

Modern philosophers have interested themselves in the different jobs which words can be used to do and, in particular, in the fact that whilst superficially a sentence may have the appearance of a statement of fact, it may be, in reality, something more, or other, than that. The work of J. L. Austin[4] in this connexion has been especially influential and so I will say a little about it.

Austin introduced into the philosophy of language the notion of 'performatives', i.e. of utterances which in the appropriate circumstances amount to the *doing*, not merely the saying, of something. Some examples which he gave are as follows: 'I will' uttered in the marriage ceremony; 'I name this ship Britannia', uttered whilst smashing a bottle on the stern; 'I bequeath X to Y', in the course of a will; and so on. He worked out a classification of performatives according to the particular kinds of job which they do, as follows. *Verdictives*, i.e. utterances which give a verdict—e.g. those of a judge or umpire; *Exercitives*, i.e. utterances which are the exercising of rights or authority—e.g. appointing, ordering, warning, etc.; *Commissives*, i.e. utterances typified by promising or undertaking something; *Behabitives*, i.e. utterances which have to do with attitudes and social behaviour—e.g. apologizing, congratulating, commending, cursing, etc.; *Expositives*, i.e. utterances which make plain how our utterances fit into the course of an argument or conversation—e.g. 'I reply . . .', 'I concede that . . .', etc. Austin did not claim that his classification is exhaustive or that there is no overlapping between its members.

He differentiated the three aspects of any and every speech act, as follows:

> The '*locutionary act*' is simply the act of saying something.
> The '*perlocutionary act*' is what a speaker is doing *by* saying something in the sense of the effect which he intends to produce in his hearers (or possibly himself) by saying what he says.
> The '*illocutionary act*' is what a speaker is doing *in* saying something, in the sense of which kind or kinds of performative his speech act is.

Austin illustrated the difference between these three acts from the example of the speech act, 'Shoot her'. Reports of the three different acts which could all be occurring concurrently in this speech act might read as follows:

> Locutionary act: he said 'Shoot her!'
> Perlocutionary act: he persuaded someone to, he made someone, shoot her.
> Illocutionary act: he urged, ordered, advised, etc. someone to shoot her.

My interest in this work of Austin's at the moment is that it helps to bring out what I have in mind when I speak of the complex character of the language in which religious belief is expressed. Many philosophers[5] have pointed out recently that what appear to be simple statements of putative fact concerning god, at least as these occur within Christianity, e.g. 'God is our father', 'God made the world', 'God sent his Son to save sinners', etc., etc. are really complex performatives. When a religious believer says such things *qua* believer his illocutionary acts go beyond merely stating things to be the case. They are typically expressions of trust or acknowledgment. This is seen when we imagine someone saying, for example, 'God is our Father, but don't trust him!' or 'God sent his Son to save sinners but don't let him save you!' If we heard such remarks we should not say that they were expressions of religious *belief* coupled with recommendations to react to the religious facts in certain ways. Rather should we say that, if they were anything, they were satirical or cynical ways of expressing *unbelief*. Expressions of religious belief are typically commissives (the placing of trust in god or submission to the authority of god) or behabitives (the acknowledgment or commendation of god as meriting trust or obedience). They may indeed have other performative aspects but into these I need not go. Enough has been said to make the point which I wish to make: that insofar as religious belief can be described in terms of what a believer as such says, it must be recognized that what he says goes beyond the mere statement of putative facts about god.

Recently some philosophers have called attention to this by pointing out that religious belief is 'belief in' rather than 'belief that'.[6] As the Apostles' Creed goes: 'I believe *in* God the Father Almighty ... and *in* Jesus Christ His only Son ... *in* the Holy Ghost, the Holy Catholic Church ...' An analysis of the expression 'belief-in' and its cognates shows that it is used typically in two ways (a) as a commissive utterance expressing trust and (b) as it has been put, 'to make and withdraw an existence claim'.[7] An instance of use (a) would be 'I believe in Mr Heath'; an instance of use (b) 'I believe in abominable snowmen'. The former expresses trust in the Prime Minister and his policies. The latter indicates that the existence of abominable snowmen is a matter about which there is great difference of opinion but that the speaker holds that they *do* exist. When believers say that they believe in God I think that both uses are involved. The existence of God is a matter about which there is widespread doubt and the believer, when he says 'I believe *in* God' is affirming (cf. (b)) that nonetheless he believes that God exists. But he is also saying (cf. (a)) that he trusts God.

For my own part, I do not go along with the view, which some seem to hold, that because religious belief is 'belief in', philosophical doubts about whether or not it is the case that God exists can be dismissed as misconceived. Believing-in God implies believing-that he exists. How could I say that I trust him and at the same time refuse to say that he is there to trust? Nevertheless, I am in full sympathy with the recent remark of one philosopher: 'a "belief *that* God exists", if it was logically independent of any and all ways of regarding him, would be of no interest, not even to God'.[8] Participation in characteristic 'ways of regarding' god is a logically essential part of religious belief. The most cursory analysis of the language in which the latter is expressed will make this abundantly clear.

Two things, then, have emerged from my reflections upon the meaning of the word 'religious', in the expression 'religious education': (i) that religious discourse is constituted by the concept of god; and (ii) that religious belief, if expressed at all, is expressed in performative language which places trust, acknowledges a claim, etc. Certain things follow from this as to what religious education must (logically) be. We shall come to them in due course.

'Education'

Turning now to the word 'education', I do not intend to attempt a comprehensive definition. Even if I were competent to offer one, it would go beyond the purpose of this paper to do so. What I shall try to do is to fasten on one or two of the defining characteristics of education which will be especially relevant when, in the next section, we come to the question of whether or not religious education is a contradiction in terms.

To begin with, education is a process of initiation.[9] If anyone is receiving an education, then it can be said that he is being initiated into some pursuit, or pursuits, theoretical, practical, or both. Religious belief is one such pursuit. A religious education will therefore be initiation into religious belief. This seems obvious enough but it is, I think, rather important to bring out precisely what it means.

Confusion about this may arise because there are all kinds of pursuits which may take religion as their subject-matter, e.g. history, psychology, sociology, philosophy. One can be educated in how to think in these varying ways *about* religious belief. But all such pursuits must be carefully differentiated from religious belief itself. It is no doubt a necessary part of a liberal education to initiate people into some, or all, of these different ways of thinking about religious belief and the mark of an educated man that he has some knowledge of them. But this is not specifically *religious* education. The latter is education *in* religious belief. I fastened above on two logical features of religious belief, viz. that it is constituted by the concept of god and that the language which expresses it has a complex performative character. Now, if this is correct, initiation into religious belief will necessarily be initiation into these two features, or aspects, of it. For convenience, I will refer to them as *theology* and *devotion* respectively. I realize that it may be a little dangerous to use these terms because both have overtones which may put the reader off. To speak of theology in the classroom, or devotion in the assembly hall, may strike him as odd, if not archaic. But they are the best words for my purpose and so I shall use them, without apology, in the following clearly defined senses.

By theology, I mean conceiving of god and thereby putting oneself in the way of the explanations and experiences which this concept constitutes. By devotion I mean engaging in those ways of committing oneself in trust and obedience to god, which are characteristic of the expression of religious belief. Of course, the particular brand of theology and the particular forms of devotion will depend upon the particular kind of religious belief concerned. But the point which I wish to make is simply that religious education is necessarily initiation into some form of theology and devotion. This fact must be faced.

It is fashionable in some quarters to speak of religious education without theology. If this means that there can be religious education without embroiling those who receive it in bitter or abstruse doctrinal controversies which are largely unintelligible to them, then of course I agree. But if it means that there can be religious education without initiation into the ways in which god is conceived of according to the religious belief in question, then I claim that this is logically impossible. Since religious belief is constituted by the concept of god, one cannot be initiated into it without learning how to conceive of god.

Again, it is fashionable to speak as if there could be religious education in the absence of initiation into devotion, where 'devotion' includes *speech acts* expressive of trust or obeisance. Examples of such acts of devotion are public or private prayers, reflection on what is God's will for one's life, etc. I claim that it is logically impossible for there to be religious education in the absence of initiation into such pursuits. In asking the question: is religious education possible? I am therefore asking whether initiation into theology and devotion is logically possible. To this question we return below.

If the answer is yes, as I think it is, that does not, of course, settle the problem whether such initiation can properly be called education. Initiation is a necessary condition of education; there cannot be education without it. But it does not follow that initiation is a sufficient condition of education; that initiation into any pursuit at all can properly be called education.

Two further defining characteristics of education must be noted, viz. the pursuits into which it initiates must (a) fall within the rational tradition and (b) must allow for independence of mind. I take them in turn.

The rational tradition That into which education initiates must fall within the rational tradition. It must do so in two respects: (a) it must be an activity, or activities, and so offer scope for reasoning; and (b) of all possible activities those into which education as such initiates must be ones in which there is widely deemed to be good reason to engage.

It is possible to reason *within* an activity or *about* it. One can, for instance, give reason why a certain thing is done as part of the activity called soccer; one can, again, give reason for or against engaging in this activity at all. The former reason is *internal* to the game. Why a free kick now? Because the rules of the game—which constitute this activity called soccer—require one in circumstances such as these. The latter reason is, by contrast, *external* to the game. Why play soccer at all? Because it is good for health, earns one high fees, or is a beautiful pursuit in itself. The two former reasons treat soccer as a means to some desirable end (health, money); the last of the three treats it as an end in itself.

Now, I am saying two things: (a) That into which education initiates must fall within the rational tradition in that it is an activity constituted by rules of procedure which can be invoked as reasons for what is said or done. (b) The activities into which education, as such, initiates must fall within the rational tradition in the sense that there are reasons for engaging in them which are widely held to be good reasons. I will try to bring out more fully what I mean in each case.

(a) Compare education with forms of conditioning such as hypnosis or subliminal advertising. The behaviour into which such processes initiate their subjects allows for the operation of *causes*. The subject, for instance, sees something and the response which he has been conditioned to make to it occurs. But, by contrast, any pursuit into which one can be educated proceeds in accordance with reasons. There is reason why this word rather than that is spoken in a language, the reason being a meaning-rule for the use of the word in question. There is reason why this act is performed rather than that in activities such as scientific enquiry, building, or whatever, the reason being that this is the recognized way to do what the subject, who has learned how to do science, to build, or whatever, intends to do. I call these pursuits into which education is possible activities to bring out that they allow for the application of reasons not just the operation of causes.

As an activity into which education initiates becomes more complex, what to say or do may well be a matter which has to be reasoned out carefully. Is this the best way of doing what one intends to do? Opinions may vary. But insofar as the activity concerned allows scope for reasoning, the correct opinion can be sought through reflection or debate.

Within any universe of discourse certain questions will not be possible matters of reflection or debate. Whether or not there is any point in moral evaluation, for instance, is not a question which can be thought or argued about within moral discourse because that whole way of thinking proceeds on the assumption that there is. But it can be considered in some wider context. We may ask whether as an end in itself, or a means to some end beyond itself, moral evaluation has a rationale. The scope of the reasoning is, therefore, dependent upon the scope of the activity into which one is being initiated. If moral education is the activity in question, then the reasoning will be confined to what has positive or negative moral value. But if a wider education is being given then this will initiate into activities which may well afford scope for reasoning *about* moral evaluation, not simply in terms of it.

At this point it may be useful to note a difference between rationalism as such and education. A rationalist, it is often in my view rightly claimed, is a man who holds all his beliefs, *including the presuppositions in accordance with which he is thinking* at any given time, open to abandonment or change if he finds good reason to abandon or change them.[10] An educated man, by contrast, is to be defined as one who has been initiated into activities where reasons will exist for thinking or doing one thing rather than another *given certain presuppositions*. The activity of moral evaluation, for example, proceeds on the presupposition that there is moral value. What I am saying is that for a man to be *morally* educated is for him to be able to reason in moral terms. It is *not* for him to be open to argument which may lead him to give up thinking morally. To speak of education into an activity does not imply willingness to abandon that activity, as to speak of being rational about an activity might. But it does imply that one is shown how to give reasons for what is said and done appropriate to the activity.

(b) Turning now to my other point about what it is for an activity to fall within the rational tradition, it is a contingent matter in any community what particular activities are widely regarded as ones in which there is good reason to engage. As ends in themselves activities may, or may not, be considered things to do; or as means to ends beyond themselves, activities may, or may not, be thought effective. Take the question for example: why play soccer? It is perhaps widely held in some community that doing so is an effective means to keeping fit. Or again: it is perhaps widely held in that community that playing soccer is a thing to do for its own sake. In either case, this is what it means to say that it is held in the said community that there is good reason to play soccer.

By a good reason for engaging in an activity, then, I mean a reason external to the activity itself ('external' here marking the contrast with reasons 'internal' to the activity as noted above under (a)). Such good reason may refer to the relevant activity when considered either as end-in-itself or means-to-end beyond itself. The reason consists in the intrinsic value of the activity as end or the effectiveness of the activity as means to an intrinsically valuable end. Which activities are deemed valuable as ends or effective as means is a contingent matter. It happens to be the case that certain activities are thought things to do for their own sakes, or effective as means to things to do for their own sakes, in any given community. In our society, for example, the pursuit of knowledge is widely deemed a thing to do for its own sake; the building of libraries, a thing to do because it is a means to the pursuit of knowledge. It is thus widely held that there is good reason to engage in the activities of pursuing knowledge or building libraries.

Those activities in which there is thought to be good reason to engage constitute part of what I mean by the rational tradition of the community concerned. Now, what I wish to say here about education is this. Education must (logically) initiate into activities which, as a contingent fact, are ones which it is widely held that there is good reason to perform. It is implied in the meaning of 'education' that, as used by members of any community, it refers to initiation into activities which, in that community, are widely held to be ones in which there is good reason to engage.

The point which I have been making here can be put in this way. 'Education' is one of those words which are said to have both an emotive and a descriptive meaning (others with which it may be compared are 'democracy' and 'civilization'). The emotive meaning is constant; to call anything 'education' is to express approval of it. But the descriptive meaning may vary or change: what is described as education by one man, or group, or age, may not be so described by others. This duality in the meaning of 'education' and other such words makes possible what has been called 'persuasive definition'.[11] People sometimes commend what they wish to see done by claiming that it is 'what "education" really means'. Relying on the emotive meaning of approval which 'education' bears, they seek to attach this word to activities which they want to see practised or taught, thereby commending the latter. Such a move would not be possible unless to call anything education were, in effect, to express approval of it. This is what I have been pointing out: the activities into which one *can* (logically) be educated *must* (logically) be activities which there is widely held to be good reason to perform.

Independence of mind The other defining characteristic of education which it seems to me important to mention is that its purpose is to enable those who receive it to think about its subject-matter for themselves. To give them independence of mind. This is one respect in which education differs from indoctrination. A successful in-doctrinator is someone who inhibits thinking for oneself in those whom he indoctrinates. The object of his exercise is to get people to hold opinions, or do things, without question or criticism. But education aims to produce people who can, and do, form their own judgments. A child is educated in mathematics when he can do sums for himself; he is educated in science when he can work out for himself why things happen as they do. Professor R. M. Hare[12] insists, rightly in my view, that even moral education should not aim at persuading a child to accept certain moral opinions or conventions, but at enabling him to think for himself in moral terms (what is just, good, etc.) so that he can arrive at his own conclusions. This idea of independence of mind as the end-product of the process seems to me to be built into the very concept of education.

II. Is 'religious education' a contradiction in terms?

We turn now to the question: is 'religious education' a contradiction in terms?

Let me recapitulate briefly what we have seen so far. Education is initiation into activities, theoretical, practical, or both; and specifically religious education is therefore initiation into such of these activities as constitute religious belief. These are of two kinds which I designated theology and devotion. We noted that the initiation to which I referred is a necessary, but not a sufficient, condition of education. The activities into which one is initiated by education, we saw, must fulfil certain other conditions, if the process is to be properly called education. Of these I extrapolated for special consideration the following conditions: (i) The activities concerned must fall within the rational tradition in the senses that (a) they offer scope for reasoning and (b) are activities which it is widely held that there is good reason to perform. (ii) Initiation must aim at producing independence of mind in the pursuit of the a ctivities concerned.

The issues, then, which I think we have to consider in deciding whether or not 'religious education' is a contradiction in terms are as follows:

(i)   Is initiation into the activities which constitute theology and devotion logically possible?

(ii)   If so, does such initiation fall within the rational tradition in the senses (a) that theology and devotion allow scope for reasoning; and (b) that it is widely held that there is good reason to pursue these activities?

(iii) Is it logically possible for religious education to aim at producing independence of mind in those who receive it?
I will take these questions in turn.

Initiation into theology and devotion

I see no difficulty in the idea of initiation into theology and devotion. Both can be taught. By theology, I mean thinking in terms of god in those ways which are characteristic of the religion into which one is being initiated. Initiating people into a theology simply means acquainting them, at a level of completeness appropriate to their age and background, with the concept of god as it has been understood within that tradition and allowing such scope for reading, questions, discussion, etc. as may be necessary for them to assimilate what they are being taught. There are, no doubt, many practical problems concerning the best methods to adopt in order to do this but these are not our present concern. All I want to establish is that the notion of teaching pupils how to do theology, i.e. how to think and speak in terms of god, is no less intelligible than that of teaching them a science or a language.

The same is true of devotion. I said above that the language in which religious belief is expressed is performative. In saying, for instance, 'God is our Father', a Christian as such is not simply stating what he takes to be a fact; he is reposing his trust in god, acknowledging his duty to god, or whatever. Religious belief is belief *in* god, not merely belief that god exists. Because this is so, I claimed, initiation into religious belief must include initiation into the activities of reposing one's trust in god, acknowledging one's duty to god, etc.—activities performed by religious language and to which I gave the composite description, devotion. I see no problem in the idea of teaching people to be devout insofar as devotion consists in certain forms of behaviour. Putting one's trust in god, acknowledging one's duty to god—these are ways of behaving; they consist of speech and the activities with which it is interwoven, in contexts where religious belief finds expression. Again, the notion of devotion being sincere, insofar as it can be cashed in terms of behaviour (and surely every advocate of religion would say that it can) presents no difficulty. People can be taught how to be sincere. No doubt there are effective and ineffective methods of initiating people into devotion, as into theology, but these are not our concern. All I wish to point out is that devotion consists of activities into which people can be initiated.

The first of the questions posed above is, therefore, easy to answer: initiation into theology and devotion is logically possible. There is no self-contradiction in the idea of religious education up to this point.

Religious belief and the rational tradition

The second question which we have to consider is: does initiation into theology and devotion fall within the rational tradition in the senses (a) that these activities offer scope for reasoning and (b) are widely held to be ones in which there is good reason to engage.

I want to emphasize that the rationality of religious belief is in question here only in these two senses. I am not suggesting that, before there can be religious education, there must be some justification of religious belief which will show that there are good religious or non-religious reasons for believing in god's existence. I do not think that this justification could be provided. Above I advanced the opinion that religious belief is a universe of discourse comparable to physical science or morality in that it is constituted by a concept (or set of concepts). Just as physical science is thinking in terms of physical objectivity and morality, of obligation, so religious belief is thinking in terms of god. Each of these constitutive concepts is *sui generis* and cannot be reduced to anything other than itself. If one is asked: does god really exist? where does one go for an answer? Not to religious belief itself for within that universe of discourse the question of the existence of god cannot arise because god's existence is presupposed by everything said within it. Nor to any other universe of discourse (e.g. physical science) because the concept of god would have to be reduced to something other than itself for the question to be answered. Within physical science, for instance, there are ways of determining whether any X does, or does not, exist as a physical object. But god is by definition not a physical object, so it would be meaningless to treat the question of god's existence as a scientific one. The same is true *mutatis mutandis* whatever universe of discourse is substituted for science.

We do not have to say, then, that religious belief must fall within the rational tradition in the sense that god's existence can be proved, before religious education is logically possible. Whatever constitutes falling within the rational tradition here, it cannot be that a question which it is logically impossible to answer should be answered.

There are, however, the respects mentioned above, in which religious belief must fall within the rational tradition if it is to be a subject of education.

(a) The first of these is that it must offer scope for reasoning. We saw above that the activities into which education initiates must do so. They must not be simply conditioned reflexes in which causes alone operate, but activities within which what is done or said proceeds in accordance with reasons.

Do theology and devotion offer scope for reasoning? Are they activities within which what is characteristically said or done occurs because those involved are conditioned to say or do it, or because there are reasons for saying or doing it? Clearly the latter. To initiate a pupil into theology is not to put him in a position where certain causes will produce certain effects in him; it is to instruct him in how to reason in terms of god, just as to initiate him into physical science is to teach him how to do so in terms of physical objects. To initiate him into devotion is similarly to show him the way to do certain things just as to initiate him into, say, gardening or building is. There are meaning-rules for religious terms as for terms of any other kind, and recognized ways to perform religious acts as to perform those of any other sort. As in other subjects of education, points may come in religious belief when what to say or do is a matter which has to be reasoned out carefully. Religious belief allows scope for such reasoning.

There is however a limit to this reasoning. Within religious belief, as we have noted, god's existence cannot be questioned because this whole universe of discourse presupposes it. Therefore, one must not say that religious education is not education unless it allows, as part of the process of such education, for the abandonment of religious belief. However desirable it may be on other grounds to create a context in which the abandonment of religious belief for what seem to be good reasons is possible, it is not part of the concept of religious education to do so. But it *is* part of that concept that the activities which constitute religious belief shall allow for change and development of opinion or practice. Religious education could hardly, as such, lead one to stop thinking in terms of god because, being initiation into religious belief, it is initiation into that which presupposes the existence of god. But it could—it must—allow for reasons to think one thing rather than another in terms of god and for the exercise of open-mindedness in seeking for, and following, such reasons.

(b) The second respect in which religious belief must fall within the rational tradition is that there must be reasons for engaging in theology and devotion which are widely held to be good ones. As an end in itself religious belief must be widely deemed to have intrinsic value; or as a means to some end beyond itself it must be widely held to be effective. If it is to be a part of education, it must be considered one or the other, or both.

Is it either? There are, one must acknowledge, many people who would say not.

The chief end of man has been defined within Christianity as: 'To glorify God and enjoy him for ever'.[13] Whatever that may be taken to mean in precise terms, it undoubtedly involves the activities which I have called theology and devotion. It recognizes these as ends in themselves which have intrinsic worth. But nowadays even some religious believers would deny this. It is fashionable within religious circles to denigrate theology and devotion, at least as these activities have been traditionally understood. Man 'come of age', to use a phrase favoured by *avant-garde* religious thinkers, must, it is said, learn to get on without the god of traditional Christian thought and devotion. Explanations and experiences, constituted by the concept of god, as traditionally understood within Christianity, are out. So far from being ends in themselves, traditional Christian theology and devotion are hindrances to true spirituality. They are 'religion': a term of derogation. In their place what is called 'religionless Christianity', or 'holy worldliness', is advocated.[14]

The difficulty in such views is to see what room they leave for anything identifiable as religious belief, which is distinct from secular humanism. Some authors quite cheerily assert that they have no desire to leave any such room, but it is puzzling when they go on to speak as if it were some great Christian achievement not to do so. They seem to have stipulated a meaning for Christianity which is so radically different from its traditional meaning that it is unintelligible why they should have chosen that term for what they have in mind rather than any other.

Religious belief has come in for no less suspicion when regarded as the means to ends beyond itself. Take three possible ends, for example, about each of which I will say a word, viz. knowledge, mental well-being, and particular goals. The knowledge I refer to is knowledge of god. Theology and devotion, considered as means to this, might be effective enough, if there is any such end to be achieved. But many now hold that knowledge is an end which it is impossible for religious belief to attain because claims concerning god simply cannot be established in the way that what is called knowledge is normally established. Again, religious belief as a means to desirable states of mind, such as freedom from anxiety, or at a higher level, blessedness or bliss, would now be affirmed by many to be ineffective. Religious belief is a source of neurosis, they would say, or at least is potentially so. When I spoke of particular goals, I had in mind the kind of thing sought through petitionary prayer. Many now have lost all belief in prayer as a means of achieving such goals.

How widespread is this rejection of religious belief as end or means? We need to know because it is implied in the meaning of the word 'education' that one can be educated in religious belief, only if the latter is not too widely rejected as end or means. One cannot (logically) be educated in an activity unless it is accepted widely as an intrinsically valuable end or an effective means to such, or both. If the day has come, or ever does come, when religious belief is widely enough regarded as neither such an end nor such a means then religious education will not be logically possible.

For my own part, I do not think that that day has come. Religious belief has not lost its point in the sense which I have defined here. As a matter of contingent fact—and I emphasize that this is what is at issue—the view *is* still widely held that religious belief, as an end in itself, or as a means to other desirable ends, has point. Widely enough held, at least, for it not to be logically odd to speak of religious education. Opponents of religious education may have all kinds of reasons which they can advance for abandoning it. All I am saying here is that they cannot claim, as one of those reasons, that the expression 'religious education' is self-contradictory on the ground that religious belief is widely considered to have lost its point.

Religious belief and independence of mind

It is, we have seen, a further defining characteristic of education—as distinct from indoctrination—that it aims to produce independence of mind. The activities into which it initiates must therefore be ones in which the exercise of independence of mind is possible. They must be ones in which people can think and decide for themselves what to say or do. I see no reason to suppose that independence of mind is any less possible within religious belief than it is within science or morality or any other generally accepted subject of education. Note, of course, that insofar as specifically religious education is concerned, this will be independence of mind *within* theology or devotion as distinct from *about* these subjects. In some wider sense of 'education' it will no doubt be desirable to promote independence of mind *about* theology or devotion. And it has to be conceded that education ought perhaps to be one and indivisible: that we should not say 'You must learn to think for yourself about god but not about this whole business of thinking about god'. I am not denying that but simply pointing out that it is not part of the concept of religious education as such to encourage this critical attitude *about* theology and devotion. The encouragement, on the other hand, of an attitude of critical exploration *within* religious belief certainly *is* part of the concept of religious education. If what is in process is properly to be described as religious education, then it will actively encourage those who receive it to investigate the

187

concept of god and the experiences of devotion for themselves in order to discover what has particular significance for them. Logically, there is a distinction between what you must accept in order to engage in religious belief at all (viz. the concept of god and the specific performative character of the language which expresses religious belief) and what you may think or say for yourself within that universe of discourse. But chronologically it is not necessary to divide religious education into initial periods when pupils are encouraged only to accept what they are told and later periods in which they are encouraged to think for themselves. From the first the exploratory approach can be encouraged. The skilled teacher will try to latch what he says or does in religious education on to aspects of the youngest child's experience—his sense of wonder at the world around him, for instance—so that the way is open from the start for him to explore for himself the significance of what he is being taught.

I think the approach which I have described here—encouraging independence of mind—is characteristic of *all* education correctly so called and therefore of religious education in particular. I should make it clear that so far as the latter is concerned I am not putting a premium on heresy or non-conformity and suggesting that the educated religious believer must (logically) engage in either. He may be very traditional and conservative in his beliefs. But he will have been encouraged by those who have educated him to make these beliefs, if he holds them at all, his own; to see their point more and more clearly as life unfolds for him and as, in different situations, he discovers the relevance of such theology or devotion as he has been taught. Thinking for oneself, making the subject one's own, being able to reason for oneself within it—these seem to me to be defining characteristics of religious, as of all, education.

III. Misuse of the expression 'religious education'

We come then to the question: to what extent is the expression 'religious education' misused? I have attempted a definition of this expression and, given that definition, I have contended that religious education is logically possible. When, however, we consider what actually occurs, or is proposed, in the name of religious education, how far does this conform to what I have taken 'religious education' to mean?

Education about *religion*

It is important to remember the distinction, of which I have made much, between initiation into religious belief and initiation into various ways of considering it. Education may be either *in* religious belief or *about* it. But only the former is, strictly speaking, religious education. Now, there are those who seem to think that religious education in schools should acquaint pupils with, say, the literature and history of religion to the degree that these subjects are likely to be understood by, or of interest to, them, but that it should not initiate them into the activities of theology or devotion. These later activities, it is felt, call for a degree of commitment which the pupil should be left free to decide for himself whether or not to evince, when he is sufficiently mature and well informed to do so.

I doubt, by the way, if such a programme could in practice be carried out. Can one simply impart information about religion without at least risking that those to whom it is offered will begin to have religious thoughts and adopt religious attitudes? But even if this programme were possible without these effects, it would not amount to religious education. Valuable as some instruction in the Bible, for instance, considered simply as literature or history, may be, when part of a general education, it is a misnomer to call such instruction religious education. Those who advocate that 'religious education' in schools be confined to such instruction *about* religious belief are almost always avowed unbelievers. Their enthusiasm for it supports my contention that this is not religious education.

'*Implicit religion*'

There is an approach to religious education which is fashionable nowadays called the 'implicit religion' approach. Religious beliefs are held to be 'implicit' in both the experience of the child (e.g. in his feelings of wonder, need, gratitude, etc.) and in the subjects (science, geography, or whatever) which form his school curriculum. One advocate of this approach, for example, writes: 'Science is concerned with the structure of crystals, religious education is concerned with wonder and delight, the response of the human spirit as microscopy throws up this beauty . . .'[15] Carried to extremes, this approach denies that there is any such thing as religious education, distinct from education in general. Every activity into which one may be initiated by education is implicitly a religious one; and religious education, if it is about anything, is about everything. To quote again: the content of religious education is said to be 'the depth, the realisation of everything, the experience of the whole, the living, and the human . . .'[16] Or yet again: study of the Bible 'must start from the position that the Bible is not about the Bible but about the human situation . . .'[17] It is hard to avoid the conclusion that this is an approach to religious education which evacuated the expression 'religious education' of all meaning. It is no doubt an excellent thing to awaken wonder in the young, to interest them in living things, to introduce them to the human situation, etc. but why call all this 'religious education'? Some advocates of the 'implicit religion' approach say 'Why indeed?' But when they do, their response is not a genuine one. They want to get rid of the expression 'religious education' but they are not really advocating a non-religious approach to experience. They are claiming in effect that religious belief is *implicit* in all experience. And what does that mean?

It is important to draw a distinction between the following:
(a) The view that from non-religious premises (e.g. statements about crystals) one can argue logically to religious conclusions (e.g. statements that god made the crystals).
(b) The view that any aspect of nature, history or experience can (logically) be talked about in terms of god.

The former view is mistaken; the latter, correct.

Once we are thinking or speaking in terms of god we can have a theology of anything and make a devotional response to anything. But it is important to see that *logically* the concept of god constitutes this way of speaking or thinking. It is one thing to say that there are crystals; another that god made them. The frontier between the two is passed if, and only if, the concept of god is accepted. That concept is not logically reducible to anything other than itself, not even to the concepts of wonder or delight.

The notion that religious belief is 'implicit' in all experience, therefore, seems to me to be misleading. I am not, of course, suggesting that one must—or should—begin religious education in schools with definitions of 'god' and, only when they are clearly in mind, encourage one's pupils to look at the world around them with interest or sympathy. But I am saying that religious education cannot (logically) be other than initiation into theology and devotion, and that these activities are essentially religious activities and cannot (logically) be conceived simply as wonder or delight at the way the world is, or sympathy with one's fellow creatures in their happiness or need. Insofar then, as the 'implicit religion' approach expresses a desire to dispense with theology or devotion it is, I think, as misconceived as the view that religious education can consist only of instruction about religion.

All I have said leaves open the question whether or not it is *psychologically* best to introduce children to religion by pointing out certain features of the world around them or of the human situation. If one is going to speak to them eventually of god as creator of the world, for instance, then the significance of this will depend in part on what they know of the world and it may be the most effective method of introducing them to the doctrine of creation to extend their appreciation of the wonder or beauty of the world first. But the distinction which I draw above between (a) and (b) is still valid and important. It is an illusion to suppose that if only one tells people *enough* about the world or human experience they will eventually see that it follows logically that god exists and has certain attributes. The logical gap between non-religious premises and religious conclusions remains, and no matter how you pile up premises on one side, you do not bridge it. For good or ill, if anything is religious education it is logically grounded in the concept of god. It is a misuse of the expression to apply it to anything grounded elsewhere.

Religious education and indoctrination

The third example of a misuse of the expression 'religious education', which I wish to note, is when indoctrination is so described. I think the difference between religious education and indoctrination can be put in this way. Religious education initiates into a certain *form* of belief, whereas religious indoctrination initiates into a certain *content* of belief.[18] By 'form' here I mean simply the logical form of thinking which is constituted by the concept of god and the complex performative character of the language in which religious belief is expressed. By 'content' I mean particular theological beliefs or devotional practices. Of course, I am not saying that in the actual teaching of pupils one can ever dispense with a certain content. It would be quite unrealistic to suppose that one could teach religious belief in the abstract. Religious education must always be grounded in some particular tradition through which those being taught make their first acquaintance with the concept of god and the practice of devotion. But what is essential to education, as against indoctrination, I think, is that the object of the exercise is not to get one's pupils to accept any particular content, but to initiate them into theology and devotion as such, the content of these being open to change or development as the pupil begins to think for himself in terms of god. It was said of Lord Shaftesbury that his nurse impressed her own religious beliefs on him so firmly that he never changed them and at the age of eighty he believed exactly what he had believed at the age of eight. The aim of religious education is not to produce that kind of stability in belief. It is the aim of indoctrination to do so, but religious education, by contrast, aims at the independence of mind which will lead those initiated into religious belief to explore that universe of discourse for themselves. It encourages them to consider contents other than those with which they were first acquainted; to look at what religion has meant to people outside the nursery; to compare the religious opinions or experiences of others with their own; to retain a properly inquisitive attitude towards any content which is given to theology and devotion. The *form* remains and limits the scope of the exploration. But this only in the way that the scope of scientific enquiry is limited by the fact that it is enquiry concerning physical objects, or moral enquiry by the fact that it concerns moral value. The limit in religion is that it has to do with god and how god shall be conceived of and responded to. That is as fascinating an area of exploration as any could be. Or so a religious believer would claim. Anything properly called religious education must aim at launching a pupil on his own voyage of discovery into that dimension of life.

Conclusion

My answer to the question with which we began is 'yes'. Religious education is logically possible. In arriving at that answer, I believe that I have taken the expression 'religious education' in a sense which accords perfectly with the normal use of the words which form it. I have not placed an idiosyncratic meaning on 'religious' nor have I invented an unusual definition of 'education'. Putting these terms together in their ordinary senses, I have tried to show what is logically implied in the idea of giving anyone a religious education. I have insisted on two things: (a) that any such education must be unashamedly designed to initiate its recipients into theology and devotion; but (b) that it must also allow for, and indeed encourage, openness of mind in the widest possible exploration of what can be thought or experienced within the religious universe of discourse. How best these two ends can be served in practice is a task for professional educationists to work out. But it would, if I may say so, be, in my opinion, a great gain in the present muddled state of thinking about religious education if those responsible for it could see clearly that *both* initiation into theology and devotion *and* the encouragement of openness and independence of mind, are essential to the meaning of the process and not one to the exclusion of the other.

Postscript

All I have written so far in this chapter has been concerned with the possibility—as distinct from the necessity, or even the desirability

—of religious education. It may be objected that this leaves the really important question unanswered. So, it may be said, there *can* be religious education: but *ought* there to be? Is this a necessary element in our educational programme for schools or colleges? Is it even desirable that the young should be initiated into religious belief?

These are, indeed, important questions but any full discussion of them would call for another, and a different, chapter. What I have written here is relevant to them in this respect: all I have said to the effect that religious education is possible shows that these questions cannot be answered in the negative simply on the ground that religious education is a logical impossibility. But it is nonetheless true that they cannot be answered in the affirmative simply on the ground that religious education is a logical possibility. When it has been shown that something *can* be done, the question is always open as to whether or not it *ought* to be done. And so, at the end of this paper the question, 'Is religious education a necessary, or even a desirable, element in a general education?' does remain open.

I want, however, to note one or two possible approaches to it for those who feel that this chapter leaves them with it. The 'ought' in 'Ought there to be religious education?' can be interpreted in at least two ways. It may be either a *moral* or a *logical* 'ought'.

If we take it as a *moral* 'ought', at least three positions are possible.

First, most religious believers consider that they have an obligation to initiate their children, or have them initiated by others, into religious belief. They think that they would be failing in their duty to God, and to the children themselves, if they did not ensure that this was well done.

Second, unbelievers, of course, do not share any sense of the former duty, viz. that to God, but as to the latter, viz. that to their children, two views are current among them. Some unbelievers think that their children ought to receive a religious education so that they can react to religious belief for themselves without having the issue prejudged for them by their parents. The religious question, as we may call it—i.e. whether god exists or not, whether there is any point in religious devotion or service—is widely regarded in our society as one to which the answer is not, perhaps cannot be, *known*. That is why many who are not themselves believers consider that the possibility that their children will become believers should be left open; and so they are quite happy to have them subjected to a process of education, the aim of which is initiation into theology or devotion. Insofar as this process is effective—i.e. as their children's participation in religious belief becomes actual—they respect such belief and do not deliberately attempt to undermine it.

Third, over against such unbelievers are others who hold that they are morally bound to prevent their children from being initiated into religious belief because it induces maladjustment to life in the form of fantasy, even neurosis.

The differences of opinion among these three types of people have to do, at least in part, with matters of fact. Does god exist? Unless he does it makes no sense to speak of our duty to him. Can it be known whether or not he exists? Unless the answer is that it cannot, it obviously makes no sense to say that we should stop children receiving religious education because it cannot. Is it true that religious belief induces fantasy or neurosis? Unless it is, it makes no sense to give that as a reason for preventing children from being initiated into theology or devotion. I think it is important to see that many, if not all, the points at issue between holders of the three opinions which we have noted (i.e. believers and the two types of unbelievers) are factual. It is differing beliefs about matters of logical or empirical fact which divide them, not about what is morally right or wrong. Holders of all three opinions would agree that we ought not to give our children an education which makes them neurotic, that we ought to respect truth, that we ought not to leap to conclusions too hastily, etc. The disagreement is about what does in fact induce neurosis, what is true, which questions are open etc. Now it may be too much to hope that these questions of fact will be settled some day beyond all doubt, but at least it is conceivable that some of them will be. For instance, the question of logical fact as to whether or not it can be known that religion is untrue, or the question of psychological fact as to whether or not religion induces neurosis, could conceivably be settled. It is, therefore, at least conceivable that insofar as the question of the necessity or desirability of religious education is a moral question, it could be settled when certain relevant facts are known.

I said that the 'ought' in 'Ought there to be religious education?' could be interpreted, secondly, as a *logical* 'ought'. In other words, that the answer to this question could be a matter of logical implication. What I have in mind is this. If it is the case that education in general is necessary or desirable, then it may be the case, by logical implication, that religious education is also. Mr Langford speaks in his contribution to this volume of education as learning to be a person. Let me adapt this to learning to be a human being and then claim that whatever is involved in learning to be a human being will be involved in education.

The life of a human being, as such, I want to claim, consists, not only in possessing a certain physical constitution, but in participating, within human society, in a number of universes of discourse or 'forms of life', as Wittgenstein might have called them. For example, moral and aesthetic judgments. At the most un-sophisticated levels of human life, human beings work with some conceptions of what is right or wrong, beautiful or ugly. Would anyone be a human being who did not understand at all what it meant to approve or disapprove of things in moral or aesthetic terms? Ability to participate in such universes of discourse, at least to some minimal extent, is part of what it means to be a human being. Someone who did not at all understand what moral obligation is, or who had no conception whatever of what beauty is, would surely, to that extent, be sub-human. If, then, participation in these universes of discourse is part of what it means to be a human being not that, insofar as 'education' means learning to be a human being, it logically implies initiation into these universes of discourse.

Very tentatively, now, I hazard the view that the religious universe of discourse can be regarded in the same light. Religious belief, in one form or another, has been—and still is—so character-istic of human beings that unless, to some extent, one knows one's way about in this universe of discourse, one is less than human. It may be, of course, that, having ventured into this religious universe of discourse, one will decide that it is a vast illusion; but in order to do that one must know what religion is. A human being who really had no acquaintance with religious belief whatever would, it seems to me, have lost touch with a dimension of human thought and experience which is definitive of humanity, as such.

So, may we not say that, insofar as there is education and insofar as education is learning to be a human being, there ought *logically* to be religious education. Such education is implied in the concept of learning to be a human being. I am not, of course, saying that in order to be a human being, one must be a religious believer, but simply that one must know what it is to be one. One cannot know this unless one has undergone some education *in* religious belief and not simply *about* it. And so, religious education is a necessary element in the education of human beings as such. That is to say, it is—as a matter of logic—necessary and desirable, insofar as education *sans phrase* is necessary and desirable.[19]

Notes

1 Cf. G. E. Moore, *Principia Ethica*, Cambridge, 1903.
2 For a recent discussion see M. Durrant, *The Logic of 'God'*, London, 1972.
3 Cf. my *Ludwig Wittgenstein*, London, 1968, pp. 33–41 and 'Tran-scendence', *Theology*, 6, 9, March, 1966. For comment on my views

see K. Nielsen, *Contemporary Critiques of Religion*, London, 1971, pp. 120–5.

4 See J. L. Austin, *How to do Things with Words*, Oxford, 1962.

5 E.g. D. D. Evans, *The Logic of Self-Involvement*, London, 1963.

6 E.g. H. H. Price, *Belief*, London, 1969.

7 See J. J. MacIntosh, 'Belief-in', *Mind*, 1970.

8 N. Malcolm, 'Is it a religious belief that God exists?' in J. Hick (ed.), *Faith and the Philosophers*, London, 1964, pp. 107–8.

9 Professor R. S. Peters's word: cf. his *Ethics and Education*, London, 1966, ch. II.

10 Cf. W. W. Bartley III, *The Retreat to Commitment*, London, 1964.

11 Cf. C. L. Stevenson, *Ethics and Language*, New Haven and London, 1944.

12 R. M. Hare, *Applications of Moral Philosophy*, London, 1972, ch. 5.

13 Westminster Shorter Catechism, 1647.

14 After D. Bonhoeffer, *Letters and Papers from Prison*, London, 1953.

15 H. Loukes, quoted in *Religious Education in Secondary Schools* (Schools Council Working Paper 36), London, 1971, p. 35.

16 *Ibid.*

17 *Ibid.*

18 Here I acknowledge my indebtedness to a similar view put forward by Hare concerning moral education: cf. note 12 above.

19 I discuss some of the problems in the philosophy of religion, touched on in this paper, more fully in *A Philosophical Approach to Religion* (forthcoming).

Aesthetic education I I

Diané Collinson

Let us suppose two persons, A and B, both of whom are intelligent and, in general, well educated. They differ, however, in one important respect; one of them, A, is in my judgment aesthetically educated whereas the other, B, is not. The question I wish to consider in the first part of this chapter is this: what is it about a person that leads me to say of him that he is or is not aesthetically educated? In asking this question I am assuming that talk of aesthetic education makes sense and that practical steps can be taken to bring it about. In the last part of the chapter, therefore, I shall make some suggestions about the sort of methods which might be adopted in educating people aesthetically.

What is it, then, that leads me to say of a person that he is aesthetically educated? To help answer this question I shall introduce a distinction between *aesthetic involvement* and *aesthetic commentating*. The aesthetically educated person is not so much the person who is able to talk about, describe or *comment* on certain objects and situations in a certain way, as the person who in fact has a capacity for experiencing, understanding and becoming *involved* with them in a certain way. A, I maintain, is capable of aesthetic involvement and this means that he is able to enter into some kind of union with works of art. He may or may not possess the different ability for aesthetic commentating, which I define here as an ability to make certain sorts of remarks about works of art. Thus, if we suppose that B, whom I judge not aesthetically educated, does in fact have a capacity for quite fluent aesthetic commentating, but that A has not, then in an actual situation of, say, looking at a painting, B may be making remarks about things like 'impasto', 'colour masses' and 'technique', while A stands before it apparently passive and unresponsive. Of course, we do not know from A's stance of inertia that he *is* aesthetically involved, just as B's eloquence does not assure us that *he* is, but what I have to say is directed towards arguing that A's stance is one that is at the very least compatible with, and at the most a typical feature of, many cases of aesthetic involvement. That is not to say that it is the only such feature. If A does speak to us out of his aesthetic involvement then what he says can be distinguished from aesthetic commentating of the sort of which B is capable because it can be seen to be talk that is a corollary to his aesthetic involvement. He speaks as someone who sees rather than as someone who observes. I hope to make this point clearer as we go on.

I have said nothing yet about what it is to be aesthetically involved, or indeed, aesthetically anything. However, in posing a situation in which A and B look at a painting I have taken it for granted that aesthetic experience is closely connected with the arts; I have assumed it is in experiencing works of art in a certain way that we are likely to encounter the shining examples of the aesthetic moment. Yet, one has to say immediately, it is not only works of art that are fit matter for aesthetic contemplation, for we speak also of the aesthetic enjoyment of nature and of many other things not subsumable under the title of art. And it has been argued, for example by Bullough, that aesthetic experience is not so much an experience characteristically engendered by a certain class of objects—works of art—as a certain *kind of experience*, theoretically possible in respect of anything at all.[1] On this view we might think of ourselves as having a pair of aesthetic spectacles to put on at those times when we wish to see something from the aesthetic point of view. It would follow from this that an account of the difference between one's experiences when wearing spectacles and one's experience when not wearing them would provide us with the distinguishing marks of the aesthetic moment. But this approach says nothing about the fact that certain kinds of objects are peculiarly apt for aesthetic regard, and indeed command it. In what follows, therefore, I shall take cases of our experiences within the arts as paradigm cases of aesthetic experience, and I shall not specifically discuss the aesthetic enjoyment of nature. What we may usefully remember is that the concept of the aesthetic is in some respects wider than the concept of art, in that it can embrace more than works of art, and that the concept of art is in some respects wider than the concept of the aesthetic, in that not all our dealings with art are aesthetic dealings.

Besides taking it for granted that the aesthetic mood is significantly to do with our experience of art I assumed something else also. I assumed an agreement about the essential nature of aesthetic experience; that is, I spoke of aesthetic *enjoyment*, taking it that it is some sort of delight or pleasure that characterizes the aesthetic experience. If this is correct it follows that it is a mark of A's being aesthetically educated that he has a capacity for enjoying works of art, a capacity for delight in them. This is not to say that he is able to enjoy all the arts in all their manifestations, but in describing A's abilities I can say that he is receptive and open to the arts, is both welcoming and respectful towards them. He gives a work of art time and attention, so that it has the opportunity to inhabit his consciousness. He is, to use a word used by Gabriel Marcel in the context of talk about the moral life, disponible in respect of the arts.[2] And if A is sometimes seen as blank and unmoving in the presence of a work of art, it is generally because he is admitting it totally to his awareness.

There are questions to be asked about the notion of delight or enjoyment as *the* mark of an appropriate experiencing of works of art. For it certainly is not the case that one experiences delight in the presence of all the works of art one is capable of experiencing appropriately. Our particular experiences may range from those of pure terror or grief to convulsive mirth.

Certainly it is delight, a kind of sweet inward rapture, that comes with the reading of just one line of poetry like Laurie Lee's:[3]

the hedges choke with roses fat as cream.

Delight, too, from these lines:[4]

they're wrong who say that happiness never comes
On earth, that has spread here its crystal sea.

Yet not delight, but perhaps a sorrowing tenderness from Philip Larkin's poem about the young mothers who take their children to the recreation ground:[5]

Before them, the wind
Is ruining their courting places . . .
Their beauty has thickened.
Something is pushing them
To the side of their own lives.

And turning to painting for our examples, those, say, of Francis Bacon, then it is nothing like delight that is felt in the presence of these works, but rather a fearfulness, a fearfulness that if we look again more carefully we shall be gazing upon what is unendurable. This does seem to be true equally of a painting such as his study of a dog, which portrays no obvious grotesqueness, as of 'Fragment of a Crucifixion', in which menace and deformity are more explicit.[6] Again, the sustained horror-tension of a play like *Waiting for Godot*[7] cannot be said to engender delight. Nor does Marlowe's Faustus, with his last anguished words as he waits to be taken by the Devil:[8]

See, see where Christ's blood streams in the firmament.
One drop would save my soul, half a drop: ah, my Christ . . .
O soul, be chang'd into little water drops,
And fall into the ocean ne'er to be found.

Yet it is true to say that I am as glad to have seen *Godot* or *Faustus* or a painting by Francis Bacon as I am to have read Laurie Lee, even though I am harrowed by the first three and entranced by the fourth. It is this that shows us how the term 'aesthetic delight' is applied. It is not that it describes the character of every appropriate experience in the presence of works of art, but that it is characteristic of ultimate aesthetic approval. It is a delight that clarity has been achieved, that something matchless, intelligible and illuminating has been present to us.

Of course, a work may express delight and also engender delight in the beholder, as well as evoking the delight characteristic of ultimate aesthetic approval. Laurie Lee's line about the roses does just this. We have first the poet's own delight in the roses, articulated through words that evoke the reader's delight in them; then we have a further delight in the words appreciated as a new object of experience. This further delight is in fact a rejoicing over the perspicuity with which the poet's vision has been presented. It is that perspicuity which has arrested and commanded our attention so that we dwell on the poet's vision. Moreover, our delight in that perspicuity forms the core of our evaluation of the work of art.

The aesthetically educated person comes readily to the kind of participation described here. I have already spoken of him as welcoming and open to the impact of the arts, but there is more to it than that. For the work of art, first encountered, is a new object of experience. So it is not only that A is pronouncedly able to follow through the way the poet or artist has taken in making his work so that he comes to a vantage point indicated by the poet, but that in doing this he reveals a further capacity, a capacity for taking certain risks: he reveals a willingness to undergo the hazards of experiencing something new by participating in the exploration and discovery of the maker of the work.

In giving these further details of what I hold to be the marks of the aesthetically educated person, I have generated a number of questions which are essentially philosophical. One such question is a question about the exact nature of aesthetic experience. If it is some kind of clarity of perception that the arts offer us, how precisely is aesthetic experience different from, say, a straightforward acute observation of some physical object, or a detailed factual description? After all, if one places a crystal under a microscope, is there not a certain perspicuity about what is then displayed to me?[9]

Another such question is about what a work of art *is*? To what class of things may we assign works of art? It is not enough to lump works of art in with the class of physical objects. One criterion of something's being a physical object is that it cannot be in two places at once, yet we speak of works of art in a way that suggests that they do not satisfy this criterion. You can, for instance, have Chaucer's *Canterbury Tales* on your table at the same time as I can have it on mine, or can see a play in Edinburgh at precisely the same time as I see it in London.[10]

A further question arises from the claim that it is our delight in the perspicuity of what the artist presents that forms the core of our judgments of works of art. What kind of standing can such judgments have, based as they are solely on one's pleasure in the work? Indeed, are they properly to be called judgments? For I may be delighted with what I hold to be the arresting perspicuity of something which to you is merely vulgar and silly, while you are entranced by a work which affords nothing but obfuscation to me. And if it so happens that we are both ripe in experience of art, is there anything further to be said in the matter? Is it not after all just a question of taste, in the simplest sense of that word?

I have raised these questions because they are quite evidently questions that come before, in that they are logically prior to, any account of the content of an aesthetic education. If my claim that A is aesthetically educated is to carry any weight at all then my description of him must be backed by a clear account of what essentially constitutes an aesthetic attitude. Nor could one begin to foster, by education, a capacity for aesthetic experience without some idea of what it is to have such an experience. One cannot encourage involvement with works of art unless one knows what kind of thing it is that a person is to be involved with. One cannot nourish aesthetic discrimination unless one understands how we *tell* what is valuable from what is not. And in addition to all this, if we are to be in any way clear about the notion of aesthetic education, we need also to understand the place of art and of the aesthetic in the larger scheme of human life.

We have before us four immense and fascinating topics: one, aesthetic experience; two, the nature of the work of art; three, aesthetic judgment; and four, the significance of the aesthetic mode in human life. Any account of aesthetic education must follow from some sort of understanding of these. But for the present I want to pursue in some detail the topic which I take as central to the concept of aesthetic education: aesthetic experience. I have raised and stated the other questions because any discussion of aesthetic experience points to such questions, inviting our consideration of them. We should therefore keep them in mind.

Let us return, then, to the subject of aesthetic experience and to the distinction I drew between aesthetic involvement and aesthetic commentating. What I suggested was that an ability for commentating on works of art was not a necessary ingredient of aesthetic involvement, so that B, whom we supposed to have this ability, is not thereby judged to be aesthetically educated. This is not to denigrate B's ability for commentary but simply to distinguish it from aesthetic involvement so that it is not mistaken for it, and because it is an activity that quite often alternates with aesthetic involvement. B, when commentating in his uninvolved way, is perhaps exercising historical understanding, or knowledge of techniques, or connoisseurship. A, still and engrossed, presents us with something far more indicative of aesthetic involvement. For one mark of the aesthetic moment is that the work seen or heard arrests and holds us within its orbit. We are, at best, rapt or entranced, poised or passing back and forth in mind only within the limits and evocations of the work itself. Insofar as our immediate absorption is aesthetic we do not learn lessons from the work, make practical applications out of it or calculatingly relate our experience of it to the everyday world. That is to be less than rapt, less than totally available to the emphases, the illusions, the illuminations provided by the work once it has a certain shaft of our attention.

This is not to say that ideally we would bring nothing with us to the contemplation of a work of art. But the difficulty now lies in saying what must and what must not be brought to it for proper contemplation. It would be absurd to think that we should, or could, come to a work of art as a *tabula rasa*. We require a past and we require experience in order to recognize what is before us when we contemplate anything at all. It is obvious that I need my experience of roses, and of many other things as well, if I am to make anything at all of Laurie Lee's line of poetry. What I have to do then, is to bring myself as an appropriate recipient of what works of art offer, and in order to see what is appropriate here I shall try to think back and forth from what a work of art is, and what it accordingly demands, to the kind of attention and esteem that we give it.

If A is totally absorbed in a work then that work has all of his attention and his attention is confined to the work. More than this, his attention, if it is aesthetic attention, is bounded by the aesthetic features of the work. In contemplation of a painting of, say, a Virgin and Child, we are admitted to the point of view that the painting offers to us. The painter's work is, to epigrammatize, *his-vision-for-me*, and if I am an appropriate recipient of what he offers, then my activity is in contemplating his vision by the means he offers. It is perhaps truistic, but worth saying, that I will not come to the artist's vision except by *seeing* it, and this by means of the artist's token that stands between him and myself. It will not help my seeing of his vision, as present to me in this particular painting, to contain alongside it within my consciousness the images of other paintings. Nor is the attention that I direct upon this painting intensified if I reflect on, say, the explanation of some mannerism in the execution of the fall of the drapery. Rather, I must look to the fall of the drapery, so that I see *it* and do not turn my mind away to an explanation of why it is there or how it is as it is. Other paintings, and explanations of a vision, are not themselves that vision.

If an artist's work is his-vision-for-me, the work of a person for a person, then it is as a person that one must come to a work of art. One brings oneself as one is in one's essential nature and as one is as the result of one's accumulated experience. We bring ourselves as persons with pasts, but do not bring the rationally conjectured accounts of those pasts that are our personal and social histories. For the kind of attention that is required for aesthetic contemplation is not compatible with an awareness of our historical selves or the historical past, although it is dependent on our being such selves and having such a past. Aesthetic contemplation requires that we regard what is before us as a self-contained and self-validating entity; that we do not regard it within a shaft of consciousness that holds an awareness of history that invites comparisons, so that the work that is before us becomes classified as one of a kind. What is required is that we narrow and intensify consciousness so that it is wholly pervaded and informed by the object. The scope of this attention cannot contain simultaneously a rationally conjectured account of the past *and* aesthetic awareness of the work of art.

Thus, if we are contemplating, for instance, da Vinci's 'Virgin, Child and St Anne', as soon as we dwell on some such matter as Leonardo's predilection with vulture-like shapes, along with the possibility that his predilection is the outcome of infant traumata, or, in reading a poem, ponder the fact of the special poignancy for ourselves of some shred of a line being the result of a link with an old memory, we have turned away from attending to the work of art as a self-sufficient and self-validating entity.[11] By linking it with incidents in the artist's history or in one's own, we place it in a relationship of dependence with historical events that is irrelevant to its aesthetic significance. This kind of relationship tends to explain the work in terms which are only contingently related to the work itself.

Of course, any object, aesthetic or otherwise, may be placed in a historical or practical relationship with other objects, past and present, but the essential character of aesthetic appreciation is such that it requires the suspension of such considerations. The value we place upon a work of art, is not a value derived from comparisons; aesthetic judgment is not a grading of goods. It is a judgment upon a particular combination of elements. Yet, as I have said, we do need experience and the past if what we experience is to be intelligible. It is not my case to argue that we should never reflect upon or turn scholarly or speculative attention towards Leonardo's 'Virgin, Child and St Anne' or towards our own psychological propensities. Such studies, along with connoisseurship, iconography and many other activities, when thoroughly assimilated, can only enrich our perception and enjoyment of the arts by providing the possibility of more points of contact with works. Yet they remain no more than possible channels of aesthetic consciousness: means rather than the manner of perception. Properly deployed towards aesthetic contemplation they sharpen our vision of a work, providing both greater clarity and greater significance. When they are not properly deployed so, they are distractions that lead us away to incidental connexions, diffusing our attention so that its aesthetic aim is deflected and its unity dissolved. This is why it is sometimes said that the only proper answer to the question: What does it mean?, when asked of a work of art, is to point again to the work. The work of art means itself, and this aesthetic meaning is not to be elucidated by reference to its place in a temporal sequence or its maker's psychological development.

The past we need, then, is the past that is the necessary condition of personhood, and it is as persons that we come to a work of art. We may reasonably enquire whether the confrontation by a person of a work of art is analogous to an encounter between persons. I think there is an analogy and that it is worth pursuing, but we need to know precisely the ways in which these two sorts of confrontation are alike and the ways in which they are different. The proper attitude between two persons is one in which both have a readiness for the experiencing of new facets of the other. Built into the attitude between persons is the recognition of the possibility of some entirely fresh understanding or perception of each other. I am not a person in confronting others unless this is contained in my attitude to them, nor do I treat others as persons unless it is there. Wittgenstein[12] describes this attitude, although in a different context, when he says: 'My attitude towards him is an attitude towards a soul. I am not of the *opinion* that he has a soul.'

Here, then, are similarities between the attitude under discussion: that absence in a person of a disposition to classify what the other does by reference to preconceived ideas is analogous to the exclusion of historical comparisons in aesthetic contemplation; and just as a readiness for fresh illumination and a willingness to venture into new experiences is part of A's aesthetic sensibility, so is it part of the attitude between person and person.

There is a further similarity, and it is one that fills out the account already given of aesthetic involvement. When I put forward the idea that rapt attention is one important feature of aesthetic involvement, I cited an instance of it in A's mental and physical stance before a painting. But this, as I indicated, is not the whole story of aesthetic participation. The next similarity between the confrontation of persons and the confrontation of a work of art by a person gives more of that story.

The similarity becomes plain if we think again about the attitude appropriate between persons. For then we come to say that persons engage in exchanges and replies, giving back uniquely, although not necessarily with originality, one to the other. There is reciprocation between persons.

One might tend to think that no such engagement could possibly take place in the confrontation of a work of art, that in that kind of case one simply absorbs what is before one. But this is not so. In the presence of a painting, A's seeming inertia may be succeeded by a more active contemplation which is an exploration of the painting's possibilities. The exploration may take the form of stepping back from the work, of moving closer or to one side of it, in order to obtain different vantage points. If it is possible, A may place the painting in a different light or at a different level. He may try turning away from it and then wheeling round to see it suddenly and afresh from a new angle.

A poem may be explored in a similar way. Consider a line from Gerard Manley Hopkins's poem, 'God's Grandeur'[13]:

It will flame out like shining from shook foil.

The line may be spoken out or spoken in the mind's ear and enjoyed for its sibilant passion or its declamatory force. Or it may be brooded over quite slowly, so that one dwells on its radiant images, passing indecisively from mental sight of a cascading shower of gold to the other image of a gleaming sword flashed forward in a challenge. All this is active exploration. Much of it takes place quite quietly; some of it involves physical movement. What we may note is that there is little room in this activity for what I have called aesthetic commentating.

Turning now to differences between the attitudes under discussion, there is first of all the quite obvious difference between a person as the recipient of the attitude in one case and the work of art as recipient, or more properly as its object, in the other. Works of art and persons cannot replace each other, even though a work of art may be an intensely personal embodiment of a person's vision; they are not logically substitutable one for the other. If a man presented us with a work of art *qua* human being, or with a human being *qua* work of art, what he did would provoke puzzlement as well as moral and aesthetic repugnance. We would think that such a man had made a mistake in believing that he had effected a transformation, when in fact he had merely brought about a transmogrification.

A further difference becomes plain if we think about the ways in which our encounters with persons and our encounters with art respectively figure in our daily practical lives. Participation in the aesthetic life is something we may take or leave as we please, but participation in the moral life, the practical life between persons, is unavoidable. Even choosing to opt out of personal transactions is a choice both presented and made within the moral life, whereas choosing to opt out of the aesthetic is not in itself an aesthetic choice but a practical one again.

However, it does not follow from the pervasiveness of the moral life, nor from the non-intrusiveness of the aesthetic, that full-blooded aesthetic experience is less profound or less influential than our encounters with persons. Nor is it in the end tenable to assert without qualification that the aesthetic treats characteristically of extremes, the bizarre, the tragic, the ecstatic, and so is essentially at the fringes of our lives. For against this it may be protested that encounters between persons may be utterly strange or terrible and entirely remote from the centre of one's daily life, while illumination through art may take place at quite the domestic level. Yet it is true to say that art, through its encapsulating power, and because it is illusion, frequently takes us to matters and moods from which timidity or circumstances or ignorance might keep us, were they actually to spring up between persons. Art can afford to treat of extremes of which daily life cannot stand the cost. If I meet and talk with someone and in consequence become hopeful and pleased, or at peace, then *that did happen*, and I and that person were agents in it; but if I see *Hamlet*, and experience his anguished sensibility, then all that *Hamlet* did not in a like sense *happen*, and if it had then I would probably spend the rest of my life under the shadow of the event. Yet both my meeting with another person and my experience of *Hamlet* provided the possibility for some growing edge of my personhood to be cultivated, and it could have been the case that *Hamlet* was the stronger nourishment.

There are now two things to be done. First, I want to return to an earlier part of my account of aesthetic experience in order to make some comments and qualifications in respect of it. Second, I wish to turn attention to the question of aesthetic education and ask how a capacity for aesthetic involvement is best fostered.

To return, then, for comment and qualification concerning the account of aesthetic experience. When I described A's ability to become aesthetically involved, I made no mention of the actual exercise of that ability. But part at least of our understanding of it must rest on certain facts connected with its exercises, and the first fact is that its full exercise is both difficult and rare. However eagerly A, and indeed most of us, seek aesthetic involvement and participation, we often find ourselves dull and insensible, or incapable of detaching ourselves sufficiently from distractions. The experience is not readily to be had.

Next, there is a diversity of ways in which the experience can, so to speak, take hold of us. This diversity does not offend the require-ment for seeing the work in a particular way, that particular way being to see it as a particular thing. There are those occasions of encounters with works of art which seem to move us not at all, which at the time provide no sense of arrest, but which subsequently come to mind again and again, accumulating at each recurrence a wealth of significance that is in the end a revelation. Even more typically, there are occasions when one's regard alternates, shifting rapidly from the purely aesthetic to the practical, historical or analytic. And perhaps this last, hybrid attitude is the one which most of us find ourselves adopting in the presence of works of art, and especially in the presence of those, such as paintings, which command only one of the senses.

Obviously, then, many of our encounters with art fall short of that engrossment that marks A's attention at its best. The occasions of entrancement are rare and one begins to question whether the concept of aesthetic involvement as expounded here does not give an impression of an altogether too glaring and blinkered con-centration; one that quite ignores the idea of an experience that is spontaneous and effervescent in its exercise.

If so, the balance must be redressed. We can do this and so liberate ourselves from the apparent straitjacket imposed by the formal requirements of aesthetic contemplation by turning attention in a specific and detailed way to what precisely takes place in particular cases of aesthetic contemplation. We shall find that the formal requirements are capable of containing a rich and in-exhaustible content.

Here I want to take up something discussed by R. K. Elliott in a paper called 'Aesthetic theory and experience of art'.[14] Elliott suggests that some works of art are capable of being experienced as if they were human expression. He does not mean by this that we experience expression in the way in which we experience or perceive an object, but we can experience it as the thought or speech of another person and thereby can make it our own. A work, he says, may be experienced 'from within' or 'from without'.[15] Experience from within is experiencing the work as if one were the poet or artist; from without it is experiencing it still as expression, but not one's own. A lyric poem is the sort of poem in which we are quickly given an understanding of the situation of the poet and Elliott says:[16]

> the lyric 'I' functions as an invitation to the reader to place himself, in imagination, at the point from which the poet is related to the situation in the poem . . . the reader is able, eventually if not immediately, to take up the lyric 'I', invest himself imaginatively with the poet's situation, and experience the poet's expression and the emotion expressed from the place of the expressing subject rather than from the place of one who hears and understands the expression from without.

There is a short poem by Gerard Manley Hopkins which I think provides us with this experience:[17]

> I have desired to go
> Where springs not fail
> To fields where flies no sharp and side hail
> And a few lilies blow
> And I have asked to be
> WHERE NO STORMS COME
> Where the green swell is in the havens dumb
> and out of the swing of the sea

Elliott's claim is that to experience a poem like this at all, one has to assume something of the standpoint of the 'I' in it. If one does this, it does not mean that the longing contained in the poem is in fact one's own longing, although the longing is imaginatively present in oneself in experiencing the poem. This point is well brought out by the Gerard Manley Hopkins poem once we know its title, which is 'Heaven-Haven', and its sub-title, which is 'A nun takes the veil'. For knowing all this does not diminish our ability to experience the poem from within, although the knowledge may provide us with quite precise mental images we would not have otherwise found. Elliott speaks of the emotion of a poem as being present to the reader, but not predictable of him or her.

Even where no lyric 'I' invites us to the poet's stance, we may experience a poem from within. This is the case with Philip Larkin's

'Going'. In this poem we are gradually drawn from a calm outward gazing on field and sky into a tight confinement within something like personal terror:[18]

> There is an evening coming in
> Across the fields, one never seen before,
> That lights no lamps.
>
> Silken it seems at a distance, yet
> When it is drawn up over the knees and breast
> It brings no comfort.
>
> Where has the tree gone, that locked
> Earth to the sky? What is under my hands,
> That I cannot feel?
>
> What loads my hands down?

In reading this poem we are able to encompass the shades of difference in experiencing from within so carefully described by Elliott:[19]

> In experiencing a poem from within, the reader keeps more or less explicit contact with the poet. Sometimes he seems to be there with the poet, as if they inhabited the same body and as if the poet were speaking or thinking with the reader's voice; sometimes the reader seems to be there in place of the poet, expressing and experiencing the poet's emotion as it were on the poet's behalf; sometimes the reader seems even to have supplanted the poet, but still without experiencing the expressed emotion as the product of his own fantasy.

Experiencing a work from without is experiencing it as expression but not as if it were one's own. In this case the aesthetic qualities are perceived or witnessed rather than lived. In discussing this Elliott makes a point I am eager to underline since it supports my attempt to display something of the variety and indeed the naturalness of aesthetic involvement. This is the point that there is no ground for supposing either mode to be 'unaesthetic'. He says:[20]

> Each (mode) is a way of making the work available to aesthetic awareness. In one case the poem arises as a complex content entirely at the objective pole of consciousness; in the other it is realized as an experience, the description of which involves a reference not simply to an objective content but to a subject.

I cannot with any confidence quote a work here and then bring it about that we experience it first from without and then from within. But I can draw an analogy that may be useful. Suppose we read an obituary notice, well written, sensitively phrased and passionate, in praise of a good man. We commend it as fine and appropriate writing about someone who seems to have been a noble and joyous person. Then we learn the name of the dead person, and find he was someone we held in the greatest esteem and affection, so that at once we feel a sense of loss and mourning. We turn again to the obituary notice and this time we read it 'from within'. And now it is not simply a fine expression of respect and praise, whereby we are enabled to understand the quality of another's mourning. This time it is a vehicle of our own praise and sense of loss, an expression in which we participate from the point of view of the writer.

What is plain is that works of art are not given to us as problems, although we do find some problematic. There is not, for instance, in Larkin's 'Going', some strange subliminal depth that we have to plumb or analyse in order to comprehend the meaning of the poem, although there may be elements in the poetry that work in us subliminally. We do not have to *answer* the poem's questions:

> What is under my hands,
> That I cannot feel?
> What loads my hands down?

Rather, we have to be able to ask these questions, or to come to know what it is to ask them; and the poem itself enables us to ask the questions and to recognize their urgency.

It is time now to turn to the question to which all I have so far written is a prologue. This is the question about what should be going on in an aesthetic education. I shall try to say what basic conditions are required for fostering an ability like A's.

1. First, <u>time</u> must be given to aesthetic education: time for looking, listening, reading, watching, time for contemplation and reflection and then for returning again to the work. Although the impact of some works of art, notably paintings and lyric poems, may be immediate so that the artist's or poet's vision is swiftly and transparently displayed, other works acquire significance only after long acquaintance and through a gently persistent familiarity. Again we may draw something from the analogy of getting to know another person. The attention we give to someone we have just met is spoilt if a third party stands alongside delivering information about the person one is trying to get to know. This is not the way in which we can best get to know another person, nor is it the best way of approaching a work of art that is new to us. In the case of persons meeting, the conduct of the third party is somewhat insulting,

however well meant; moreover, it misses the point of personal encounters. In the case of a person and a work of art, the delivering of information about the work is likewise misplaced. Let the work be presented or made available in an appropriate setting, in an unhurried way, with the opportunity for dialogue. This is the situation I count as fundamental to aesthetic involvement. But although it is fundamental, it is not the only worthwhile situation. A third party, and indeed a fourth, fifth and more may be importantly and valuably involved in a single aesthetic situation; for not all the best encounters are dialogues. I shall return to this in a moment.

All the time in the world is of little use if we cannot also, as part of aesthetic education, foster the two qualities of mind I found so commendable in A. These two qualities are open-mindedness and a willingness to explore. They are more crucial for understanding and enjoyment of the arts than for any other branch of culture or knowledge, because in the arts we are so often required to confront something which is not only new to us but which is also original, and so perhaps quite strange. A work of art, and by this I mean as I have throughout, a *good* work of art, has a particularity and originality the significance of which one could not presume to recognize with certainty at a first encounter. But if our intention in approaching works of art is to come to new visions and experiences, we need not be anxious to grade and classify what we see, nor need we be greatly concerned with observing our own mental states. Our aim is fully to behold what is offered, and for this we need open minds with no tendency, at any rate at the outset, to know what we like or like what we know.

The second quality of mind, a willingness to explore, is important because of the demands made by originality and uniqueness in works of art. We have to be prepared to follow through the way the artist went in order to reach his vision. For the artist, this is not a matter of following a set of rules which, properly enacted, enable him to produce some specified object. The artist has to discover, as he explores, what is the right gesture or rhythm or sound for externalizing his vision in an intelligible form. It is a question of trying or rummaging, and this is sometimes described as the *bricoleur* element in artistic activity.[21] Often it is only by exploration into his medium that an artist can come to any substantiation or determination of his vision. So his work is not a matter of recognizing something in the medium that expresses his vision, like recognizing a piece of jigsaw as correct because it is the shape of the gap one has, but like trying a piece in the gap and then finding it *is* right, of finding that *that* is what one was after. A truly original vision requires an original expression; yet if it is also to be intelligible it must be in some way a rule-governed expression. A good work of art is both original and intelligible: we do not count original nonsense as works of art. But the artist's concern is always with the particular, not with stating *that* he has experienced a certain kind of emotion or vision, but with conveying the precise quality of what he has experienced. Yet no general rule can convey such particularity, and so the artist makes a new rule which precisely determines his particular expression.

It is by a following through of the artist's exploration in paint, word or sound that we may come to his standpoint. It is in this way, too, that we judge of the artist's success in externalizing his vision. We judge through knowing the elements internal to the work, by seeing what is actually done to reveal what it particularly expresses, and our judgment is by means of our delight in the fittingness of the work. If we think of following through for the first time the steps of a theorem, of our recognition of each successive and undeniable conclusion, we have, I think, a model for the internal consistency to be found in works of art. In the *Remarks on the Foundation of Mathematics*, where he is discussing the way in which one comes to the understanding of a mathematical proposition, Wittgenstein wrote: 'I find not the result, but that I reach it.'[22] It is typical of aesthetic understanding, too, that we do not find a result, but that we reach one. It is through a willingness to explore that we do reach it.

So much for the desirability of fostering open-mindedness and exploration in aesthetic education. But my picture so far of this kind of education is not a very positive one. We have our subject-matter, works of art, and we may suppose its students. We have also various suggestions as to what state of affairs should be the result of the education: the apprehension of the artist's vision and delight in its perspicuity. But what has been said about the work of the educator here, beyond a hint to produce works of art in appropriate environments and then absent himself as quickly as possible from the scene? Is there nothing more than this to be said?

I think there is a good deal more. If we now ask what exactly is to be done to foster an aesthetic attitude and to develop qualities of open-mindedness and a willingness to explore, we may answer the question by returning to the subject of talking about works of art. What I said was that a situation allowing for something like a dialogue between a person and a work of art was the fundamental situation for experiencing the work, but although this was a fundamental situation it by no means excluded the possibility of there being other sorts of valuable aesthetic situations. Such a situation may be one involving a third party.

The third party best able to educate us aesthetically is the critic. Of course, he must be a good critic, and the role as I shall now describe it is that of the ideal critic. I do not see this role in a different way from most writers on aesthetics. It goes almost without saying that the critic must share A's capacity for involvement with works of art. But he must have further abilities as well. He must be able to bring us to see, in the very widest sense of that word, what we might otherwise miss in a work of art. If aesthetic experience of works of art consists in coming to the artist's vision, then it follows that the critic's skills are the ones eminently suited to directing our gaze. Yet I have deplored the imparting of information about works of art as a means of fostering aesthetic awareness. How then does a critic bring about our illumination?

The seeing we require, that is, seeing in the sense of becoming illuminated, is not a special kind of refined sensory perception or sensitivity, although it is a kind of sensibility. It is not a skill in the detection of fine nuances, a kind of wincing preference for subtleties, delicacy or the exquisite. Critics, as such, do not have special eyesight, or privileged in-group access to the minds of artists or to hallucinatory drugs. What they do have is wide experience in the arts, imagination, and a marked ability to communicate their imaginative activity. We make a mistake if we equate heightened or disturbed sensory activity with imaginative sensibility. Perhaps this distinction is a clue to the disappointment and insatiability that seems to attend the taking of hallucinogens, in that their takers are in search of the latter but find only the former. This is not to say that works of art do not stimulate the senses, but that sensory stimulation is only a part of the means to rich imaginative activity in experiencing a particular sensuous object that is intelligible, coherent and expressive. In contrast, the sensitivity brought about by hallucinogens is experienced in respect of everything encountered by the hallucinated person and so, in the end, is experienced in respect of nothing. It is attached to no particular object and so results in a multiple sameness which, in turn, generates a psychological need for some singular, entirely idiosyncratic involvement with something indomitably personal and particular.

Although the critic's ultimate concern is not with the refinements of sensory perception, he is not barred from pointing to straightforwardly physical properties of works of art, for these themselves may constitute a work's aesthetic significance. This is well brought out by Miss Ruby Meager in a paper in which she quotes some words of Norbet Lynton, reviewing an exhibition of paintings by Robert Law in 1968. Lynton wrote:[23]

213

Each colour is allowed to bleed into the next colour's field, so that there is a hint of time sequence and thus also a kind of colour hierarchy, but Law's chief concern would seem to be with the intensity of his colours; his yellows are intensely yellow, his blues richly blue.

Miss Meager points out that it is the colours themselves that are aesthetically powerful for Lynton. She goes on to imagine him before the paintings:[24]

'How intensely yellow! How richly blue!' we hear him murmuring to himself as he stands entranced. The yellowness here, the blueness, certainly *make* the paintings live, are the *reason* for, the explanation of their challenge, their aesthetic force.

Through his words Lynton invites others to look at the blueness and yellowness in Law's paintings. He does this in such a way that attention returns to them with its attitude shaped by the adverbs 'intensely' and 'richly'; the spectator has the chance to see the paintings as Lynton does, and so gain access to their significance. This kind of talk about a work is consequent upon the critic's own involvement with the work; it can lead a spectator into discussion that is undertaken not for the sake of coming to some conclusion but, as Professor Stuart Hampshire has said, 'for the sake of what one might see on the way'.[25]

This single example of how a critic may work scarcely begins to give an account of his skills. Yet it may serve to suggest the kind of guidance appropriate in an aesthetic education. One easy thing remains to be said here, and this is that there is another sort of opportunity for gaining insight into works of art in trying oneself to paint, to write, to sculpt or to compose. The possibilities of expressiveness in the various media of the arts may be more fully understood if one has worked in them oneself, striving with the difficulty of making something of clarity and meaning, something that says what one wants to say. The quality of what is produced may not be very high, but the rewards of this striving are reaped through a sensuous familiarity with the materials, the textures and the qualities fundamental to art objects. Here, too, it is an open mind and the willingness to explore that takes us forward, and which on occasion leads us to make fools of ourselves and so undergo yet another experience that is a proper part of any education.

Notes

1 Edward Bullough in E. H. Wilkinson (ed.), *Aesthetics*, London, 1957.

2 See F. Copleston, *Contemporary Philosophy*, London, 1956, pp. 145, 170.
3 Laurie Lee, 'Home from abroad', *My Many-coated Man*,
   London, 1955.
4 Ann Ridler, 'A letter', *A Little Treasure of Modern Poetry*,
   London, 1947, p. 342.
5 Philip Larkin, 'Afternoon', *The Whitsun Weddings*, London,
   1964, p. 44.
6 Several of Francis Bacon's paintings are in the Tate Gallery,
   including the 'Study of a dog'. Reproductions of the works referred
   to in this chapter may be found in Russell, *Francis Bacon*,
   London, 1964.
7 Samuel Beckett, *Waiting for Godot*, trans. Beckett, London, 1956.
8 Christopher Marlowe, *The Tragical History of Dr. Faustus*, *Plays and
   Poems of Christopher Marlowe*, London and New York, pp. 157, 158.
9 For a discussion of perspicuity as a requirement of works of art see
   J. N. Findlay, 'The Perspicuous and the poignant', *British Journal of
   Aesthetics*, vol. 1, no. 7, January 1967.
10 For a detailed discussion of the ontological status of a work of art see
   Richard Wollheim, *Art and its Objects*, New York, 1965, pp. 1–11.
11 S. Freud, 'Leonardo da Vinci, and a memory of his childhood',
   Selected Essays, 11, London, 1957. In this paper Freud interprets the
   shapes of the dark heads of the women in the painting as resembling
   a vulture which frightened Leonardo in infancy.
12 Ludwig Wittgenstein, *Philosophical Investigations*, trans. G. E. M.
   Anscombe, Oxford, 1968, 11, 4, p. 178e.
13 Gerard Manley Hopkins, 'God's Grandeur', Penguin edition, p. 27.
14 R. K. Elliott, 'Aesthetic theory and experience of art', a paper
   delivered to the Aristotelian Society, 13 February 1967.
15 *Ibid.*, p. 112.
16 *Ibid.*, p. 113.
17 Gerard Manley Hopkins, 'Heaven-Haven', Penguin edition, p. 5.
18 Philip Larkin, 'Going', *The New Poetry*, Penguin edition, 1962, p. 102.
19 Elliott, *op. cit.*, p. 114.
20 *Ibid.*, p. 115.
21 A *bricoleur* is a kind of junk man who rummages around and makes
   things out of his finds. See Wollheim, *op. cit.*, pp. 37, 131, 132.
22 Ludwig Wittgenstein, *Remarks on the Foundations of Mathematics*, *11.47*.
23 Quoted in Ruby Meager's 'Aesthetic Concepts', *British Journal of
   Aesthetics*, vol. 10, no. 4, p. 321.
24 *Ibid.*
25 Stuart Hampshire, 'Logic and appreciation' in W. Elton (ed.),
   Aesthetics and Language, Oxford, 1960, p. 165.

I 2   The problem of curriculum sequence in mathematics

Christopher Ormell

In recent years a curriculum sequence in mathematics based
essentially on the categories of mathematical logic has been
introduced into many schools. What does it mean to claim that
such a change represents a 'radical reform'? When a proposal as
radical as this is made, how can we distinguish it from
an ideology?

I. Introduction: some problems arising from curriculum reform

It is generally agreed that the subject which set the pace in the
curriculum reform movement of the last fifteen years was mathematics. An interesting research project would be to trace the spread
of current ideas about curriculum development, by stages, from
their epicentre in 'new mathematics' to a widening circle of school
groups, subjects and activities. But 'new mathematics' which has
sometimes been the envy of curriculum innovators in other fields,
has characteristic problems of its own. Many of these may be seen
to stem from the fact that the 'new mathematics' movement
acquired a striking degree of support, authority and momentum
almost as soon as it had begun. One of the penalties of such swift
success was the widespread acceptance by teachers who joined the
'new mathematics' movement of an uncritical, summary, even
naive, conception of what the curriculum change was all about.
Today the movement has reached the stage at which it is evident
that many awkward and intractable problems remain;[1] some
critics even go so far as to claim that the new scheme of things has
deficiencies of a kind, which are *different* from those of the traditional
scheme it deposed, but no less serious taken as a whole.[2] In trying to
disentangle this situation, clarity of analysis about what is wrong is
obviously the prerequisite of progress. However, there is little sign of
a sustained attempt on the part of the leading curriculum innovators
to conduct such an analysis. Those who have identified themselves
most closely with the movement, and are most aware of current
criticisms and difficulties, generally have been inclined to look for
the answer in directions like inadequate primary and nursery work,

indifferent teacher training, lack of teachers of sufficient quality, and poor teaching methods.[3]

Meanwhile the situation of a partially-successful reform—which has achieved much in terms of books used, courses started, conferences held, etc.—but which seems to have failed to have *indisputably* improved the quality of the mathematical understanding of the average youngster, remains. A few of the leading innovators have had second thoughts,[4] or have begun tentatively to re-examine points of doctrine close to the roots of the reform. Looking ahead it seems unlikely that an unresolved situation of this kind will continue indefinitely, though a substantial realignment of thinking may have to await the emergence of a new reform programme strong enough to challenge the 'new mathematics' paradigm right across the board.[5]

It seems important, therefore, to look carefully at some of the issues underlying the conceptual confusion which at present hangs around the problem of curriculum sequence in mathematics. Why is there such a degree of confusion in this area? What are the factors which generate this confusion? In a previous paper on the subject I looked at the problem mainly from the point of view of the social aspects of reform and ideology.[6] A preliminary analysis of the features of the 'new mathematics' movement led, I argued, to the notion that the doctrine of *logical sequence* lay at, or near, its centre: and a discursive survey of this doctrine presented many of the features we associate with the term 'ideology'. In the present chapter I shall attempt to carry this analysis forward by asking what it would mean to say that the proposal to adopt logical sequence is a proposal of 'radical reform'. I shall attempt to draw a contrast between 'logical sequence' and alternative views about curriculum sequence in mathematics.

II. Logical and evolutionary sequence in mathematics

'Logical sequence' may be defined as a way of ordering the main steps in a mathematical curriculum (especially in the early years) which broadly follows the hierarchy of formal concepts used by professional pure mathematicians. Such a curriculum sequence commonly begins with *sets*, and the *relationships between sets* (including equivalence).[7] The concept of *mapping* leads to that of *isomorphism* and hence to sets which are *similar*.[8] From this the concept of cardinal number can be developed. Another line of development from sets leads to *ordered sets*, *product sets*, *binary relations*, and hence to *groups*.[9]

The ideas of groups can then be (partially) applied to the operations $+$, $-$ and $\times$, $\div$ on cardinal numbers. To complete the pattern we need to construct the sets of *integers* and *rational numbers*, both of which may be defined as equivalence classes of number pairs.[10] And so on . . .

To some readers this terminology may be a meaningless jargon: but it is quite likely that their children, or younger brothers and sisters, will have encountered it, and that they already assume uncritically that this is what 'mathematics' is all about.

Many variations on the theme are possible, but the level of discussion on which we are engaged is very general; it is enough to say that the main arguments will apply with equal force to a wide range of syllabuses of this kind. When one calls such a scheme of learning a logical sequentialist 'curriculum sequence' one uses the term to cover situations in which, for example, the concepts of 'set', 'mapping', 'relation', 'ordered pair', 'isomorphism' are introduced prior to (and as a prerequisite to) the introduction of fractions. In practice, a curriculum scheme of this kind can be defined by a precedence diagram which allows the teacher a considerable degree of freedom in selecting his or her teaching sequence. And it is not necessary for us to define precisely *which* collections of concepts are to count as belonging to such a scheme. For example, a curriculum based on the same kind of approach using Polish notation[11] (in place of the intuitive notation) for operations will be of the same *general kind* as that sketched above.

It needs little special knowledge of mathematics to see that this kind of mathematical curriculum is quite different from one based on the traditional curriculum sequence—in which natural numbers are first added, subtracted, divided, multiplied; in which work is then done on fractions, decimals, money sums, mensuration, etc. Here, too, many variations are possible, and—at least in the hands of good teachers—the main topics are usually extensively enriched with cognate activities such as measuring, map making, solving puzzles, descriptive drawing and geometry, model making, etc.

This kind of approach may be said to embody *evolutionary sequence*, since it roughly retraces the main steps by which mankind has painfully acquired its mathematical concepts.

Few curriculum schemes in England can be said to be wholly logical sequentialist in character. Indeed, one of the strengths of curriculum reform in England has been the development, within a broadly child-centred framework, of apparatus, practical work and concrete illustration in the early years.[12] Many schemes, probably the vast majority, are hybrids, composed of elements of both logical and evolutionary sequence.

Another point may be mentioned. Some secondary projects offer curricula which, apparently writing off most of what the child has learnt before 11 +, begin a fairly straightforward logical sequentialist curriculum at 11 +. This may be called 'delayed logical sequence'. Other projects delay logical sequence (in effect) to the sixth form stage (16–18).[13] Thus in England compromises have been struck between the two main types of curriculum sequence. There are relatively few here who would accord logical sequence the kind of unqualified acceptance it enjoys in some circles on the Continent and in the United States.

This should not be taken to imply that logical sequence is a negligible force as a curriculum idea in England. It is, on the contrary, a potent force, held in check only by the realism and good sense of the teachers and the curriculum innovators. Many teachers feel that they *ought* to weave in as much of the logical sequentialist material as possible; though the limitations of their pupils' capacity (for abstraction) necessitate some straying from this rather stony path of virtue.

III. Radical reform versus ideology

To say that the doctrine of logical sequence is an 'ideology' is of course to make a pejorative comment on it. The gist of the comment is that it is unrealistic: that those who accept and promote it see the situation in a stereotyped way which leads them to oversimplify issues and to fail to respond sensitively and constructively to the scale and quality of the competences, insights and responses actually generated by children in the classroom. The danger of an ideology is the danger of a leviathan which plunges ahead blindly, because no effective channel of communication exists which could lead those in command to reverse engines. In the case of the doctrine of logical sequence the danger is that those who accept it may see the strategy of logical sequence, not as a hypothesis, but as being beyond criticism 'because it embodies the structure of modern mathematics'. Some evidence that this is in fact the way in which many logical sequentialists see their position was adumbrated in my previous paper.[14]

The danger springing from the lack of sensitivity implied by the criticism is that teachers imbued with an absolute conviction of the rightness of logical sequence will impose this view on their classes and will fail to see—or at least fail to recognize as significant—signs of dwindling understanding, motivation, and involvement.[15]

It is possible to believe that logical sequence is the best curriculum sequence for mathematics, and to argue that it will produce in those who follow it a clearer understanding of mathematics, a greater appreciation of the subject and a new creative style of work.

Presented in this way it begins to sound much more like a 'radical reform programme'. What, then, is the difference between logical sequence as an ideology, and logical sequence as a radical reform programme?

The answer is that in the latter case it is not being held that logical sequence is beyond argument; what is implied is that logical sequence has beneficial results, viz. clearer understanding, greater appreciation, increased creativity. ... So here some feedback channels are being allowed. *If* it became clear that youngsters were *not* acquiring a clearer understanding, a greater appreciation, etc., the logical consequence of this would be that the hypothesis underlying the reform was mistaken.

Some uncompromising logical sequentialists profess to hold their view of logical sequence, in the approved manner, as a radical reform programme. The issue, 'ideology versus radical reform', having been brought into the open, they are hardly likely to opt for ideology! And to support their position they tend to make claims like those listed above. But ... when it comes to putting these claims to the test it soon becomes apparent that it is logical sequentialist criteria which they propose to employ. If the test employed for detecting 'clearer understanding' is one which rates an imperfect grasp of the structural hierarchy above lucid exposition of intuitive ideas, the issue is never really going to be in doubt. If this is the kind of test to be employed, the notion that the claim 'that logical sequence promotes clearer understanding' is an earnest of its non-ideological character is seen to be a chimera. That logical sequence—effectively used—promotes clearer understanding is a tautology, if we mean by 'clearer understanding' a degree of awareness of logical sequence.[16]

In other words a conceptual mesmerism with logical sequence, as the panacea for some of the more deep-seated difficulties of mathematical education,[17] can manifest itself in sophisticated as well as simplistic forms. It is possible for a logical sequentialist to convince himself that he is a reformer rather than an ideologist, and yet fail to see that the tests he proposes to establish empirical content are pseudo-tests. The danger of this sophisticated form of ideology is the same as that of the simplistic one: that no channel of genuine feedback has been allowed. It appears that the reform doctrine is open to confrontation with reality: but under closer inspection we see that these channels are individually subtly blocked. The danger of the leviathan blundering on, regardless of the inappropriateness of the curriculum to the actual needs and strengths of real children, remains.

IV. Logical sequence as 'modern mathematics'

Clearly the study of philosophy is concerned to a great degree with freeing ourselves from the mesmeric effect of certain powerful one-sided generalizations.[18] The doctrine of logical sequence possibly presents us with a prime, substantial, 'live' example of such conceptual mesmerism. It may be that a large-scale outbreak of conceptual mesmerism occurred in 1957 with the launching of the 'new mathematics' movement. On the other hand it may be said that opposition to the logical sequentialist position is itself a form of conceptual mesmerism, and that the doctrine of logical sequence is a harmless, inevitable adjustment of mathematical curricula to bring them into line with the best modern thinking about mathematics. This argument leads us to the point of view that modern mathematical criteria will 'of course' be applied to determine whether the expected beneficial results of the new curricula are being realized: should those who are prompting the new syllabuses deliberately renounce modern ideas and re-embrace old-fashioned ideas about mathematics, before judging the outcomes of the new curricula?

This question itself embodies a typical example of the kind of rhetoric frequently employed in the current situation. It presumes that the doctrine of logical sequence is one which reflects modern ideas about mathematics, while evolutionary sequence reflects old-fashioned ideas. The question therefore arises as to what degree an acceptance of modern ideas about mathematics entails the logical sequentialist position. The same question is implicit in judging the results of logical sequentialist courses by 'modern mathematical criteria'. Do 'modern mathematical criteria' entail a logical sequentialist point of view?[19]

Many theorists assume that the answer to these questions is that the entailment clearly exists. Indeed we may infer that many hardly consider that any discussion of the connection is needed, the issue being apparently so self-evident. Yet one may question whether the issue really is as simple as this.

In the first place it may be questioned whether the term 'modern mathematics' is sufficiently clear, definite and objective to act as a starting point for satisfactory discussion, that is, to enable us to define exactly *what* is being maintained.

In the second place it is unclear why such importance should be attached to *modernity*. Mathematics, it might be argued, is the one subject (with logic) in which the truths are eternally true, and in which the practitioners may be expected to be least susceptible to the temptations of current fashion.

In the third place, even if an identification of, say, the Bourbakist treatment of pure mathematics[20] and 'modern mathematics' could be established, it is far from clear that this entails that we should adopt a particular strategy for promoting conceptual development. Surely the best way to find out how to lead youngsters to identify with a particular kind of mathematical purpose, and to achieve the greatest assimilation of a particular kind of mathematical material, is to consult the actual accumulated experience of educators and psychologists.[21] It can hardly be analytic that the shortest distance from A to B is also the quickest way to get there. Yet it appears that such a naive choice of strategy underlies, and is implicit in, the logical sequentialist position.

In the fourth place even if an entailment could be established between 'modern mathematical ideas' and 'logical sequence', it is not self-evident that the social purpose of mathematical education is identical with the achievement of these ideas.[22] It may be that the reason why society insists on youngsters receiving as much mathematical education as they can take, is *not* that it desires to promote 'mathematics' for its own sake, but as a *means* to their personal numeracy, and as a basis for their future studies in economics, engineering, science, etc.[23] Certainly these aims have been widely canvassed in the past. It is far from clear that they can be dismissed with a wave of the hand, or that the *raison d'être* of a mathematical education is to study mathematics as an end in itself.

We turn now to consider these points in more detail.

(1) The term 'modern mathematics' and its variants seem to embody the claim that there is a unique, structured body of mathematics which can be called 'modern mathematics' and which is justified in calling itself this. There *is* a unique, structured body of mathematics (defined by its use of formalization, axiomatics and semi-formal meta-language) but it is far from clear that we are justified in calling this body of thinking and material 'modern mathematics' without further qualification. If we do so we imply that it is the *only* body of mathematics which could possibly be a serious claimant for the title. But it is not. There is another body of mathematics, which may be called 'computer-based applicable mathematics' which is identifiable by its use of mathematics to model situations and thereby to explore their predictable implications.[24] There is a certain degree of overlap between the two bodies of mathematics (e.g. in linear algebra) but by and large they are pursued by different people,[25] with different purposes,[26] and with the aid of different styles of formalization,[27] manipulation[28] and meta-mathematical discussion.[29]

It therefore begs the question to pre-empt the title 'modern mathematics' for the first group and to deny it to the second. Some theorists argue that the first body of mathematics is more 'fundamental', more unified in ideas and method, and more substantial in weight, than the second. But against this it can be argued that the second body of mathematics is less artificial, embodies a clearer sense of purpose, employs a more powerful executive instrument (the computer) and is infinitely more useful, than the first. These arguments may be reasonably held to cancel out, and to justify the general use of two distinct terms 'modern abstract mathematics' and 'modern applicable mathematics' to cover the two areas.[30]

(2) Is modernity important? In the rhetoric of the logical sequentialist movement the contrast between 'modern' and 'old-fashioned' notions of mathematics is frequently drawn: and clearly this kind of rhetoric exerts a pressure. The question therefore arises whether this pressure is a mischievous or a genuine one; whether it is based on values which are, in the last analysis, relevant to the case, or not. It is clear enough that there is no virtue in including material in a mathematical curriculum just because it is modern, nor in excluding material just because it was discovered a long time ago. Fragments of modern mathematics presented out of context might easily upset the youngster's conceptual digestion,[31] whilst the omission of age-old ideas like algorithm, axiom, zero, proof, would hardly recommend itself to anyone.

What, then, is the meaning of the recurrent reference to modernity in the logical sequentialist rhetoric? It seems clear that this rhetoric exerts a pressure on the average teacher, headmaster, board of governors, education officer, etc. How does the pressure arise? The answer seems to be that the teacher who is not teaching 'modern mathematics' risks—it is implied—being left behind by the march of progress. The telling aspect of the aggressive reiteration of the *modernity* of the new curricula is not primarily its reference to the content of the courses, but to the style of the material, the concepts and language used, and the method of organization.[32] Taken together these features of the material do, or seem to, provide access to a central body of modern thinking possessing inexorable power.

(3) The notion that *if* we are agreed that an initiation into modern abstract mathematics is the objective of mathematical education, *then* we must necessarily choose a logical sequentialist strategy, is very odd, It seems to reflect a judgment of the nature of the task of education which overlooks some important factors which operate at the local level. The main factor it overlooks is the need for a credible form of motivation. How are the sophisticated mental styles and purposes of modern abstract mathematics to be woven into the homespun fabric of thinking which the youngster acquires from his

general experience? It is sometimes said at this point that making the material fully palatable is, of course, the main pedagogic problem facing the new mathematics curriculum. Following this it is claimed that, with the passage of time, teachers will find ways of blending the material into the fare of ordinary thinking and so generate the required motivation. But this overlooks the fact that the 'fare of ordinary thinking' has qualities which are contradictory to those of the mathematical material.[33] If such a 'blending of opposites' creates a temporary motivation by suggesting the involvement of this kind of mathematics in life, technology and science, it must lead inevitably, sooner or later, to a crisis of credibility: does the presentation reflect the inner purpose of the material or not? This poses the movement with a dilemma: either to develop the involvement, and so move gradually away from the original logical sequentialist blueprint, or to let it lapse by degrees, and disappoint the hopes originally raised.

In other words to present modern abstract mathematics to the youngster via its involvement in elementary applications is to fail Bruner's test that the reduction exercise should result in an 'intellectually honest' treatment. The essence of the modern abstract approach to mathematics is that one pays virtually no attention to the modes of thought needed to grasp and thoroughly understand empirical situations,[34] but concentrates on the clean-cut logic of the internal isomorphisms of the structure of mathematics.

The logical sequentialist programme is, however, only one strategy for producing an awareness of modern abstract mathematics at 16+, 18+, or 21. It is a comparatively rigid one.[35] It provides the teacher with little room for manoeuvre, since it lays down the main steps to be taken in building up the awareness. But it is not the only possible route to the objective. The mathematicians who developed modern abstract mathematics were, after all, themselves educated by teachers who followed traditional evolutionary sequence. In most cases the curriculum sequence was 'evolutionary' up to first degree level, and only at the post-graduate stage did the serious study of the internal isomorphisms of mathematics arise. In England 'modern abstract mathematics' was not found in many first degree courses prior to 1945, and after that it was some years before it could be found in the courses offered in all the universities. Yet there is no doubt that this very roundabout approach to modern abstract mathematics was successful for a majority of the few who followed it, i.e. undergraduate mathematics specialists.[36] It was from among their ranks that many of the teachers were drawn who were later persuaded to introduce modern abstract material into the school course.

We know, therefore, that logical sequence is not the only way to educate mathematically-talented youngsters to achieve an awareness of abstract modern mathematics at 21. It is possible to reach the same end-point at 21 via an evolutionary course. And since the questions which modern abstract mathematics was developed to answer are implicit in the mathematics of the eighteenth and nineteenth centuries[37] it may be argued that an evolutionary sequence is the *best* way to reach the objective.

On the other hand, whether a satisfactory awareness[38] of abstract modern mathematics can be achieved by *any* route at $18+$ or $16+$ is open to doubt.[39] But supposing that it is possible, it would be surprising if logical sequence were the only way to do it. Any scheme of education which provides answers to questions which have not been allowed to emerge and establish themselves in the youngster's mind as *real* questions is likely to encounter difficulties. From this it may be argued that the stage which should ideally precede the abstract modern approach is a stage based on a sample of the calculus, algebra and co-ordinate geometry of the eighteenth and nineteenth centuries. But to reach the preliminary stage we can hardly avoid some form of evolutionary sequence.

The essence of the matter is that logical sequence has qualities which strongly appeal to many adult professional mathematicians, and which seem to them to provide a very straightforward logical scheme of work for the youngster to follow. The question is whether those who appreciate the qualities have also had sufficient insight to realize that it, or any other scheme of mathematical education, looks extremely different from the youngster's point of view. The qualities of economy, elegance, precision, rigour and abstraction, which appeal so strongly to the adult, are in fact ones which carry little weight in the mental framework of the youngster.[40] If—as much of the evidence indicates—logical sequentialists believe that logical sequence is 'necessary', on the grounds that it embodies these qualities, the belief is a complete mistake. The embodiment of these qualities, far from guaranteeing the 'necessity' of the sequence, makes it an extremely difficult sequence to follow.

It can be held that, contrary to appearances, the strategy of logical sequence works. To establish this one would have to point to empirical evidence, such as groups of youngsters who had acquired impressive degrees of conceptual facility, problem-solving capability, etc. after following such a scheme.[41] But in the act of marshalling such evidence one would implicitly retract the claim that logical sequence is 'necessary'.

(4) Even if abstract modern mathematics were the only respectable variety of modern mathematics, it is not clear that there is an

a priori need for youngsters to acquire an awareness of this at a certain academic level. In other words, even if one accepted all the premises of the logical sequentialist case, the question remains how far the average youngster should be expected to go along this road, or whether he should travel on a different road.

What is the underlying reason why mathematics has been, and is, so strongly represented in the school curriculum? It can be argued, with reason, that it is that mathematics is the chief *integrative* subject in the curriculum, and that it is needed mainly, in the first instance, to provide access to the study of all sciences and technologies.[42]

This point of view may be challenged. But whatever the underlying reason, it is far from obvious that the 'reason' applies equally to the old syllabus and the new.[43] One can argue therefore that *even if* logical sequence were 'necessary' as a route to modern abstract mathematics, it has not been established that any of the points on the logical sequentialist route reflect the kind of mental equipment society previously promoted school mathematics to provide. One might say that what society needs in the school syllabus, is not 'mathematics' in the pure sense indicated above, but an *im*pure variety, such as 'elementary intuitive mathematics' or 'elementary applicable mathematics'.[44]

The conclusion of this part of the argument is therefore that the logical sequentialist case—as it has been commonly presented—hinges to a great extent on what seem to be verbally deceptive and epistemologically misleading arguments. It may be that a good case can be made out for the logical sequentialist position. But such a case will not imply that modern abstract mathematics is the only direction of progress for modern mathematics, that the modernity of the material is a major relevant factor, that logical sequence is 'necessarily' the only way to approach modern abstract mathematics, or that the justification for inflicting *n* hours of mathematics per week on the average youngster must necessarily apply unchanged to the new curriculum.

V. Logical sequence as radical reform

The burden of this chapter has been that the doctrine of logical sequence is not a minor internal adjustment of school mathematics syllabuses, but a major, daring educational/psychological hypothesis. It is clearly important that such a hypothesis should be put to the test. The only caveat one would wish put in here is that we should not be blinded by the heady nature of the enterprise into applying the test inadequately, or prejudging the answer. We need to look much more soberly than we have hitherto done at precisely *what* tests are appropriate to the case; at what signs and evidences we should seek out and scrutinize. This means, in effect, rethinking the logical sequentialist movement as a radical reform movement. By asking ourselves what we expect of a radical reform movement in general we can equip ourselves with a yardstick against which to measure the logical sequentialist movement.

One expects of a radical reform movement, first, that it presents a weighty preliminary case, both in terms of empirical evidence and in terms of the central body of theoretical insights available in the discipline. The greater the change which the reform involves the greater the 'weight' needed in the preliminary case. In the instance of logical sequence one expects both a clearly argued, cogent analysis of the motivational advantages which can be expected to flow from adopting a value system within which qualities like economy, elegance, abstraction, precision, rigour are promoted to an unusual pre-eminence, and also extensive empirical evidence that the analysis is correct. If, as in the present case, the analysis is counter-intuitive, it is all the more important that the empirical case should be established.

One expects, second, that a radical reform movement should operate in an open way, looking carefully at reasoned criticisms, alleged counter-examples and difficulties. Its leadership should eschew doctrinaire attitudes and remind itself as often as possible that truth is hard to come by—that it is rare for any single group to possess its monopoly.

One expects, third, that fundamental changes in objectives should be justified by reasoned arguments which take into account the full range of the repercussions the changes are likely to entail; and that, in particular, a dialogue should be conducted with those who will be, or believe that they may be, adversely affected by the change.[45]

One expects, fourth, that a thorough evaluation should be carried out to ascertain whether the effects of the change have been, in fact, those which were predicted.

This is a brief summary of the rules we expect a radical reform movement to follow. To say that the logical sequentialist movement '*is* a radical reform movement' is to say that it does observe these rules.

When we begin to apply three of the above rules in the present instance we find ourselves concerned with 'the empirical case', 'the truth' and 'whether the effects have in fact been those . . .' And here we face a central difficulty: *how* to determine 'the empirical case' objectively; *how* to assess whether the expected results have materialized. At this point we come across a phenomenon similar to that which Lakatos has described in detail in relation to scientific research programmes.[46] Those who are committed to a certain scientific hypothesis naturally prefer to deal with awkward or ambivalent evidence in the first instance by protecting their hypothesis. In the same way those who firmly believe in a curriculum hypothesis, such as logical sequence, may be expected to protect their hypothesis and to put the blame for any apparently adverse results on to other factors. It would be a feeble form of radical reform which abandoned its position at the first whiff of grapeshot. If society is not satisfied with these protective explanations it is up to society to put the reformers in the position where they are obliged—to re-establish credibility—to restate their claims in clear, definite, verifiable terms. Society can put pressure on a questionable radical movement in order that it may see whether the movement's hypothesis is in a progressive, or a deteriorating, problem shift.[47] When one says that 'it may see whether', one means that a set of claims has been made previously for which the reformers have admitted that they are accountable. No such claims, of course, are ever completely well defined: there are always likely to be unforeseen factors which intervene. Nevertheless, over a period of time a mass of *definite* predictions can be checked against performances. It can be seen that some failed predictions do not count, because of the presence or absence of known or postulated factors. It can be seen whether the problem shift has acquired a definite momentum in the 'progressive' direction, or whether it has lost momentum and is visibly deteriorating.

The essential difference between the straightforward case of a scientific research programme and the development programme of a curriculum reform movement is that in the latter case there is no automatic commitment of the innovators to make verifiable claims. It is up to society to insist that radical curriculum reform movements progressively redefine their aims in verifiable particulars, ensuring that a problem shift occurs, and bringing the results into the objective domain where the quality of the problem shift can be publicly inspected and discussed. Some commentators have remarked that it is odd that logical sequentialists should confidently claim that their courses promote a deeper understanding of mathematics, yet refuse to allow that this deep understanding can be expected to materialize in the form of definite skills and pattern recognitions. It is tempting, of course, for a movement of radical curriculum change to operate under ideological, rather than under radical reformist, rules; it makes life easier for the participants. But such movements can operate in the long run under ideological rules only while society allows them to do so; in other words when and whilst it is unaware that its own general interest is involved.

In the last fifteen years the logical sequentialist movement has enjoyed what may appear in retrospect as a long honeymoon, during which it has been virtually free from serious criticism. The time is now, however, overdue when we should begin to ask searching questions of the movement: questions which, if they win sufficient support, should tend to edge the movement away from its ideological stance, towards the more open stance of radical reform. The main reason for recommending this is, of course, that the education of a whole generation of the world's most intelligent children is too important to be left to the whims of an unchallenged ideology. A subsidiary reason is that much of the groundwork has now been done on an alternative style of mathematical education, placing its emphasis on intuitive understanding, imagination, application to new situations, manipulative confidence and evolutionary sequence.[48] This may also claim to be a form of 'modern mathematics', thus making clear, by concrete example, that modernity alone is not enough, and undermining the premise implicit in much discussion of the situation, 'that there is no up-to-date alternative'. Finally, the situation itself is surely one of considerable interest to the student of the persuasibility of human nature. Here is a live, contemporary issue in which *either* the case for the 'reform', *or* the case against, must reflect an extreme form of conceptual mesmerism. And challenging conceptual mesmerism of all kinds is, at least a major part of, what philosophy is all about.

Notes and references

1 That there are 'problems' for the movement is self-evident. Whether they are appropriately described as 'awkward' or 'intractable' is open to dispute (because it seems to imply a vote of no confidence in the movement). For a discussion of difficulties in relation to teaching see D. H. Wheeler, 'The role of the teacher', *Math. Teaching*, 50, 1970, pp. 23–9. Wheeler says on p. 23: 'Judging by results rather than intentions—and what else is there to go by?—SMP and Leicestershire primary schools, say, move us an inch when we need to go a mile.'

2 Some articles which are critical of 'new mathematics' on general grounds are the following: Morris Kline, 'Logic versus pedagogy', *American Math. Monthly*, 77, 1970, pp. 264–82; J. M. Hammersley, 'On the enfeeblement of mathematical skills . . .', *Bull. Inst. Math. Appl.*, 4, 4, 1968, pp. 3–22; D. B. Scott, 'The modish maths', *Advancement of Science*, 44, 1968, pp. 135–42.

3 See, for example, *The First Report on the Supply of Teachers*, I.M.A., 1969. Also D. H. Wheeler, *op. cit.*

4 See, for example, J. M. Hammersley, *op. cit.* and M. Beberman 'UICSM looks at elementary school mathematics', *Math. Teaching*,

55, pp. 26–8. Beberman says (p. 28): 'I now think that it is a fallacy of mathematics curriculum development *for young children* that logical organisation of the subject determines its pedagogical organisation'. (Author's italics.)

5 Using Kuhnian terminology. See T. S. Kuhn, *The Structure of Scientific Revolutions*, Chicago, 1962.

6 See C. P. Ormell, 'Ideology and the reform of school mathematics', *Philosophy of Education Society of Great Britain*, vol. 3, 1969, pp. 37–54. For a reply by Dr W. M. Elliott see *op. cit.*, pp. 55–65.

7 A set of objects is, in ordinary language, a 'collection' of objects. A set of biscuits, B, can be discussed mathematically without mentioning the number of biscuits in the set. For example, if B contains a mixture of plain and chocolate biscuits and if C is the set of chocolate biscuits, C is a subset of B. This is written $B \supset C$.

8 Sets are 'similar' when their elements can be put into 1–1 correspondence; in ordinary language, when the elements of the first set can be *paired off* with the elements of the second. If the sets happen to be finite, this entails that they have the same number of elements. For example, the set of Wonders of the World is similar to the set of Days of the Week. If the sets are infinite we can have the odd situation of a set being similar to one of its own subsets. The set of even natural numbers is similar to the set of natural numbers, because we can pair them off like this:

$$
\begin{array}{ccccccccc}
1 & 2 & 3 & 4 & 5 & 6 & 7 & 8 & \ldots \\
\updownarrow & \updownarrow & \updownarrow & \updownarrow & \updownarrow & \updownarrow & \updownarrow & \updownarrow \\
2 & 4 & 6 & 8 & 10 & 12 & 14 & 16 & \ldots
\end{array}
$$

The kind of curriculum issue which arises here is whether, in the interests of mathematical generality, we should introduce children to similarity as the basic concept first, or whether, in the interests of practical understanding, we should limit the area of interest in the early years to finite cases. If the latter we allow ourselves to talk in an uncomplicated way about the number of Wonders of the World and Days of the Week being the same: if the former, we insist that these numbers are equal *because* the sets are similar.

9 A *group* may be regarded as a set of operations of a certain kind. For example, the set of permutations of the names

(Tom, Dick, Harry)

forms a group.

If X represents the operation 'put the first name at the end, and move the other names up one place each' we can see that doing this three times (XXX or X^3) leaves the set unaltered. So we write

$$X^3 = 1.$$

Also $X^4 = X$. This leads to the idea of an algebra of group operations. Another operation in this group, Y, can be defined as 'exchange the second and third names'. It can be shown that $(XY)^2 = 1$.

10 For example, 3/5 can be written as (3,5), representing an *ordered set* of two natural numbers. (6,10) and (36,60) are also ordered sets and the set of all ordered sets of the form (3k,5k) is called an 'equivalence class'. This equivalence class can be regarded as a precise definition of 3/5. Should we introduce fractions to children in an intuitive way with reference to simple images (like slices of a cake), or should we insist that the only way to understand fractions 'properly' is via this fairly sophisticated modern scholasticism?

11 In Polish notation $3+5$ is written $+3,5$: the operations prefix the operands. There are advantages in using this notation in some contexts in formal logic and in designing computer languages.

12 So much so that the theme of 'relevance of the environment' is the dominant theme in some schemes at the primary stage which are commonly described as 'modern mathematics'. Another point arising here is that many evolutionary sequentialists accept that certain words such as 'set', 'mapping', 'space', and certain symbols such as '$\Rightarrow$', '$\exists$', '$\cap$', can be very useful in a minor but not delimited *instrumental role* from such time as the need occurs.

13 An example of this is the MEI project which has not so far developed a syllabus below the $15+$ level.

14 C. Ormell, *op. cit.*, pp. 45-6.

15 Assuming that such symptoms occurred in the first place.

16 Assuming that the programme is not a *total* failure.

17 Particularly a lack of logical sensibility among ex-mathematical sixth formers.

18 Some of the special features of *ideologies* as one-sided generalizations are discussed in my previous paper, *op. cit.*, pp. 40-1.

19 I.e. if one accepts modern criteria about what 'counts as mathematics' is one committed to a logical sequentialist curriculum strategy?

20 The 'Bourbakist treatment' is that of a group of French academic mathematicians who set out to write a unified account of the main branches of mathematics under the *nom-de-plume* 'N. Bourbaki'.

21 Some psychologists have convinced themselves on *a priori* grounds that logical sequence has psychological advantages. We may, however, distinguish between this *a prioristic* psychological theorizing and the 'accumulated experience' of educators and psychologists.

22 I.e. with the acquisition of these ideas (and some fluency of use) by a fair proportion of each cohort.

23 Not necessarily actual. To have studied mathematics to a certain level safeguards the option of further study in these fields.

24 See, for example, 'Mathematics in the community', *Int. J. Math. Educ. Sci. Tech.*, 3, 1972.

25 See, for example, J. Heading, 'Revival in applied mathematics', *Bull. Inst. Math. Appl.*, 7, 1971, pp. 262-8.

26 See W. W. Sawyer, *A Path to Modern Mathematics*, Penguin, 1966, Introduction, p. 11. Sawyer says: 'In some countries, at an early stage in the educational debate, mathematicians have been asked what

they thought important, and it seems to have been assumed that their answers would automatically provide material relevant to the problems of industry and attractive to young children. But the evidence for this mystic harmony is hard to find. Indeed there is considerable evidence in the opposite direction.'

27 These styles are sometimes referred to as the 'highbrow' and the 'lowbrow'. See W. W. Sawyer, *op. cit.*, pp. 17–18, for a defence of the 'lowbrow' functional notation.

28 I.e. manipulation by computer programme, including the use of heuristic and 'non-rigorous' methods. See J. M. Hammersley, *op. cit.*

29 In the one case, the discussion is mainly concerned with the security of the deductive logic used: in the other, with the security of the inductive logic on which the model rests. See C. P. Ormell, 'Mathematics, science of possibility', *Int. J. Math. Educ. Sci. Tech.*, 3, 1972, pp. 329–41.

30 Similarly 'new abstract mathematics' and 'new applicable mathematics'.

31 That there is such a thing is not always recognized. Some theorists talk as if it were impossible to upset the youngster's conceptual digestion: that every approach will do some good. The admitted failure of some early experiments in logical sequence must however suggest to even the most sceptical observer the possibility of digestive upset.

32 This remark applies particularly to the situation in some courses in which a considerable part of the previous *content* remains in the syllabus. It is, however, treated in a very different way. It is this factor which tends to generate the feeling of a closed 'society of the initiated' and the implied threat of exclusion from this 'society'.

33 For example, imprecision, low level of generality, complexity, unpredictability. See M. Kline, *op. cit.*

34 This of course results from the fact that its objective is mainly internal security and organization, not external application.

35 That is, in comparison with evolutionary sequence.

36 'Successful' in the sense that a high proportion did assimilate the new ideas, in spite of a lack of well-written elementary texts.

37 See W. W. Sawyer, *op. cit.*, pp. 8–9. Sawyer says, p. 8: 'To present the mathematics of this century without any reference to the previous century is like presenting the third act of a play without any explanation of what is supposed to have happened in the first two acts.'

38 This is difficult to define, but most modern mathematicians would concede that if one considers a succession of less and less competent students there comes a point at which one finds a threadbare grasp of modern concepts which has virtually no value. (It is in this kind of recognition that the greatest hope of breaking the closed circuit of justifications associated with logical sequence lies.) A 'satisfactory awareness' will be one which is clearly better than this.

39 There is no *a priori* reason why it should be possible to accelerate the

average youngster's maturity of outlook sufficiently to do this. To expect to be able to do it *may* be as unreasonable as to expect a a three-minute mile.

40 The underlying point here is that these qualities in the material are, for the youngster, insufficiently grounded in his or her own experience. The youngster does not know enough about either intuitive mathematics or high level academic purposes to see just how 'elegant', 'economical', 'precise', etc. the new style of material is, at least in relation to these purposes. (In relation to utility many would say that the material is over-elegant, over-economical, over-precise.) The 'lack of insight' referred to in the text is a failure to see this situation in perspective, i.e. to see that, in the absence of the familiarities and the purposes, the youngster experiences the learning situation as an imposition of factual and value judgments.

41 It is not generally realized how little evidence of this kind has been produced. D. H. Wheeler's (*op. cit.*) comparison of intentions (a mile) to achievements (an inch) is not of course intended to be taken literally, but it does reflect the kind of gap which exists.

42 This does not presuppose that every youngster will want to study these subjects beyond *n* years, but only that the possibility of her or his doing this should be left open.

43 Other reasons for the presence of mathematics in the curriculum are its effect on stabilizing the imagination, and the need for all children to appreciate the role of mathematics in the development of scientific theories and technologies.

44 'Impure' of course carries an emotive overtone. 'Integrated mathematics' as opposed to 'dissociated mathematics' is another way to talk about the same issue.

45 The absence of such a dialogue between the mathematicians and the physicists has led many physicists in England to feel that the mathematics syllabus has become less helpful to the physicist than it used to be.

46 See Imre Lakatos, 'Criticism and the methodology of scientific research programmes', *Proc. Arist. Soc.*, 69, 1969, pp. 149–86.

47 This is a term defined by Lakatos (*ibid.*) which is very useful. A 'progressive problem shift' is roughly one which increases the credibility of the programme.

48 See, for example, M. Kline, 'A proposal for the high school mathematics curriculum', *Math. Teacher*, 59, 1966, pp. 322–30; C. P. Ormell, 'Mathematics through the imagination', *Dialogue*, 9, 1971, pp. 10–11; F. L. Knowles, 'An approach to applicable mathematics', *Mathematics Teaching*, 56, 1971, pp. 50–3.

I3   Philosophy of education and the place of science in the curriculum

P. H. Nidditch

1.1. In this chapter I shall, after dwelling on a number of other germane matters, move forward to raise and arrange a selection of questions and of possible answers about the study of science in secondary schools and universities, and in other educational institutions and settings that offer values similar in kind to theirs. For simplicity and definiteness I shall largely limit myself to English[1] conditions; there are, I recognize, other, and more varied, possible frameworks and contexts. The reader can go quite a long way towards overcoming the limitations of my presentation by taking seriously the select bibliography which I have appended at the end; this bibliography should be regarded as an integral part of the contents of this chapter: the discourse that precedes it can hardly be more than a foreword to such further reading—prolegomena to the philosophy of education concerning science.

2.1. I want, to start with, to indicate my conception of philosophy in general, and also of philosophy of education; these remarks will serve to explain my view of the province of academic philosophy of education concerning science, my subsequent approach to the topic of science education, and how I view the status of judgments in discussing this topic.

2.2. I distinguish between the discipline of philosophy ('disciplinary philosophy') and other sorts of philosophical exploration and assertion. Disciplinary philosophy is comparable in its standards to the generally acknowledged canons guiding practice throughout scholarship and science, for example respecting concern for evidence, possible counter-considerations, accuracy, and stringency of argument; associated with these canons is the quest to assist the Advancement of Learning. Other sorts of philosophy involve the rejection or distortion of some of these standards. Instances of them may—some, I think, do—have estimable values of their own, but they are not academic values. Their pursuit, except as recreation, should therefore be left outside academic institutions along with that of the creative arts.[2] It is deleterious to confound logic and *Wissenschaft* with expressionism and vague *apriorism* (i.e. reasoning from non-mathematical notions to their causes, conditions, or consequences too much on the basis of abstract assumptions and by too little reference to the empirical).

2.3. Such expressionism and *apriorism* may take the form of systematic speculation and asseveration, or of conceptual analysis. The latter was perhaps first methodized, and methodologized, by Ramus in the sixteenth century: much in the recent phase of Anglo-American philosophy can usefully be understood as Neo-Ramism.[3, 4]

> Like a non-Ramist, to find 'arguments' a Ramist went to the headings furnished by dialectic—genus, properties, whole, parts, conjugates, and so on—but he characteristically thought of these as implementing a 'logical analysis' of a subject, enabling him to draw material out of the subject itself. The Ramist felt less need to rely on the collections of material culled from authors in commonplace books, for he thought of himself as securing his arguments from the 'nature of things', with which his mind somehow came into direct contact. Thus he felt he would find arguments against disloyalty by simply understanding disloyalty and 'analyzing' its genus, species, conjugates, and the rest, rather than by finding under the headings of the various 'places' what had been said about it.

The Neo-Ramism of today does not, like its forerunner, contrast 'analysis' with the citation of authors; its mode of 'analysis' is to be contrasted with what is functionally analogous to such citation: a due consideration of actual or possible empirical evidence. Ramism constituted a step—although more a kick than a pace—towards the empiricism (in the sense of concern for evidence) first apparent in modern times in the generation of Bacon, Galileo, and Kepler: the Ramist rejection of external authorities helped to clear a way for the rise of an empiricist method, for which Ramism's cognitive vacuousness still left a crucial gap. But Neo-Ramism seems to serve no purgative purpose. And its complacent *aprioristic* doctrine 'that all the evidence which bears upon [philosophers'] problems is already available to them'[5]—to quote the words of a distinguished adherent —is hardly compatible with an empiricist method. For arguments have contexts that change through changes of circumstance and consciousness, and so do concepts and their constellations; and in at least many important cases alertness to contents and developments of activities and disciplines outside philosophical reflection as such is materially relevant to an understanding and evaluation of arguments and concepts. For instance, the past record shows that philosophical reflection on 'the ordinary concept of matter' or 'the ordinary concept of probability' yields nothing for the Advancement of

Learning in comparison with the work of the physical scientist and the mathematical probabilist or statistician. Rather than being inward-looking very much, philosophy should be outward-bound.[6]

2.4. The chief business of disciplinary philosophy, as I see it, is, first, the history of cognitive ideas and methods; adjoined to which is the history of philosophical epistemology, and of educational thought and systems, pertaining to such ideas and methods; and, second, Logic (the logics of deduction and empirical enquiry), which is, partly and roughly, what used to be designated as 'deductive and inductive logic', dealing with all fields of investigation, and their statement-making, to which public rules and evidence are directly and powerfully relevant, e.g. natural science, technology, geography, history, and comparative and historical linguistics; and partly the evaluative application of the principles and techniques of the logics of deduction and enquiry to particular areas and types of argument. Apart from this chief business, the only other matter I would add to disciplinary philosophy is the reflective examination of its general scope.

2.41. I should give here a few further comments on bits of what I have just been saying. First, 'history': three sorts of this may be counted in disciplinary philosophy. One is textual criticism: establishing reliable 'classic' texts and, relatedly, collating variant readings of their manuscripts or printed versions; such collations are especially important when, as in the case of Alexandre Koyré and Bernard Cohen's edition of Newton's *Principia*[7] and—if I may be allowed to intrude myself—my edition of Locke's *Essay concerning Human Understanding*,[8] one is dealing with an author's successive and extensive revisions of a major work. Another sort, not necessarily exclusive of the first, is giving a running elucidatory commentary on an individual work or an individual's work, possibly at the same time indicating, in the light of progress, its defects and deficiencies in respect of facts and arguments adduced in it; examples are W. D. Ross's edition of Aristotle's *Prior and Posterior Analytics*, Derek Whiteside's of *The Mathematical Papers of Isaac Newton*, and R. A. Fisher's notorious 1936 paper ('Has Mendel's work been rediscovered?')[9] on Mendel's original published account of his genetic experiments. The third sort of history of the cognitive and what pertains to it is more wide-ranging and synthetic; well-known books that are illustrative of this are E. A. Burtt's *The Metaphysical Foundations of Modern Physical Science*, R. G. Collingwood's *The Idea of Nature*, and the Kneales' *The Development of Logic*, but also—unlike those in not being avowed philosophers—Herbert Butterfield's *Man on his Past*, Gertrude Himmelfarb's *Darwin and the Darwinian Revolution*, Mach's

Die Mechanik in ihrer Entwicklung, historisch-kritisch dargestellt, and Vucinich's volumes on *Science in Russian Culture.*

2.42. I subsume under Logic what I shall call 'applied logic': the application of presumed canons of rationality to individual fields of investigation and to particular arguments or clusters of arguments. The term 'applied logic' should not be taken to signify that all the canonical details of this activity are satisfactorily embodied in already worked-out schemes of Pure Logic; the relationship is not unlike that of applied to pure mathematics. Of course, consideration of meaning or alternative meanings arises in doing applied logic; its semantical propositions, however, are only contingent and there is no question, contrary to Neo-Ramist 'analysis', of reaching and issuing a network of '*a priori* truths'. The groundwork for a case of applied logic may take the form of an ordering of some questions, and possible answers, on a given topic. Books which extensively provide examples of applied logic include D. H. Fischer's *Historian's Fallacies,* Kroeber and Kluckholm's *Culture: A Critical Review of Concepts and Definitions,* and Morris Weitz's *Hamlet and the Philosophy of Literary Criticism.*

2.43. I have referred to 'cognitive ideas and methods'. What do I want 'cognitive' to embrace? The cognitive has two distinct components; one is Logic and pure mathematics, while the other is *Wissenschaft,* covering all the disciplines concerned with specific regions or types of matter of fact, such as natural science, technology, geography, history, and comparative and historical linguistics mentioned above (2.4).

2.44. I suggested that Pure Logic could roughly be identified with what used to be called 'deductive and inductive logic'. Why 'roughly'? For two reasons. One is that logics of deduction, including meta-mathematics, many-valued logic, and other modern innovations, transcend the coverage of how deductive logic used to be conceived. The other reason is that what I have called the 'logic of empirical enquiry' is not to be restricted to inductive processes, where these consist of generalizations justified by appeal to ante-cedently known particular cases; to make only a couple of simple supporting points: not all empirical disciplines necessarily have generalizations as their conclusions, e.g. history, and several empirical disciplines commonly follow the non-inductive procedure of elaborating and using an abstract model, hopefully fruitful for classificatory, explanatory, and/or predictive purposes.

2.5. What, now, of the philosophy of education? Which practices in this make a part of disciplinary philosophy and which ones lie without it? For one thing, certain aspects of educational matters fall within the purview of disciplinary philosophy insofar as they are related to the history of cognitive ideas and methods: socio-educational considerations are relevant to an understanding of all branches of knowledge; it is through socio-educational means and media that the perpetuation and development of each branch are made possible and that, more specifically, the traditions, the already secured gains, and the urge towards innovation and new discovery are continually communicated and maintained. In the second place, applied logic that deals with educational proposals and arguments falls within the purview of disciplinary philosophy; thus analysing and evaluating from the standpoint of Logic educational claims and aims as argumentatively propounded by educationists, ideologists, politicians, and others is philosophy of education of the disciplinary kind. And, third, the reflective examination of philosophy of education—what should its subject-matter, procedures, and objectives be?—belongs to the disciplinary philosophy of education, in accordance with my previous account of the discipline of philosophy. Hence, insofar as the present chapter is itself to be an example of disciplinary philosophy, in particular, disciplinary philosophy of education, it can proceed along any or all of the three lines I have just described, but not along any others.

2.6. On the other hand, there are two familiar sorts of philosophy of education whose ambitions and tactics are non-disciplinary. One is the programmatic sort as found in Plato's *Republic* and *Laws*, Rousseau's *Émile*, and Dewey's *Democracy and Education*. Such works advocate certain authorially preferred educational ideals, which are recommended to the reader by emphatically rhetorical devices. This advocacy is comparable to claiming particular new religious, moral, social, or political changes, outlooks, and courses of action to be desirable; their supporters make these claims recognizing as a rule (I surmise) their controversial nature, which leads them to exercise the arts of persuasion in the attempt to overcome the inertia of established and differently motivated habits, the weakness of will, or positive oppositions that stand in their way: the urge 'to a new order' has a challenging and polemical character, enjoyed by missionaries. Their propounding what they think *ought to be* occurs only when what is actual in human affairs *is not* to their heart's desire. Programmatic works share two connected features. They insist that certain states of affairs which do not and, without efforts, would not, prevail *should* prevail; hence what they say substantially is not objectively descriptive, is neither true nor false, but is recommendatory. And, further, their methods of backing up their proposals largely exclude conformity with the canons of Logic, whose utilization involves a co-operative and cumulative enterprise, as Bacon realized, rather than single-handed combat for victory over competitors; and it involves self-criticism. It also involves allowing for alternative possibilities, and recognizing that on occasion the most suitable way of handling them is by adopting a syncretic treatment, and constructively trying out a degree of mutual adjustment, of them. What I have in mind here is a point that was nicely expressed by the late Evert Beth in relation to the foundations of mathematics:[10]

> My own personal position on the different questions studied will not be defended. This is because my viewpoint is characterized by the continual effort to understand every other viewpoint as reasonable. I strongly dislike doctrines which oblige us to reject any other opinion as 'meaningless'. At the same time, I am of the opinion that the different traditional concepts concerning the foundations of logic and mathematics are all inadequate in the present situation. Thus it seems to me that we must accept the necessity of a kind of doctrinal synthesis of the different contemporary tendencies, a synthesis which will probably be established as these tendencies are exploited to the utmost.

I certainly do not deny that holding strong opinions, and the formation of striking new plans and policies, are needed in educational as in other practical spheres of life. What I object to is confounding these things with the strenuous objectivities and canonical constraints of science and scholarship emergent in academic disciplines. To confound the programmatic with the disciplinary is deleterious to both, enfeebling the creative boldness of the programmatic side and deforming and prejudicing the rigorous and fact-finding temper of the disciplinary side.

2.7. The other sort of non-disciplinary philosophy of education is an outgrowth of the predominant movement in philosophy since the Second World War; this is the currently familiar phase of what I have earlier labelled 'Neo-Ramism'. Although at least the immediate ancestry of this phase located itself in polar opposition to the programmatic constructions (and speculative systems) favoured by so many philosophers from the time of the ancient thinkers of the Greek world, many present-day philosophers of education (and, indeed, of religion, morals, society, and politics) have—intentionally or otherwise is usually left obscured—reverted to the recommendatory habits of the programmatic writers. Although supposedly limiting themselves to discerning and describing what they call 'conceptual truths' or (even) 'logical truths', these philosophers of education continually commit themselves to highly controvertible evaluative propositions about education *as if their statements were truths of the discipline of philosophy.* What they say about the upbringing of children and about educational arrangements are intended to be *a priori* truths which exclude from possible experience and actualization all other possibilities. But, at best, if they were to succeed in registering linguistic or mentalistic facts about these matters, their accounts would only reflect and add another presentation of certain established views and attitudes among members of a (usually very ill-defined) population—which may be a rather small class. All the evaluative questions about the upbringing of children and about educational arrangements would remain open to new answers in the future even if (contrary to what seems to be the case empirically) there were universally agreed answers now: would-be descriptions of 'the educational concepts' that are used are generalizations from what are, hopefully, data in psychological and social history; neither the data themselves nor the generalizations can control, however much they may be geared to influence, future valuations. But at present, possibly more than in many past generations, *diversity* of view and attitude about the fundamentals of upbringing and education unremittingly exists; accordingly, on his own ground too, the 'conceptual analyst' should admit that he has no warrant in making rigid claims about what education *must* (ought to) be on the basis of what *is* (i.e. is said or thought in 'using the educational concepts'). That diversity is illustrated in a wealth of current educationist literature.

2.8. I remarked above (2.7) that many present-day 'analytical' philosophers of education commit themselves to highly controvertible evaluative propositions about education. Let me give two examples, taken from the typically named book *The Concept of Education.*[11] Notice in the following quotations the use of the first person plural in ways that are without any warrant that is given in them or in any other place; this is representative of Neo-Ramist practice, whether about education or otherwise. ('The question is often put to philosophers when they have done some conceptual analysis: "Whose concept are you analysing?" The first answer, obviously enough, is *our* concept. For concepts are linked indissolubly with the social life of a group . . .'[12]—the authors, sincere and modest thinkers—fail to specify the relevant social group and presuppose *a priori* a much greater—if not Aristotelian—conceptual uniformity among human beings than has been empirically justified. The matter is more complex, subtle, and multi-dimensional when attention is to be paid to notions, such as those of education and being educated, which have extensively changed through past generations.) And notice the unargued-for nature of the assertions about what the process of education ought to achieve or consist in;

and what some educationists would regard as the quite unduly restrictive emphasis on knowledge and thought, with a neglect of the non-cognitive aspects of what it is to be educated, in particular e.g. the affective, aesthetic, and conduct aspects (' "education" implies that a man's outlook is transformed by what he knows'; 'To be educated, one must be able to participate in the great human traditions of critico-creative thought'). Of course, some people reading this are likely to have preferences that coincide with those of one or both the quoted writers; it would, nevertheless, be illegitimate for you to infer that the shared preferences can be properly stated as universally valid 'conceptual truths'.[13, 14]

(a) We would be disinclined to call a man who was merely well-informed an educated man. . . . It is possible for a man to know a lot of history, in the sense that he can give correct answers to questions in classrooms and in examinations, without developing a historical sense. For instance, he might fail to connect his knowledge of the Industrial Revolution with what he sees when visiting Manchester or the Welsh Valleys. We might describe such a man as 'knowledgeable' but we would never describe him as 'educated'; for 'education' implies that a man's outlook is transformed by what he knows.

(b) An educated man—as distinct from a merely 'cultivated' man—must be, let us agree, independent, critical, capable of facing problems. But these qualities, while necessary are not sufficient; many uneducated nineteenth-century radical workmen possessed them in abundance. To be educated one must be able to participate in the great human traditions of critico-creative thought: science, history, literature, philosophy, technology, . . .

2.9. The immediate upshot, for the present purpose, of what I have been suggesting in this section is that if my treatment of the topic of science in education is to proceed in accordance with the requirements of disciplinary philosophy, then, first, it must be in terms of the history of cognitive ideas and methods or/and in terms of Logic (especially, in practice, applied logic) and, second, insofar as I myself make any evaluative, educational judgments and recommendations, I should clearly declare that this is their status and that they are not being offered as truths, nor as universal, necessary, or incontrovertible pronouncements. An academic philosopher could treat the topic otherwise, disclaiming to be speaking *qua* academic philosopher and avowing that he is speaking *qua* parent, educationist, politician, ideologist, or whatever. It is my intention to embrace this alternative in 3.1 and 3.2 only, which, however, also display the motivation impelling the concern with the use of applied logic occupying the subsequent paragraphs.

3.1. Voicing an outlook and a stance on the general issues of education is unavoidably to speak rhetorically. Thus rhetorically, I say (if I may repeat in this paragraph the words I used on a previous occasion; see [Nidditch], p. 4) that educational processes should bequeath to the next generation the totality of a civilized heritage together with a preparation for improving what has so far been attained. These educational processes have six principal aims: (1) the effective employment of the intellectual powers in all the relevant business of life; (2) the transmission of knowledge; (3) an enthusiasm and respect for truth and for the advance of efforts towards finding it; (4) an awareness of the potentialities and inter-connections of the different branches of knowledge; (5) the further-ance of humane feelings and ideals; and (6) an appreciation of the aesthetic. Academic institutions of all levels should concern themselves with the achievement of all these purposes, which can be given many different degrees of stress. It should be made clear that institutions and individuals have carefully, in applications, to adjust the values reflecting those purposes one to another; the values can mutually co-operate, and conflict. Also, while a balance of them is excellent, allowance must be made for the frequent if regrettable insistence of creativeness to be immoderate in its demands.

3.2. I distinguish between academic institutions, which include secondary schools and universities of the current patterns, and institutions that, like colleges of music, architecture, accountancy, or law, primarily limit themselves to an interest in a single domain and to the purpose only of teaching a professional competence. The following remarks are about academic institutions. I assume, provisionally, that the student who has latently creative power in, e.g. physics, will not have that power impeded (but possibly, on the contrary, effectively promoted) by his being prevented from specializing until he is half-way or further on in studies in a tertiary-level setting. (If this assumption turned out to be wrong for persons of really profound creativity—of the calibre, in twentieth-century theoretical physics, of, e.g. Einstein, Heisenberg, and Dirac—I would be driven to amend it.) On grounds of what I see as being attractive in individual cultural development and, through in-dividuals, in social cultural accumulation and advance, I would, ideally, wish the scholastic system to be such that all students would learn and would continue to learn a diverse range of 'subjects' (not necessarily only subjects hitherto recognized as such) instead of, as is now common in England, concentrating on at most three, often cognate disciplines once they reach the age of sixteen or seventeen;

and the university (etc.) system to be similar to that during at any rate the first two years of (full-time) study instead of, as now, its not only permitting but positively forcing each of its students to concentrate on just one or two disciplines for all or the greater part of their time. Apart from the collapse of the assumption I have mentioned, I do not think that the arguments that have been put forward in the Crowther Report and elsewhere in favour of 'the English principle of Specialization' can outweigh the importance, for a young person growing towards maturity, of continuing to experience a reduction in his wide spread of ignorance, and progress in his appreciation of the varieties of civilized skills and attainments and in his understanding and assessment of inter-relations between and limitations of different disciplines. The range of 'subjects' should, I suppose, incorporate several which are, looked at in a broad comparative perspective, markedly different in their orientations and in their judgmental and intellectual demands. I shall in the next section sketch a critique of an argument, from the Crowther Report, that runs in a direction contrary to this; it is, I think, fair to consider the Crowther argument as representative of arguments in support of specialization.

4.1. The Crowther Report's argument[15] for sixth form specialization has five stages whose contents appear to be of dubious general validity as they stand. I shall specially attend to its bearings on science. I shall consider its proposals concerning complementary elements in 4.6.

> The first step in the argument for specialisation is that able boys and girls are ready and eager by the time they are 16—the ablest by 15—to get down to the serious study of some one aspect of human knowledge which, with the one-sided enthusiasm of the young, they allow for a time to obscure all other fields of endeavour.

Not only is it historically and currently false that all able pupils in science want to limit their studies in the upper school to science; but were they to want to do so would still leave three questions to be answered: (1) Is it 'natural' that they want to do so, or is it the result of certain English scholastic traditions and policies? Is it true of able pupils in science in, for example, the U.S.A., France, or the Soviet Union? (2) Is it desirable that they be allowed to do so? Might not their being 'ready and eager' to concentrate on a single aspect of knowledge be something to help them to restrain and modify, and something that they should substantially supplement by other school interests and activities? (If it were being ready and eager for sexual intercourse that was the given premise, would the

dignitaries who were the members of the Crowther committee
have been so ready and willing to come to the conclusion that it is
desirable that pupils have sexual intercourse?) (3) Are there only
'able' boys and girls who study science in the sixth form? If not—
and some would say that there are many who are not—what
should be their programme of studies?

4.2.

> The second step in the argument is that concentration on a
> limited field leads naturally to study in depth. The boy
> embarks on a chain of discovery; he finds that ultimately each
> new fact he encounters fits into the jig-saw. As he goes
> deeper and deeper, he acquires self-confidence in his growing
> mastery of the subject. He is emancipated from the textbook
> and goes exploring behind the stage scenery that defines the
> formal academic subject.

I confess this provokes a degree of scepticism in me. I was for seven
years a senior member of a university's school of mathematical and
physical sciences, and on the basis of my teaching experience then,
of discussions I have been present at, and of material I have read,
I doubt whether the Report's argument here is applicable as a
generalization to science undergraduates, and therefore I surmise
that it is *a fortiori* inapplicable as a generalization to science pupils
in the sixth form. More aggressively, it might be claimed, first, that
the Report's argument embodies a lot of wishful thinking; second,
that a pupil's study of a science/mathematics subject in the sixth
form does not so much consist of his going 'deeper and deeper' as of
his covering more and more—at that stage, separate—items in each
branch of study; and third, that the assertion in the argument that
'ultimately each new fact he encounters fits into the jig-saw' is
largely fictional because the 'facts' he encounters do not all cohere
in one pattern in the framework of his sixth form course (or ever?
but the *prima facie* uncertain qualification 'ultimately' definitely—if
somewhat amazingly—refers in the Report to a time within the
schooling period), and because the image of 'the jig-saw' mis-
leadingly suggests that the sciences have an independent existence
of their own, with definite borders, whereas, on the contrary, no
science has firm edges nor has any science grown without being,
in one important phase of it or another, formatively influenced by
others and, indeed, by non-scientific factors.

4.3.

> The third step in the case for specialisation is that, through
> this discipline, a boy can be introduced into one or two areas

which throw light on the achievement of man and the nature of the world he lives in. The honours school of *Literae Humaniores* (Greats) at Oxford is a classic example of specialisation or study in depth. With the aid of a precise linguistic discipline, it develops a knowledge of the literature, the history, the art and the thought of one of the great cultures of the world. At the schoolboy's much lower level, similar studies in depth, embracing more than one discipline, can be, and readily are, developed from starting points in half-a-dozen literary or scientific subjects. The science side has developed a unity which the arts side has lost, to the regret of many, with the decline of the classics.

(1) To begin with an *argumentum ad hominem* (in Locke's sense, not in that of many modern dictionaries):[16] the Report's proposals about the sixth form repeatedly elsewhere express and preserve the usual idea of a subject, which is not 'interdisciplinary'; one of the virtues among pupils that it alleges is 'subject-mindedness', which is 'one mark of the good and keen Sixth Former. He has looked forward to being a science specialist, or a classicist, or a historian' (p. 223); again, according to the Report, in the arts sixth:

> It is true that where there are separate classical, history and modern languages Sixth Forms each provides an integrated course which can compare in intellectual coherence with that given on the science side; but in the majority of schools there is commonly a free selection of three main subjects from a field of five or six. . . . Out of these diverse elements, integrated and mutually supporting courses of study can be, and are, built, but [. . . only] by arranging suitable combinations of subjects [and] by seeing that the teaching of one makes use of the knowledge which has been gained in others

'combinations of subjects': one is here a long way from the idea of a subject which in principle is analogous to the idea of *Literae Humaniores* as a subject. (2) Next, the quotations I have given make it evident that, according to the Report, efforts need not be made within the sixth former's studies in arts or science subjects (however the idea of a subject is interpreted) to take any account of facets of his subject which lie on the other side (viz. science or arts, respectively). Doubtless unintentionally, the reference to *Literae Humaniores* shows this, because even if the student of Greats does make as varied a study of the Greco-Roman world as the Report suggests (what proportion of students of Greats take seriously both, e.g. classical art and philosophy?), what he is not required and is scarcely encouraged or enabled to do in that school is to make a study, even in an elementary though persistent way, of the mathematics, natural science, technology, and medicine of the Greco-Roman world: the *Phaedo* and the *Theaetetus,* the *Nicomachean Ethics* and the *Metaphysics*—yes; the *Timaeus* and *On the Heavens*—no, any more than the writings of the Hippocratics, Euclid, Archimedes, Heron, *et al.* Of course, in view of the student's actual secondary school background, these exclusions are inevitable; but are they desirable? ought he to be better equipped to approach the scientific and mathematical modes of the Greco-Roman world? (3) I shall add a final comment on the Crowther committee's 'third step in the case for specialisation'; this is that I find it hard to see how this at all supports, or consists of, an argument for specialization; it appears to be an appeal for a certain kind of specialization rather than an argument for specialization in contradistinction to a more wide-ranging group of studies or activities.

4.4.

The fourth step in the argument is that, given the right teaching, a boy will by the end of his school days begin to come out on the further side of 'subject-mindedness'. He is hardly likely to do that, perhaps, much before 18; but, as he sees how the facts he has been handling in his own subject knit together, he begins to wonder how his subject fits into the whole field of knowledge.

Apparently, the Report admits that sixth form specialization is something to be overcome, but holds that this can, or can best, happen only by the pupil being confined to a process of specialization. Whether this and the other would-be factual presumptions on which this fourth step rests are justifiable is dubious; for example, the proposition that, when nearly aged 18, the sixth former 'begins to wonder how his subject fits into the whole field of knowledge' might be doubted either for the reason that many pupils never *wonder* thus about their subject, or do not begin to do at that time, or begin to do so much earlier; and the proposition that the science (and arts) specialist normally transcends his subject-mindedness and 'narrow as his education may have been during the last few years, he will take steps to widen it as well as deepen it' may also be doubted.

4.5.

The fifth step in the argument is that this process of intellectual growth demands a great deal of concentrated time. It virtually enforces specialisation because the time left for other subjects is bound to be small—rarely can it be more than one-third.

It seems that what the phrase 'this process of growth' refers to is what has been described immediately before, in the paragraph from which I quoted in 4.4: one is told that the pupil begins to wonder how 'his subject' fits into the whole field of knowledge and that he 'reaches out for himself towards a wider synthesis. As he enjoys the first delights of intellectual mastery of his own subject, he observes that his fellows have the same joy in their subjects, and his interest impels him to discover what lies behind their enthusiasm. If a boy turns that intellectual corner, as he often does at the end of his Sixth Form time', he will, one is assured—I have already quoted the Report's concluding words on this—take steps to widen as well as deepen his education, narrow as it has been for the last few years. What, therefore, enforces specialization is the objective of the pupil's emerging, at or by the end of his sixth form time, from his subject-mindedness. Does this transcendence of subject-mindedness generally take place? Does it only *often* happen, 'often' being the more cautious term the Report uses about the frequency of a boy turning 'that intellectual corner'? More to the point than whether it often happens, is whether it happens more often than not: if it does not happen more often than not, the process of specialization supposedly required for the emergence from subject-mindedness is justified in a rather weak way; and even if it does happen more often than not, this argument for specialization remains of uncertain weight unless and until good enough reasons are vouchsafed for believing that this majority frequency of its happening is greater than would result from the adoption of curricular arrangements of a non-specialist kind. That the latter would be more effective for the transcendence of subject-mindedness—if this is the educational goal —appears to me to be a plausible hypothesis.

4.51. A quite different possible reason for the adoption of a non-specialist academic programme of the sort I have hinted at in 3.1, 3.2 above is this: at present, about 45 per cent of university entrants choose to study mathematics, natural science, or technology as their principal field; if a diverse range of studies (including of course, some in science/mathematics) were required of secondary school pupils throughout their time at school, a larger percentage of university entrants might wish to pursue some science/mathematics studies (without necessarily fewer of them wanting to do so in a specialist way), and possibly more of them than now might possess good ability for scientific work as undergraduates, and more important, after their graduation. Whether such non-specialist curricular arrangements in the schools would actually generate these consequences is, to my knowledge, an open question; that they would do so appears to me to be a plausible hypothesis. (I have, for simplicity, referred only to university entrants, and have prescinded from any attention to, e.g. polytechnic entrants.) This argument could be viewed favourably by people who wish for a growth in the numbers and quality of those studying and practising science, whether or not they sympathize with the goal of transcending subject-mindedness.

4.6. According to the Crowther Report (p. 275) the sixth form curriculum should contain three elements: one is the specialist element, on which the pupil should spend 'two-thirds of his time in school and much the greater part of his homework' ('plus almost all the homework' is said later in the same paragraph); another is 'the common element, when scientists and arts specialists should come together' for art and music, physical education, and 'to discover and to understand the central affirmations of the Christian faith' [much unholy water has since flowed under this arch of the bridge!]; the third is 'the complementary element', whose purposes are 'to save the scientists from illiteracy and the arts specialists from innumeracy'. The complementary element is to be allotted four or five periods a week. Hence, I reckon, taking account of homework, it is to occupy about one-tenth of a pupil's time. A critic could raise some large objections to the Report's proposals about this element. Is it desirable generally for pupils—not least for those who are not intending to proceed to university—to be forced (or even allowed) to pay so overwhelming a proportion of their attention to science or arts, respectively? Does this encourage a sufficiently diversified and balanced range of knowledge, interests, and attitudes needed for the modern individual's cultural development and equipment, not to mention the needs of his future jobs and possible social and parental responsibilities? The Crowther committee, without any judicial consideration of alternatives, assigned a dominant value to the integration and mutual reinforcement of a pupil's courses; so it naturally wanted the science or arts pupil to be occupied to only a minimal extent with any disciplines deemed alien to his chief concern. (There was no support given here for a pupil's combining an arts subject with his science ones, or vice versa.) Further, is the Crowther Report's recommendation concerning the *content* of complementary element periods satisfactory? Looking solely at the content aiming at 'numeracy' for the arts specialists: the Report mentions only natural science on the sciences side in its brief and tentative discussion of this matter; oddly, mathematics, including statistics and computistics (if I may coin a term), is not mentioned, nor is technology (unless this is comprehended under the 'influence of science on society'). The critic might argue that if numeracy is as important for the arts pupil as the Report concedes, at least several periods a week should be devoted to *each* of mathematics and natural science; and that, in addition, some systematic notice (with homework) albeit in an elementary and broad way, be paid to scientific aspects of the arts topics being studied—e.g. in history, something appropriate about alchemy, physiology-cum-psychology, astronomy, the shape of the earth, geographical exploration and its discoveries relevant to natural history, etc. could be included in a course on Renaissance or Tudor times, and something appropriate about Newtonianism, changing ideas of chronology and of the history of the earth, etc. could be included in a course on the eighteenth century.

5.1. There are many further questions about science in education at the secondary and tertiary levels that deserve discussion, as do the reasons and rationales of answers to them. One cluster of questions is about the content of science studies. (As throughout, I use the term 'science' or 'the sciences' to cover natural science and technology as corpuses of principled and formulaic knowledge and of know-how, and also more widely—when it is intended to contrast science with the arts subjects or the humanities—extending that coverage to mathematics.) Among the questions about content are: under what conditions, if any, should natural science be taught and learned in a unitary way, e.g. as general science, as against through the natural sciences separately? Is an understanding and appreciation of the scientific method a legitimate objective of science education—is it even a principal objective? Should science education in the school disregard technology, or, if not, how should it take notice of it? To what extent and for what purposes should science studies involve laboratory, field, or survey work on the part of the student? However, I shall, in this essay, have to leave aside all these and other issues in order that I may, in conclusion, briefly focus on the question whether science should have a major role in the curriculum.

5.2. In Turgenev's novel *Fathers and Sons* is Bazarov, a man whose outlook and conduct are characterized in it as expressions of 'nihilism'; what this meant was that Bazarov's views and values are materialistic, utilitarian,[17] mechanistic, and bound up with the belief that the only sort of knowledge that is possible and worth having is science. In the same year (1862) that the novel was first published, the Russian radical thinker and critic Pisarev wrote an article 'Bazarov' in which he equated his own views and values with those of Bazarov and claimed that Turgenev had exactly described the outlook of the materialist younger generation.[18] Nevertheless, few of the contemporary Russian radicals besides Pisarev were happy at being classified as a nihilist—a term that stuck—because the term suggested their having no positive convictions, whereas on the contrary, as a recent historian[19] has put it, 'The "Nihilists", more than any one else, believed—blindly and violently—in their own ideas. Their positivist and materialist faith could be accused of fanaticism, of a youthful lack of a sense of criticism, but not of apathy.' On the other hand, I suspect that Pisarev interpreted 'nihilism'—he preferred the name 'realism'—in tune with his sympathies with the materialism, sensationist epistemology ('the philosophy of the obvious'), and hedonist ethic of Epicurus, and with Epicurus's anomalous recognition and love of personal freedom.[20] Pisarev was rejecting outright as vacuous and worthless all the absolutes of the established social—and educational—order; the existence of immaterial spirit, of *a priori* or religious knowledge, and of non-humanist morality. Unlike Pisarev's other scientistically-orientated contemporaries (Chernyshevsky and Dobroliubov among them), in respect of education he carried his scientism to an extreme; whereas they, in company with many moderates, advocated a combination of classical (which, for Russia, entails primarily Greek) studies and scientific ones, Pisarev desired classical studies and all that they represented to be completely eliminated from education, for which he insisted on science as being the sole fit subject-matter. To my knowledge, Pisarev is the only notable writer to have urged this extremist policy. Commonly, those who regard science as properly having a substantial or even dominant place in the curriculum have the view that science studies should be supplemented by at any rate historical and literary studies (as are involved in a classical curriculum) either because the latter studies are required for the sake of culture and of the balanced development of an individual's different sensibilities, or because and insofar as these studies can be undertaken in the same kind of disciplinary manner as science studies themselves.

5.3. What is a line of argument having a similar conclusion to Pisarev's that someone nowadays might draw? In the light of English history, one might argue like this: in Tudor and Stuart times, when certain Christian and classical works and standards were accepted nationally as the norms of learning and conduct; when the classical languages provided the key to the Christian scriptures and Fathers and other authorities and to the great original works, in European antiquity, of history, literature, philosophy, and science;—classical (especially Latin) studies dominated the curriculum of the grammar school, the remainder of the curriculum being determined by the needs of Christian learning and devotion. (The reader should, perhaps, be reminded that the grammar schools then provided (apart from some private schools) the only schooling available to boys aged from about seven to thirteen or fourteen—the old 'public' schools in the sense of the nineteenth century and after were grammar schools committed as all grammar schools were by their statutes or tradition to the acceptance and 'breeding up' of indigent pupils of ability as well as of pupils coming from better-off homes; a prerequisite of entering the grammar school was a knowledge of the rudiments of reading, writing, and calculation, which were taught at home or in a 'petty' school.) Let me make clearer what the curriculum in the grammar school amounted to by my citing an illustrative record from that time. When Charles Hoole was headmaster of Rotherham Grammar School in the earlier part of the seventeenth century, the 'constant employment' of the highest form—called (of course!) the 'Sixth Form'—was, according to his account, as follows:[21]

> 1. To read twelve verses out of the *Greek Testament* every morning before Parts. 2. To repeat *Latine* and *Greek* Grammar Parts, and *Elementa Rhetorices* every Thursday morning. 3. To learn the *Hebrew* Tongue on Mondaies, Tuesdaies, and Wednesdaies, for morning Parts. 4. To read *Hesiod, Homer, Pindar,* and *Lycophron,* for forenoon lessons on Mondaies, and Wednesdaies. 5. *Zenophon, Sophocles, Euripides,* and *Aristophanes,* on Tuesdaies, & Thursdaies. 6. *Laubegois's Breviarium Graecae linguae,* for afternoons Parts on Mondaies, and Wednesdaies. 7. *Horace, Juvenal, Persius, Lucan, Seneca's Tragedies, Martial* and *Plautus,* for afternoons lessons on Mondaies, and Wednesdaies. 8. *Lucian's* select *Dialogues,* and *Pontani Progymnasmata Latinitatis,* on Tuesday afternoons, and 9. *Tullies Orations, Plinies Panegyricks, Quintilians Declamations* on Thursday afternoons, and Goodwin's Antiquities at leisure times. 10. Their exercises for *Oratory,* should be to make *Themes, Orations, Declamations,* Latine, Greek, and Hebrew; and for Poetry, to make *Verses* upon such Themes, as are appointed them every week. 11. And to exercise themselves in *Anagrames, Epidrams, Epitaphs* [. . .], English, Latine, Greek, and Hebrew. 12. Their Catechismes are *Nowell,* and *Birket,* in Greek, and the Church Catechisme in Hebrew.

Latin studies were the staple diet of the grammar school pupils; for instance, at Rotherham School, Greek was not begun till the fourth form, and Hebrew not till the sixth form. Now, the argument may proceed that the curriculum of the grammar school in Tudor and Stuart times was quite suitable for the period of Christian neo-classicism, as is evidenced by the fact that the grammar school was the nursery of a crowd of distinguished men of letters and the learned arts, including Sidney, Marlowe, Shakespeare, Ben Jonson,

Milton, John Wallis, Locke, Newton (not to mention later writers such as Gibbon, or Parliamentarians such as Cromwell: I may remark incidentally that one of the objections made by royalists and their fellow-travellers to the curriculum of the grammar school was that it led pupils at an impressionable age to be immersed in the imitative study of Republican Rome and consequently to be possessed by erroneous and mischievous political ideas). Three big benefits may be suggested as stemming from the grammar school programme. One was the provision and perpetuation of a *common* cultural environment, frame of reference, and store. Another was the intensive educational coherence at each stage, and through all the stages, of school life: the courses did not involve a multiplicity of unrelated topics and skills or nurture fragmentation and superficiality. And third, the content of what was studied had an international standing as being matter and manner that were normative and useful for all civilized and Christian people everywhere. Inevitably, because of what was assumed to be the school's function, much was excluded from the scope of its coverage, e.g. modern languages, modern history, mathematics, and natural sciences; but it was believed, boys who had undergone a training in the polite learning of the school were prepared by it for making advances in their adolescence and maturity in other fields of learning. Analogously: now that the values of Christian neo-classicism are outmoded and we are living in an Age of Science, the curriculum of the secondary—which should reflect the key factor of modern life that is science—school should be constituted by science studies. These would provide and perpetuate a common cultural environment, frame of reference, and store. They would ensure an intensive educational coherence at each stage, and through all the stages, of school life: science courses would not (or at any rate could readily be made so as not to) involve a multiplicity of unrelated topics and skills or nurture fragmentation and superficiality. And the content of what would thus be studied has an international standing as matter and method that is normative and useful for civilization and social development everywhere. The doctrines and ethos of Christianity would be replaced by the teachings and implications of science and by humanly determined values for personal conduct and for relations *inter vivos*.[22] Formerly, the learning of the literate skills required for undertaking studies in the grammar school had been done at home or in a petty school; something similar in its results would be necessary in the new circumstances. At the other end of the educational ladder, in Tudor and Stuart times the young student at university—still in his early teens—continued to study the classics or what was derived from the classics; however, his mind was directed to Aristotelian or quasi-Aristotelian logic and metaphysics as well as to works of classical literature and the classical art of rhetoric (where again Aristotle was an important influence through the source-book status of his *Rhetoric*). Not until he had completed these classically-based studies for the Bachelor's degree could the student proceed to concentrate on a subject of his own choice—in particular, law, medicine, or theology—for 'professional' purposes; his school and undergraduate training should have prepared him, in respect of language, method, and content, for these and other advanced studies. Comparable but updated arrangements would be instituted in the scientific scheme. All undergraduates would pursue a programme of courses in the sciences (with due attention being paid to mathematics), together, possibly, with some modern Logic and even some history of science—and nothing else. After, say, two years of this, a student could move on to the pursuit of a subject of his own choice, either as a full-time or a part-time student; his school and undergraduate training should have prepared him, in respect of critical-mindedness, method, and content, to tackle properly and beneficially any subject to which he devotes himself.

5.31. Already in the seventeenth century the limitations of the contemporary grammar school curriculum (and practices) began to be emphasized and a number of sensitive thinkers—Milton[23] and Locke[24] amongst them—besides critically remarking on the established system, put forward plans for changing it. While retaining oral and written Latin as the initial subject to master, Milton and Locke recognized the values of other areas of learning for young minds; not least, mathematics, natural science, the basic medical sciences, and various sorts of technical and craft knowledge. These proposals illustrate a conviction underlying the changes in schooling that were introduced in the margin at that time (e.g. the Mathematical School of Christ's Hospital) and that later became general: the curriculum's unity and unifying character are less important than a reasonable comprehensiveness, although the latter is obtained by diluting the intensity of concentration associated with the former.

5.4. Other reasons, distinct from although related in part to those possible ones given in 5.3 may be adduced in support of the thesis that the curriculum should have only a science content and in support of any of a variety of less immoderate theses that science should have a major role in the curriculum; in respect of the secondary school, examples of these less immoderate theses are that non-science subjects directly useful to science, e.g. languages, may or should be studied, or that about two-thirds of the curriculum should be in science, the remaining one-third dealing with other aspects of things or with other needs of the pupil. The other, supporting reasons that may be adduced include the following: science is the most effective, progressive, and fruitful instrument available to man for discovering facts, regularities, and grounded explanations, about the nature of things—about physical systems and about organic systems, including human mind and behaviour. And it is an instrument, with those qualities, for altering and controlling man himself and his environment for ends that he deems to be best. This power of alteration and control makes science man's vital hope and need in his attempts helpfully to resolve problems about the utilization of human and material resources. Further, the freedom of thought, the broadening of view and comprehension, and the enlargement of the scope of action and opportunity have in the past been won primarily as an outcome of science and its diffusion, and science is man's most reliable assurance of their future continuation and growth. Science is the innocuous destroyer of superstition and prejudice, and of all that shuts mankind off from the knowledge it could achieve and of all that divides man from man. I shall mention one final reason that may be urged by proponents of the kind of scientistic thesis under consideration. It may be pointed out that the practice of science is widespread and the consequences of science are deep and extensive, nationally and internationally; it is improbable that any external forces can be applied to divert, still less to bring to rest, this massive movement. But it is undesirable to let the interests and activities of the scientists lie beyond the circumspection and critical evaluation of the non-scientists, who form the majority of the educated population. This circumspection and critical evaluation presuppose the necessity of an education that is chiefly in science.

5.5. Judged as a totality, the reasons suggested in 5.3 and 5.4 as possible arguments in favour of claims that science should have a major role in the curriculum are, I think, weighty; I find most of them forceful to some degree, without finding all the suggestions made acceptable. (For example, I doubt whether science promotes critical-mindedness, or has a record as a destroyer of superstition and prejudice, better than historical studies do; and I doubt whether science alone, or even science in conjunction with other forms of cognitive enterprise, can suffice—without appropriate modes of affective guidance—to reduce irrationality and to improve the human condition.) But weighty as a totality that the reasons suggested are, I do not regard them as justifying a claim that science should have a maximal role, or—if I may use quantities figuratively —that it should have a greater than half share, in the curriculum.

My positive conclusions have been indicated previously; they are stated in 3.1, 3.2, 4.51, and 4.6.

Notes

1 English as distinct from Scottish, as well as from French, North American, etc.

2 In general, but not inflexibly, engagement in writing poetry, plays, or novels, composing or playing music, sculpting, etc. should not, in my view, be deemed to be a proper part of academic work.

3 This association of modern *apriorism* in philosophy with certain features of Ramist doctrine and method is something of a *jeu d'esprit*— but not merely so. It might be illustrated further; compare, e.g. the modern 'contract theory of meaning' with the Ramist preoccupation with dichotomizing.

4 Walter J. Ong, *Rhetoric, Romanticism and Technology*, Ithaca and London, 1971, p. 84.

5 A. J. Ayer, *The Problem of Knowledge*, London, 1956, p. 1.

6 The latter portion of 2.3 largely repeats what is said in [Nidditch], p. 17. (References in square brackets are to items in the *Select Bibliography* that follows these notes.)

7 *Isaac Newton's Philosophiae Naturalis Principia Mathematica*, assembled and edited by Alexandre Koyré and I. Bernard Cohen, Cambridge, 1972. This is the most important edition of the *Principia* since the splendid edition of it with an extensive running commentary by T. Le Seur and F. Jacquier, 2nd revised ed., Geneva, 1760.

8 *John Locke: an Essay Concerning Human Understanding*, edited with an Introduction, Critical Apparatus and Glossary by Peter H. Nidditch, Oxford, 1973. A. C. Fraser's edition of the *Essay*, Oxford, 1894; later reprints, is an unsatisfactory work of scholarship in its textual, text-historical, and bibliographical respects; for example, its (modernized) text and its text-historical notes are repeatedly inaccurate, and it fails to record the great majority of variants to be found in the early editions of the *Essay*. The text of the *Essay* edited by John W. Yolton, London, 1961, also in a modernized form is better than Fraser's, but it contains many errata and a number of omissions some of which I have listed elsewhere: 'Corrigenda to Yolton's edition of Locke's *Essay*', *Locke Newsletter*, 2, 1971, pp. 21-9; and *ibid.*, 3, 1972, pp. 34-8.

9 R. A. Fisher, 'Has Mendel's work been rediscovered?', *Annals of Science*, 1, 1936, pp. 115-37.

10 Evert W. Beth and Jean Piaget, *Mathematical Epistemology and Psychology*, trans. W. Mays, Dordrecht, 1966, p. 4.

11 R. S. Peters (ed.), *The Concept of Education*, London, 1966.

12 P. H. Hirst and R. S. Peters, *The Logic of Education*, London, 1970, p. 8.

13 R. S. Peters in *The Concept of Education*, pp. 6, 7.

14 J. S. Passmore in *The Concept of Education*, p. 200.

15 [Central Advisory Council for Education—England], pp. 262 *et seq.*

16 In Locke's sense (see *Essay Concerning Human Understanding*, 4, 17, 21), it equals *argumentum ex concesso*. In many modern dictionaries, e.g. the *Concise Oxford Dictionary* and the *American Heritage Dictionary of the English Language*, meanings different from that, and from one another, are given.

17 The sense of 'utilitarian' here is both the broad one pertaining to an emphasis on usefulness and one pertaining to philosophical hedonism. (Let me take this opportunity of saying that wherever puns and ambiguities occur in my writing—and there are some others in the present essay—they are, I hope, intentional. The principle of interpretation that should be applied is: *each* meaning that the reader judges may be relevant *is* relevant.)

18 D. I. Pisarev, 'Bazarov', *Russkoe slovo*, 3, 1862.

19 Franco Venturi, *Roots of Revolution*, English trans. Francis Haskell, London, 1960, p. 326.

20 D. I. Pisarev, *Polnoe sobranie sochineyiy v shesti tomakh*, St Petersburg, 1894, 2, p. 96. Pisarev's conscious affiliation to the Epicurean philosophy as a whole, and not simply to Epicurean ethics, has not been noticed in the accounts of him that have been written in or translated into English, e.g. in T. G. Masaryk's *The Spirit of Russia*, English trans. by Eden and Cedar Paul, London, 1919, 1955, 2, ch. 14. The most extended account of Pisarev in English is E. Lampert, *Sons Against Fathers: Studies in Russian Radicalism and Revolution*, Oxford, 1965, pp. 272–338, 385–94 (Notes); this contains three allusions to Epicureanism (pp. 279, 318, 330), each of them, however, being only in the hedonistic sense. The most recent Russian book on Pisarev that I have seen— published to celebrate the centenary of his death—is A. N. Maslin, *D. I. Pisarev v bor'be za materializm i sotsial'niy progress*, U.S.S.R. Academy of Sciences, Institute of Philosophy, Moscow, 1968.

21 Charles Hoole, *A New Discovery of the Old Art of Teaching Schoole*, London, 1660. The title-page states: 'Written about Twenty three yeares ago, for the Benefit of *Rotheram* School, where it was first used . . .' My quotations are from the reproduction edited by E. T. Campagnac, Liverpool and London, 1913; the quoted account of the Sixth Form curriculum is taken from the part 'The Masters Method', pp. 202–4.

22 I say 'relations *inter vivos*' and not, e.g. 'interpersonal relations' because the former phrase is wider, covering also human conduct towards animals.

23 An authoritative scholarly edition of Milton's essay on education is contained in E. Sirluck (ed.), *The Complete Prose Works of John Milton*, vol. 2, 1643–8, New Haven, 1959.

24 The best modern edition of Locke's *Some Thoughts Concerning Education* is [Axtell]. However, it is by no means as satisfactory a treatment of this major classic of educational thought as could be wished. Its most serious single weakness is in its Collation (pp. 326–38), purporting to

provide a record of the development and alterations of the text of the book from 1693 (first edition) till 1705 (fifth edition); unfortunately, that Collation is thoroughly inaccurate and defective, as the results of my independent collation of the early editions, 1693–1705, have shown. (See my *A Bibliographical and Text-Historical Study of the Early Printings of John Locke's 'Some Thoughts Concerning Education'*, Sheffield, 1972.)

Select bibliography

H. O. Anderson (ed.), *Readings in Science Education for the Secondary School*, New York and London, 1969.

L. Armand, 'Machines, technology, and the life of the mind', *Impact*, 3, 1952, 155–70.

W. H. G. Armytage, *Four Hundred Years of English Education*, 2nd ed., Cambridge, 1970.

E. Ashby, *Technology and the Academics*, revised ed., London, 1963.

J. L. Axtell (ed.), *The Educational Writings of John Locke*, Cambridge, 1968.

G. H. Bantock, *Education in an Industrial Society*, London, 1963.

J. Bronowski, *Science and Human Values*, revised ed., London, 1964.

J. Bronowski, 'The educated man in 1914', *Science*, 123, 1956, pp. 710–12.

J. S. Bruner, *The Process of Education*, Cambridge, Mass., 1960.

J. S. Bruner, *Toward a Theory of Instruction*, Cambridge, Mass., 1966.

Central Advisory Council for Education—England, *15 to 18* (The Crowther Report), London, 1959.

Committee on Manpower Resources for Science and Technology, *The Flow into Employment of Scientists, Engineers and Technologists* (The Swann Report), London, 1968.

G. Compayre, *Herbert Spencer and Scientific Education*, trans. M. E. Finlay, London, 1908.

D. K. Cornelius and E. St Vincent (eds), *Cultures in Conflict: Perspectives in the Snow-Leavis Controversy*, Chicago, 1964.

L. A. Cremin, *The Transformation of the School: Progressivism in American Education 1876–1957*, New York, 1961.

S. J. Curtis and M. E. A. Boultwood, *A Short History of Educational Ideas*, 4th ed., London, 1965.

J. Dewey, *Democracy and Education*, New York, 1915.

J. Dewey, *How we Think*, New York, 1933.

J. A. Easley, Jr, 'Is the teaching of scientific method a significant educational objective?' in I. Scheffler (ed.), *Philosophy and Education*, 1st ed., Boston, 1958, pp. 154–79.

J. W. Getzels and P. W. Jackson, *Creativity and Intelligence*, New York, 1961.

B. Glass, 'Liberal education in a scientific age' in *Science and Liberal Education*, Baton Rouge, 1959, 54–85.

G. Gusdorf, *De l'histoire des sciences à l'histoire de la pensée*, Paris, 1966.

N. B. Henry (ed.), *Rethinking Science Education*, the Fifty-ninth Yearbook of the National Society for the Study of Education, Part 1, Chicago, 1960.

G. Holton, 'Modern science and the intellectual tradition', *Science*, 131, 1960, pp. 1187–93.

S. Hook, *Education for Modern Man*, new enlarged ed., New York, 1967.

T. H. Huxley, *Science and Education, Collected Essays*, 3, London, 1893.

T. S. Kuhn, 'The essential tension: tradition and innovation in scientific research' in C. W. Taylor and F. Barron (eds), *Scientific Creativity: Its Recognition and Development*, New York, 1963, pp. 341–54.

F. R. Leavis, *Two Cultures: The Significance of C. P. Snow*, London, 1962.

D. C. McClelland, 'On the dynamics of creative physical scientists', in H. E. Gruber *et al.* (eds), *Contemporary Approaches to Creative Thinking*, New York, 1962, pp. 141–74.

E. Nagel, 'The methods of science: what are they? Can they be taught?', *Scientific Monthly*, 70, 1950, pp. 19–23.

P. H. Nidditch, 'The Intellectual Virtues', Inaugural Lecture, University of Sheffield, 1970.

T. P. Nunn, 'The significance of science in education' in T. F. Coade (ed.), *Harrow Lectures on Education*, London, 1931.

T. P. Nunn, *Education: Its Data and First Principles*, 3rd ed., London, 1945.

J. Piaget (ed.), *Logique et connaissance scientifique*, 'Encyclopédie de la Pléiade', Paris, 1967.

J. J. Schwab and P. F. Brandwein, *The Teaching of Science*, Cambridge, Mass., 1962.

C. P. Snow, *The Two Cultures and the Scientific Revolution*, Cambridge, 1959. (And see *The Times Literary Supplement*, 25 October 1963, for his reply to F. R. Leavis.)

C. L. Stevenson, 'The scientist's role and the aims of education', *Harvard Educational Review*, 24, 1954, pp. 231–8.

R. A. R. Tricker, *The Contribution of Science to Education*, London, 1967.

UNESCO, *The Teaching of Sciences in African Universities*, Paris, 1964.

A. Vucinich, *Science in Russian Culture*, two volumes, Stanford, 1963, 1970.

F. Watson, *The Beginnings of the Teaching of Modern Subjects in England*, London, 1909.

F. Watson, *The Old Grammar Schools*, Cambridge, 1916.

A. N. Whitehead, *The Aims of Education and Other Essays*, London and New York, 1929; many later editions.

G. Yarlott, *Education and Children's Emotions*, London, 1972.

Index

259

Name index

Archimedes, 246
Aristotle, 164, 165
Austin, J. L., 174

Bacon, F., 199, 235
Bellarmine, R., 39
Beth, E., 239
Bradley, F. H., 12
Broad, C. D., 47
Buber, M., 34, 43
Bullough, E., 198
Burtt, E. A., 236
Butler, Bishop, 99–100
Butterfield, H., 236

Chaucer, Geoffrey, 201
Christ, Jesus, 160
Collingwood, R. G., 236
Cromwell, O., 252

Descartes, R., 12
Dewey, J., 238
Dirac, P., 242

Einstein, A., 242
Eliot, G., 136
Elliot, R. K., 207, 208, 209
Epicurus, 250
Euclid, 246

Fischer, R. D., 237
Fisher, R. A., 236
Freeman, Helen, 136

Galileo, 38, 39, 235
Gallie, W. B., 90
Gibbon, E., 252

Hampshire, S., 214
Hardie, C. D., 29
Hardy, T., 8
Hare, R. M., 42, 43
Heisenberg, W., 242
Heron of Alexandria, 246
Himmelfarb, G., 236
Hippocrates, 246
Hoole, C., 251
Hopkins, G. M., 205, 208

Jonson, B., 251

Kafka, F., 13
Kant, I., 81, 101, 103, 108, 160
Kepler, 235
Kneale, W. and M., 236
Kroeber and Kluckhohn, 237
Kuhn, T. S., 37

Lakatos, I., 227
Larkin, P., 199, 208, 210
Law, R., 213, 214
Lee, L., 199, 200, 202
Locke, J., 13, 252, 253
Lynton, N., 213, 214

Mach, E., 236
Marcel, G., 199
Marlowe, C., 199, 251
Marx, K., 91
Meager, R., 213, 214
Mill, J. S., 17, 19
Milton, J., 252, 253
Muggeridge, M., 156

Newton, I., 252